The Complete Book of
Furniture Repair
and Refinishing

THE COMPLETE BOOK OF FURNITURE REPAIR AND REFINISHING

Ralph Parsons Kinney

FULLY REVISED

by the staff of

THE FAMILY HANDYMAN magazine

Charles Scribner's Sons · New York

CONTENTS

The Complete Book of
Furniture Repair
and Refinishing

CHAPTER ONE

Furniture Restoration

You can furnish your home inexpensively and with real distinction and beauty by refinishing furniture.

New materials and methods of finishing make it possible to restore an old piece to beauty and even to enhance its usefulness. You can apply finishes that resist moisture, alkalies, acids, alcohol, heat, or abrasion. These finishes are appropriate for today's way of living, withstanding maximum wear with a minimum of care.

First, look at the pieces you have. Could you enhance their beauty and usefulness by refinishing them? Next, look for secondhand pieces of simple design and durable construction, which, if suitable for your purpose, may be bought reasonably. Explore secondhand stores, auctions, swap shops, sales from model homes, and movers' storage warehouses. Read want ads in local papers. Or you may enjoy shopping in antique shops.

Another possibility is unfinished furniture featuring beauty in grain and wood color.

RESTORING FURNITURE IS NOT DIFFICULT

The restoration of antique and other types of furniture holds a strong allure and fascination for those with a natural aptitude in the use of tools, be they beginners or expert craftsmen. Every undertaking presents a new problem, and no satisfaction equals that of its successful solution. A job well done will require all the skill and craftsmanship to which the individual can attain.

Overrestoration has ruined many a fine piece of furniture. A beginner, through lack of knowledge and an excess of enthusiasm, will often attempt to remove every scar and blemish, thus robbing the piece of all that evidence

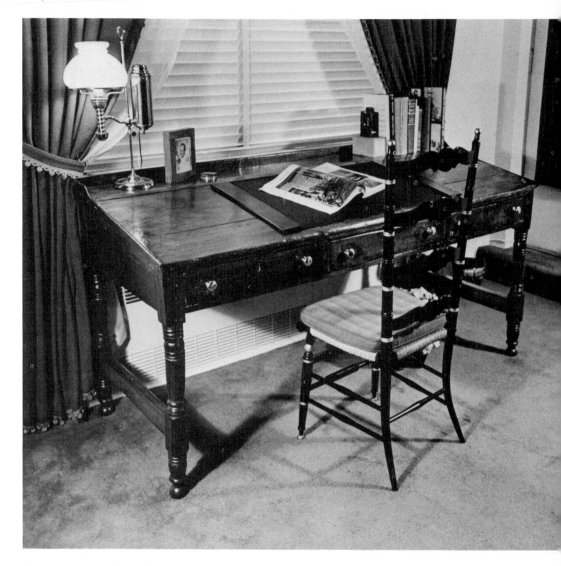

Figure 1-1. Once a sturdy work desk in a mercantile establishment, this large, handsome piece bears the scars of its long years of service. Some surfaces are distressed, and the front edge of the top shows nail holes where there once must have been fastened a small lip that prevented ledgers from sliding to the floor. The finish is a rich, deep mahogany with a high-gloss surface that gleams in the light.

which attests to its age and long usage; as a result, the piece will look like a reproduction. Of course, the question of just how far restoration should be carried is a difficult one, particularly when the piece is an antique. True lovers of antiques cherish the evidence of age in an old piece. This is lost when restoration is so extensive that the piece is actually rebuilt. Where the original finish is still intact and in good condition, no attempt should be made to remove it. A great part of the beauty lies in this old finish. A thorough cleaning and polishing will often be sufficient. Don't carry restoration too far!

There is always something new to be learned about restoration of furniture. This knowledge is acquired by the "trial and error" method. The desired result can be reached by various procedures, but those selected should be ones that have been tested and proven. This is not to say that the methods and procedures set forth herein are the only ones that will accomplish your purpose. The experienced amateur or the professional may prefer something different, and, therefore, not everyone will agree with all this book suggests. Actually, most of the work outlined herein requires only a limited supply of hand tools, and the work can be done by someone who has merely a sketchy knowledge of them. In working with old furniture, we gain great respect for that excellence of construction and craftsmanship which was accomplished with only a few crude hand tools.

Among those who read this book will be some whose interest lies in learning about restoration, even though they never intend doing the work themselves. This knowledge will enable them to direct others in their work and to recognize when a piece has undergone too much restoration. Those who plan to undertake the work themselves should read the book in its entirety before undertaking a job of restoration. Step follows step and each should be thoroughly understood, for circumstances and conditions may offer a choice of procedure, or of the sequence in which the steps should be done.

It is important to remember that furniture restoration is not difficult, even for a beginner. Time, patience, and care are the important essentials. Your first restoration project can be completely successful. Unfortunately, many people feel they have no natural talent for mechanical work and are loath to undertake anything of this kind. If such people would handle an object carefully and study it with their eyes, instead of deciding at once that it is beyond their ability, they would soon find that most of the problems they had felt were impossible for them to undertake could readily be solved.

From this it is clear that any adult person can at least attempt the work of furniture restoration. The work may not, at first, be perfect, but improvement will come quickly with repeated practice. Even though you may feel that repair work is beyond you, the work of re-

Figure 1-2. This is a lovely old dining room table that reflects all the charm and simplicity of Shaker construction. It's an extremely graceful design and was made around 1880. This piece was finished in a light color to show all the natural wood.

finishing can be done if you will follow the directions given in this book. If you feel your talents are not yet developed to a point where you want to run the risk of ruining a piece, engage a professional to do the job. The knowledge you have gained from this book will enable you to recognize that point beyond which even the professional should not go in his efforts at restoration.

The quality of the work you do yourself is in direct proportion to the painstaking effort you put into it, rather than to your natural ability as a cabinetmaker or refinisher. Careful work throughout is the only way to achieve results comparable to those of a conscientious professional.

Check the operations involved in each step with care, using the book on your workbench for reference. Don't depend on memory if you are a beginner. It is natural to forget and not do all that should be done, and such omission might cause damage or result in a poor finish. All procedures may be found in the index.

WHEN IS RESTORATION WORTHWHILE?

A piece of furniture does not have to be a collector's item to give you pleasure and have value. If the wood has natural beauty and the design is pleasing to you, if the piece fits your purpose and your home, restoration may well be worth your while. Thus, when choosing a piece of furniture for restoration, for your own use, the following factors should be carefully considered:

1. Will it be functional? How will it be used, and where will it be placed in the home? Will it fit the space?

2. Is it well designed, with pleasing lines and proportions?

3. Is it constructed from one or several woods? Does the wood have a good color?

4. Are any parts missing? Would they be expensive to replace? Can they be replaced at home with available tools, materials?

5. Is the construction sturdy? Are there any loose joints?

6. If the piece has poorly constructed or designed features, can it be remodeled to advantage?

7. Will the restored piece cost less than a new piece of furniture? (If not, it may be wiser to buy a new piece, unless it is valuable as an antique.)

8. Will the restored piece blend with my furnishings? (Woods and styles do not have to match.)

9. Does the piece just need cleaning?

At first it may be difficult for a beginner to recognize the value in an "untouched" piece of furniture because of its condition or its surroundings. A piece may be covered with dirt or a heavy layer of dust, the finish may be badly checked and cracked, it may have many coats of old paint, and its surface may be rough and scarred. It may be in need of considerable repair, and one or more of the parts missing. Often it is stored in a place where the light is poor and where it is crowded in with other pieces.

When you have had experience in restoring pieces found under these conditions, and when you have trained yourself to recognize the good and the bad, you will know which pieces to choose and which to let alone. You will have learned what can be done with a piece that, at first glance, seemed utterly hopeless. You will have developed a sense of imagination in regard to furniture that will enable you to recognize more readily those "untouched" pieces of good value. You will also have become an ardent enthusiast for the work of restoration.

If the construction or condition of a piece is doubtful and you are not certain what woods were used when it was made, there are several ways of testing and examining the piece in order to arrive at a decision regarding its value. Should the piece be tucked away in a dark corner where the light is bad, move it out into the open, if possible, or use a strong flashlight. Wipe off as much of the dust and grime as you can and proceed as follows:

1. Look for missing parts.

2. Check for necessary repairs.

3. Examine the part where the drawer sides meet the front and note the construction of these points. If these are well-fitted "dovetails" or another good type of joint, you may usually presume that the rest of the piece is well constructed and of equal quality of workmanship. (See pages 50–54 for further information on wood joints.)

4. Check the piece for loose joints by wobbling it.

5. Test the wood for hardness with your fingernail or with the point of a knife blade, unless its species is obvious. It must be remembered that several kinds of wood may have been used in the construction.

6. If the piece is covered with old paint, you will often be granted permission to scrape off a small place on the surface with a knife blade, so you may examine the bare wood for its color or species. In doing this, you can also determine how many coats of paint are on the piece; the number of coats may be seen at the feathered edge of the spot scraped off. If the piece is very old and the undercoat is red, black, or green, it will be difficult to remove. These are called *refractory paints*.

7. The ability of the wood to take a fine color, when refinished, may be tested by wetting a spot, free from paint or finish, with water or saliva on a fingertip. Old wood will usually show a rich color, while a newer wood will not (see page 126).

COLLECTING ANTIQUE FURNITURE

In recent years, the price and scarcity of good antique furniture has risen because the demand for it has steadily increased while the supply has decreased. This is particularly true of the better grades and rarer items. However, if you search patiently and diligently, many choice items may still be found.

There are many places to look for antique furniture. If you know even a little about antiques, you will get much enjoyment in hunting for them in out-of-the-way places, if for no other reason than for the satisfaction of boasting to your friends about the bargains you have thus found. When your "find" has been repaired and refinished and you have done the work yourself, your pleasure will be increased.

Buying direct from the home has become increasingly difficult, particularly in the eastern states where this field has been combed by both amateur enthusiasts and those who scout for dealers. Much antique furniture and other items of antique value now come onto the market when decedents' estates are sold, usually by means of private or auction sales. The difference between the two kinds of sales is that at an auction the items are sold to the highest bidder, while at private sales the prices are marked on the pieces before the sale. Bargains can still be picked up at either type of sale.

Figure 1-3. An antique dry sink can be easily converted into a planter, as seen here. Such units can often be found at antique auctions.

In cities, a visit to a secondhand, Goodwill, or Salvation Army store may often reward you by the discovery of a choice piece at a bargain price. However, even there, storekeepers are becoming more and more aware of true values.

The safest place for the uninitiated to buy antiques is from an antique dealer, particularly a dealer who has earned a reputation for fair prices and fair practice. Such dealers will gladly show you their stock of "untouched" pieces, and you can generally rely on their integrity.

If, after you have picked up a piece of antique furniture in an out-of-the-way place at a bargain price, and you later see a similar piece for sale in an antique store for a far higher price, you should recognize the reason for this increase. Consider the facts. Shop owners can not afford the time to hunt for and buy very much of their merchandise direct. This is particularly true if they are situated at any great distance from the source of supply. They must buy from wholesalers or dealers who attend auctions and other sales, or who buy from "scouts" who comb the countryside for them. Antiques, like other kinds of merchandise (food, luxuries, autos, etc.), move from the original source to the wholesaler, and through him to the retailer. Each takes his profit, and to this profit he is entitled. Antiques are not governed by established market prices to any great extent. Reputable dealers are content with reasonable profits.

It would be well for the beginner to hunt around in his own home to find some piece of old furniture on which to start work. Furniture that has been stored away and forgotten may often be refinished and restored to usefulness. For example, a table can be cut down in height for use in front of a couch. An "ugly duckling" can often be transformed into a thing of beauty, particularly when the removal of an old finish reveals the beauty of the natural wood.

You will be surprised at what may be unearthed in the "dump yard" of a small city or town. You may find whole pieces of good furniture or pieces of old wood

for repair. Such pieces can often be purchased at a nominal sum and, when repaired and refinished, make attractive items for your home or for gifts.

Remember that age alone doesn't make antique furniture worthy of a place in your home. Condition, workmanship, materials, and design are also important. Be cautious about buying a piece in particularly bad condition. The cost of restoring may not warrant the purchase price.

Items that are at least one hundred years old are classified by the United States Customs Department as antiques and are permitted entry into the country duty free. Collectors do not consider a piece valuable if its replaced parts amount to more than 10 percent of the entire piece, or if its original shape or design has been altered.

Most buyers choose a piece for its decorative value.

PLANNING RESTORATION WORK

When repairing or refinishing a piece of furniture, each step should be planned carefully and in advance. The work and the selection of materials and tools should follow this plan closely, except in those cases where unforeseen conditions arise during the course of the work, making necessary a deviation from the plan.

In commercial plants, the materials to be used and the sequence of the work is planned in advance and the plan set forth on written orders. The work is routed through the various departments, each of which specializes in a particular phase of the work. Restoration work must be done in separate steps, and these in their proper order. With good advance planning, many errors can be avoided. Prepare your work plan as follows:

1. Examine the piece and determine what repairs are necessary.

2. Examine the finish or paint covering the piece and decide whether it must be removed and, if so, the best method for its removal.

3. Choose the type of final finish you wish to use. This should be done from the standpoint of the effect and utility of the piece.

4. Plan in advance, when possible, to prepare the surface for the type of finish selected. This is difficult when paint must be removed. At other times, it is obvious.

Keep in mind that the condition of the piece or its utility will often govern the extent of the repairs necessary, the method of removal of an old finish, the steps required to prepare it for a new finish, and the type of new finish that should be applied.

Additional pleasure and interest in restoration work may be derived by keeping a record of time spent and materials used, as well as costs for each job. Such records are easy to keep. Their purpose is for a basis of comparison between doing the work yourself or having it done by a professional—and as a prop to your ego. You will find that what you have accomplished, and the pleasure you have had, while not completely reducible to dollars and cents, is your "excess profit." If you are interested in keeping such records, it may be done in a simple manner, as follows:

1. Keep data in a small notebook as a permanent record. Allot a separate page for each job and give it a job number. Set down the date the work is started, a brief description of the piece, and the work to be done.

2. A line or two below, write the word *Hours*. Enter here the number of hours worked on the job at different periods. (Example: 3, 1/2, 1, 2, etc.)

3. Farther down the page write *Materials*. Enter those used, together with their approximate or estimated cost.

4. Enter lower down the words *Total Cost*. Decide upon the hourly rate you think your ability warrants, compared to local professional rates. Multiply the total hours spent by this rate to get your labor cost. Add to this the approximate cost of materials. The total of the two will be the cost of the job.

USING IMAGINATION IN RESTORATION WORK

Imagination plays an important part in restoration work. By this is meant the ability to visualize what the finished piece will ultimately look like while it is still in its rough and untouched state. Imagination will aid in the selection of materials to be used, the work to be done, the color, and the approximate final finish.

Without imagination, you will find it

almost impossible to plan your work in advance, to alter a piece, or to adapt it for changed utility. (*Example:* a spinet adapted for use as a desk.) You should be able to see the finished piece in your mind's eye, to visualize what the finish will look like, and to know that to alter or modify a piece will not destroy its beauty or proportions.

In childhood, most of us have strong imaginative ability. As we grow older this sometimes wanes, but it can be developed and strengthened for restoration work by planning and thinking ahead so that we can see the results we are striving to attain. A fine example of imagination is the Spanish-Mediterranean style dining room piece that was made from a beat-up wardrobe chest circa 1920. Unquestionably the biggest aid in transforming the piece were those new plastic carvings—or castings, as the manufacturer calls them—that look, feel, and are worked like wood.

The first step was to cut off the legs and remove the scrolled piece on the top. Then, since the scribed design on the doors would give away the chest's ancient origin, the doors were rehung reverse side out, thus creating flush doors. All hardware was removed, the holes were filled, and the entire piece was sanded. Next 4-inch by 1/2-inch wood strips, beveled at the corners, were used and sanded round at the tops to hide the scrolled valance at the bottom and give the piece a heftier look. These were fastened with finishing nails and glue. Now the chest measured 42 inches

high by 36 inches wide by 18 inches deep and had lost the top-heavy look.

To provide a heat-resistant top 8-inch by 8-inch ceramic tiles of a Spanish pattern were employed. These were framed with 1 by 2 faced with quarter-round molding, to make a flush top.

The plastic carvings that were used come in the form of moldings, medallions, or plaques and are, in effect, wood. They can be cut and nailed, painted or stained. About all you have to remember when working with them is to cut or drill them from the carved side and pre-drill all nail holes. On the illustrated furniture piece, 1 1/2-inch-wide by 36-inch-long moldings were used as trim for the sides. Two lengths provided the vertical pieces on each side, a third cut the horizontal pieces in half. The double drawers were also trimmed as shown, and, with the help of some curved pieces, one of the shapes the carvings are available in, each door was decorated with a cathedral-window style design. Four medallions, placed as shown, completed the design job. All carvings were applied with silicone rubber adhesive, which has a setting time that is long enough to allow repositioning for exact placement, although any household adhesive would have worked well. The carvings were then secured with small flat-headed brads driven through pre-drilled holes. (Don't use finishing nails; when you set the nails you run the risk of splitting the carving.)

After the tiles were masked, the piece was sprayed with a coat of bright red

Figure 1-4. Three stages of the remodeling of a bureau unit

Figure 1-5. Various forms plastic carvings come in

paint. Then everything was masked but the carving which was then sprayed with gold paint and lightly wiped immediately so the red undercoat would show through for an antiqued effect. Two drawer pulls, purchased at a lumberyard, were finished separately and attached by fitting them into 90-degree pipe elbows fastened with plumbing fixture flanges. Of course, towel-bar holders would have done the trick, too.

As a final touch the three top drawers were partitioned and then lined with a colorful felt for silverware storage. The lower drawers hold table linens, placemats, and the like.

CHAPTER TWO

Furniture Repairs

Repair is the most difficult phase in restoration. If you lack the necessary tools or doubt your ability to accomplish fine work, you will do well to take the job to a professional who has the necessary skill and equipment. However, don't avoid repair work entirely. An honest trial may perhaps surprise you by uncovering a skill and aptitude you had no idea you possessed.

Comprehensive directions for furniture repair will be found in the detailed procedures of this chapter. The steps are easy to follow. Even those unaccustomed to the use of tools will not find their use too difficult, as a fair trial will prove. Actually, it's the purpose in this chapter to describe the various methods and use of materials for making *general* repairs on *all* kinds of furniture, rather than to dwell on *special* repairs or replacement of parts for *particular* types of furniture.

INSPECTING FURNITURE

The following suggestions are offered to enable you to plan your work and aid you in its execution:

1. Examine the piece thoroughly. To do this, search all surfaces for cracks, bruises, small holes, or dents and for evidence of dry rot, which may have to be cut out and patched. Check veneer for loose edges, blisters, waves, cracks, dents, or bruises, and for missing pieces. Look for missing parts that must be replaced and for damaged or broken parts that may need repair or replacement, depending on their condition. Place the piece on a level surface and see that it is in balance; if not, one or more legs may be of unequal length, which must be corrected. Long usage may have shortened all the legs so much that you may wish to lengthen them to restore the piece to its correct height.

Check drawers and doors for loose fit or bind. Make sure the hardware, such as handles, escutcheons, bolts and nuts, and hinges, are in place; if missing, they should be replaced. Check surfaces for board warps; if you find any, decide whether they are bad enough to warrant repair.

2. Rock the frame to locate any loose joints. Remove drawers, doors, and the top of the piece, when feasible or necessary.

3. Examine drawers and doors for loose joints in their construction and for any repairs or replacements that may be necessary. Keep all the hardware and fastenings, if removed, in a separate container.

4. Plan your work from the repair to the final finish.

5. Select the procedures necessary for your repair work and read and understand them thoroughly. Each and every step is important, for a step in one procedure may often be worked in with that in another. There are often optional procedures for achieving the same result, but do not deviate from the method you have selected unless unforeseen conditions arise.

6. Make your repairs before you start to refinish so the repairing will not damage the finish. The usefulness of a piece depends upon its soundness. The parts and surfaces must be intact and the alignment correct.

7. Recheck all measurements before cutting lumber. Material cut too short is unusable, and if it is slightly too long it cannot be resawed. Make allowances when ripsawing for smoothing with a plane.

8. Before putting any strain upon a recently glued joint, be sure you have allowed sufficient time for the glue to harden.

9. Have confidence in yourself. However, don't undertake work far beyond your ability. Any beginner can do simple repairs in a satisfactory manner. The rest will come with experience, but do not overestimate yourself.

10. Don't carry repair work too far. The work must be done thoroughly but it is important that you understand that point beyond which you should not proceed. Many fine old pieces have lost their charm, beauty, and much of their value because repairs have been carried too far. This is a failing found not only among beginners but also among professionals.

TOOLS AND SUPPLIES FOR REPAIRING FURNITURE

Furniture comes apart when the glue "bond" at the joints is loosened. Animal glues, generally used in mass-produced furniture, are subject to attack by fungus organisms. They also dry out and become brittle, or they may be weakened by moisture. All these changes in the glue weaken the joints, and looseness in any one joint puts extra strain on the other joints until they too become loosened.

To repair a piece of furniture permanently, you should take it apart, clean off the glue, and reassemble and reglue the joints. To do this, you should have the following tools and supplies available:

Glue (See chart on page 18 for the right glue for the job)

Clamps (rope tourniquets, C clamps, parallel jaw clamps, bar clamps)

A vise

A claw hammer, or leather or wooden mallet

A brace and bit, and a hand drill

A small saw

A sharp jackknife

Dowel sticks (the same size as missing or broken rungs)

Dowel pins (grooved pins, 3/8 inch or 5/8 inch in diameter, to mend dowel joints)

Abrasive paper and smoothing block

Newspapers

Rags

Shears

Vinegar (half pint)

Blocks of wood (to use as pads under clamps

Masking tape and pencil

Some repair jobs don't require all the material in this list; others need supplies that are not listed.

ADHESIVES

Evidence from the early days of furniture construction reveals that glue was rarely used for anything but veneers. Most furniture joints were fastened with nails, screws, dowels, pegs, or wedges.

The glue used in those days was made from hides, horns, and hooves of animals, boiled down to a jelly and then allowed to harden. This dried mass was broken into flakes or ground into coarse powder. When used, it was mixed with water and gently heated in an iron glue pot. This glue was hard, brittle, and brown in color, was not waterproof, and often left a stain on wood. In recent years, several new types of adhesives have come on the market that are far superior in holding power and lasting quality to the glues of former days. But a good adhesive must do two things— *adhere* to the surface to which applied and *cohere* to itself. On those surfaces which are porous, the glue penetrates so that it sticks to that surface. Then the glue remaining outside the pores must adhere not only to that inside the pores but to the object to which this material is to be attached. This is the way it works on wood, fabric, and leather. When you try to glue together such materials as glass, plastic, metal, and glazed tile, which have no porous surface, the glue adheres to the outside only. Then it must adhere to a similar coating of the same adhesive applied to the other material. Since not all glues and adhesives have this latter ability, you can make a poor job by using the wrong one. The rules for good gluing are simple:

1. Choose the right glue.

2. Follow the manufacturer's directions carefully. He knows his product, wants the job to turn out right so you will use it again.

3. Give the adhesive a chance to "set." Nearly all require from at least 24 to 48 hours or more to reach maxi-

mum strength in holding power. If you place a great strain on them before that time, the joint may separate and you will have to do it over. Don't risk failure by being in a hurry.

Kinds of Adhesives

Of the ten major types of adhesives on the market today, the following are generally used in furniture repair work:

Plastic resin glue (urea) is a powder that is mixed with water to form a durable adhesive for wood, plastic laminates, leather, hardboard, and other porous and semiporous materials of nonmineral composition. Although it is not waterproof, it is highly water-resistant, and is unaffected by oil, gasoline, and solvents.

Waterproof resorcinol glue provides strong, durable, waterproof and weatherproof bonds on wood, molded and laminated plastics, rubber and synthetics, and many nonporous materials. It has two components that are mixed before use, and it is applied with pressure.

Casein glue is a long-time favorite for fastening wood to wood, wood to cement and plaster, and fabric or leather to wood. It is available in powder for mix-

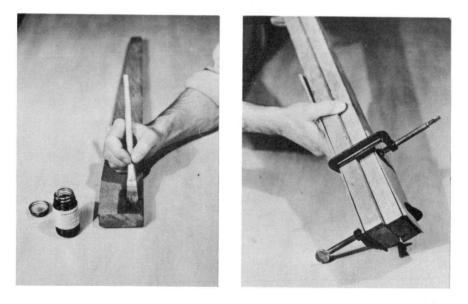

Figure 2-1. *Left:* Liquid animal and fish glues have long been used for wood joining, where they have great strength. The liquid form makes them easy to apply and to store for future use. *Right:* With liquid fish and animal glues, clamping is necessary. You can buy C clamps for a few cents each. Use scrap blocks or strips to keep the clamps from marring the wood.

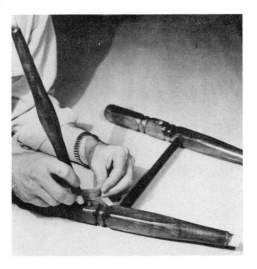 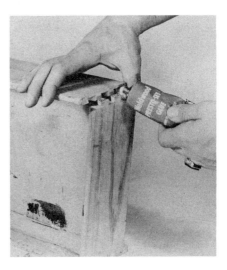

Figure 2-2. *Left:* Liquid animal and fish glues are good for furniture mending. Remove the old glue first, apply a thin coat, let it become tacky, and apply a second coat; then join and clamp. *Right:* Polyvinyl acetate glues, which are often sold in tubes, are easy to use. They are good for gluing any porous materials, but do not have great strength; they weaken under heat and moisture.

ing or in a prepared liquid mix. It sets to great but brittle strength in fairly rapid time, with good resistance to heat but little to moisture. Its color is clear to pale yellow.

Animal and fish glues are liquids used primarily for wood, paper, cardboard, leather, and fabrics. They dry slowly and with relatively good but brittle strength, and poor heat and moisture resistance.

Polyvinyl acetate is a milky-white liquid that dries quickly and colorless. It will not stain, but is not waterproof—it can be washed off. It is used for paper, cloth, leather, and wood where primary load bearing is not involved, as in furniture making.

There are three other adhesives that are sometimes used in home furniture repair work.

Contact cement is a liquid, air-drying adhesive that works immediately and permanently on contact. It does not require clamps, nails, or presses. It has exceptional initial bond strength, dead load strength, resistance to heat and moisture, and other characteristics that make it ideal for bonding such varied materials as leather, wood, fabrics, unglazed ceramics, hardboard, carpet, and floor tile (except asphalt and rubber),

USE THE RIGHT GLUE

	Liquid Hide	Plastic Resin	Casein	Polyvinyl (white)	Resorcin Resin
Advantages					
	Easy to use Keeps well Will not stain	Water resistant Very strong	Glues oily woods— teak, rose- wood, yew Fills gaps	Dries clear Easy to buy, use Fills well	The only glue that is com- pletely waterproof
Disadvantages					
	Deteriorates in moist conditions Subject to fungus attack	Not good for poorly fit- ting joints Requires consider- able clamp- ing pres- sures	Stains some woods Varies in strength Subject to fungus attack	Deteriorates in moist conditions Discolors metals	Dark glue line Complicated mixing High cost
Water Resistance					
	Poor	Good	Fair to Good	Fair	Excellent
Preparation					
	Ready to use	Mix powder with water	Mix powder with water	Ready to use	Mix powder with resin
Working Temperature					
	70°F. or warmer Warm both work and glue in colder tem- peratures	70°F. or warmer	Above freezing	50°F. or warmer Heat hastens setting	70°F. or warmer Heat hastens setting
Application					
	Thin coat to both sur- faces Let get tacky, then join	Thin coat to both sur- faces	Thin coat to both sur- faces	Coat one surface Clamp at once	Thin coat to both sur- faces
Mix Life at 70°F.					
	———	4 hours	8 hours	———	4 hours
Clamping Time					
Hardwood	2 hours	16 hours	2 hours	1 hour	16 hours
Softwood	3 hours	16 hours	3 hours	1½ hours	16 hours

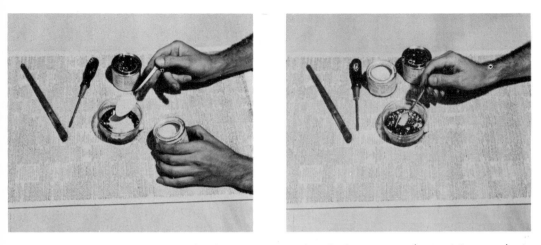

Figure 2-3. *Left:* Accurate measuring is important when mixing synthetic thermosetting resin glues. Mix the activating powder into the resin, using disposable implements. *Right:* This type of glue has a working life of about 4 hours. Don't mix too much, and, unless you can throw away containers, wash them out quickly, within the 4-hour limit.

and plastic laminates. It is easy to use, but manufacturer's directions must be scrupulously followed. While it has several important advantages, its initial bonding characteristics make it rather difficult to use in most furniture repair jobs.

Epoxy glue, a two-component adhesive that must be mixed before use, gives high-strength adhesion over a wide variety of surfaces, including metals, glass, china, ceramics, marble, concrete, brick, most plastics, and wood. It is waterproof and does not shrink. Because it is quite costly, however, it is not often used in large amounts but is ideal for repairs where a small dab will do. Since epoxies have a limited mix life, the two

components—a resin and a hardener—are not mixed until ready to proceed. Setting time can range from an hour to a full day. Due to the fact that this glue seems to work best on nonporous materials, it has never been widely employed in the furniture industry.

Hot hide glue is an excellent adhesive, but it is generally not used by the home handyman. You can buy hide glue in cake, flake, or ground forms. Soak the glue in lukewarm water overnight, being sure to make it according to the manufacturer's instructions. Use glass ovenware or metal containers, double-boiler fashion, to keep it below 150 degrees F., and apply hot. Heat only the quantity needed; frequent reheating weakens the glue. It sets fast, but requires tight clamping and matched joints for proper bonding.

CLAMPS AND TOURNIQUETS

Clamps and tourniquets are used on freshly glued furniture and other articles to hold the glued joints firmly together and in alignment while the glue is hardening.

Before clamps or tourniquets are tightened, the piece should be placed on a level surface to assure correct alignment. Joints to be glued should be checked to see that they are in the proper position. Once the glue has hardened, it is impossible to change the position without damage.

Clamps

The most common types of clamps used in applying pressure to glue joints are as follows:

The *wood clamp* (the technical name) is more commonly called a "hand screw clamp." These clamps come in various sizes with jaws from about 5 to 20 inches long and with maximum openings from about 2 to 15 inches. These clamps are important shop equipment.

The quickest and easiest way to open or close the jaws is to grip a handle in each hand and swing the clamp around. This keeps the jaws parallel as they move on the screw threads. Clamp the jaws evenly and firmly against the pieces to be held together, then tighten the outer screw to give extra tension.

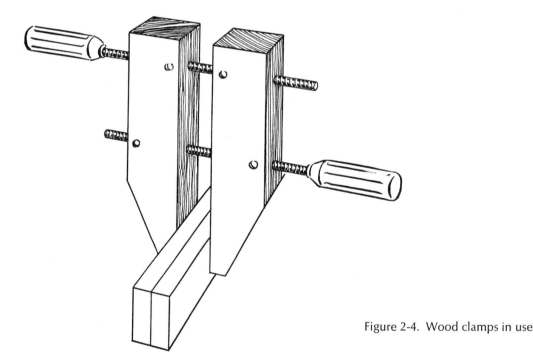

Figure 2-4. Wood clamps in use

The ordinary use of clamps is obvious. Here is an example of a more complicated use of a hand screw clamp. Should you wish to clamp a table frame to the underside of the top and hold it in place while the glue on the glue blocks is drying (or to otherwise strengthen the joint), place a stiff piece of material across and under the frame and clamp this to the top, providing, of course, that the clamp jaws are not long enough to reach into the frame.

The *C clamp* is used only for "spot clamping." Employ a folded wad of paper or a small flat block of wood under each jaw to prevent injury to the wood surface. The sizes vary, with jaw openings from about 2 to 12 inches.

The *bar clamp* is adjustable lengthwise, comes in various lengths, and is used for horizontal clamping on wide width. You will note in the illustration that there are pieces of wood under the jaws of the bar clamp holding the back slats of the chair in place. The wood strips are placed there to distribute the pressure of the clamp and prevent the jaws from injuring the chair surface. A well-equipped shop should include this type of clamp but it is not essential, as a tourniquet may often be used as a substitute.

A *pipe clamp* is often used by the handyman in place of a bar clamp. This type of clamp is available to fit either 1/2- or 3/4-inch-diameter iron pipe. Only

Figure 2-5. Bar and pipe clamps in use

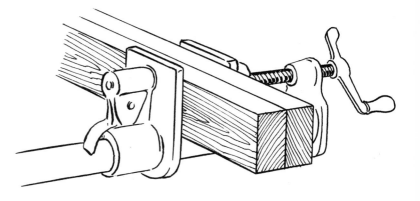

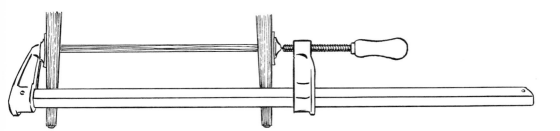

one end of the pipe need be threaded. The handyman should have several different lengths of pipe to use with his clamps. While you can use a long pipe for all jobs, this excess pipe might get in your way. It's always best to use pipe clamps, like bar clamps, in pairs.

Special clamps are made to hold pieces of wood at right angles while they are being joined. Many of these have openings in their sides through which nails or screws can be inserted.

It is possible to make your own clamps for securing work. For instance, a homemade *wedge clamp* is excellent for binding boards that are to be glued together, edge to edge. It is easy to make and use, as shown in the drawing here. Here is how it is done:

1. Construct this clamp from scrap lumber 3/4 to 1 inch in thickness, 6 to 8 inches wide and about one-half as long as the boards to be glued. On the wide side of the clamp material, mark each end at the midpoint from the sides. Now measure up and mark a point 1/2 inch above the center on one end and on the other end 1/2 inch below. Connect these two points by a diagonal line and saw through the material lengthwise along the line. This will give you two wedge-shaped pieces of the required angle, regardless of the length of the material.

2. Apply glue to both contact edges of the boards to be glued and place these edges in the correct permanent position on a level wood surface, over waxed paper, and against a backboard or butt.

3. Drive a nail that is about one and one-half times longer than the thickness of the wedges into, but not through, one of the wedges *only*, on the flat surface near each end, as shown in the drawing.

4. Put the wedges together as sawed, having on the outside and near the middle of the board the one into which the nails were driven, the other one against the outside edge of the board to be clamped.

5. Then drive the nails partly through into the surface below, deeply enough to hold the outer wedge firmly in place but leaving the nail heads above the surface in order that they may be pulled out easily later.

6. Pound the inner wedge tightly in

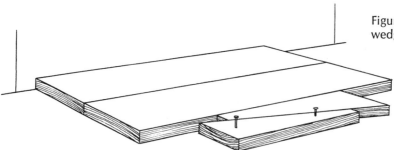

Figure 2-6. An easy-to-make wedge clamp

place from the wider end, creating a strong tension against the glued boards. If the boards to be glued are thin, it will be necessary to place a weight on them to keep them from buckling.

7. Using a damp cloth, wipe off any excess glue squeezed out on the upper surface and keep the boards clamped for 48 hours. A knife may be used later to clear the bottom side of any excess glue.

When using wedge clamps, remember that the work must be done on a level, clean surface, such as a workbench with a back or wall to butt against. A section of a wood floor adjoining a wall is an excellent spot, provided you don't object to nail holes in the flooring.

Tourniquets

The use of a tourniquet is often more satisfactory than a mechanical clamp when properly applied, as it distributes the pressure more evenly. There are two basic types of tourniquets used in furniture repair: the single and the double.

A single tourniquet is made by placing a rope once around a furniture piece, while in the double tourniquet the rope is passed around twice. The ends of the rope are tied together (a bowknot is good) and a stick (a short dowel or large spike is good) is twisted in the rope until the desired tension is obtained.

Many people use the single tourniquet. The double type, however, is better, because when a stick or spike is twisted between the two turns of the rope it can be pushed in back of some portion of the furniture to maintain the tension. In the single type the stick or spike must be tied in position. Moreover, the double type gives more even distribution of pressure.

The best rope to use is a heavy cotton clothesline, because it is soft, strong, and closely woven. There is no need to cut

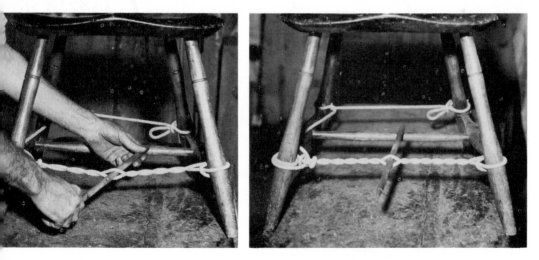

Figure 2-7. The single-tourniquet method of furniture clamping

the rope to the size needed. When two tourniquets are needed on a single job, each end of the rope may be used.

GLUING FURNITURE

There are many pieces of very old furniture that should never be dismantled at all the joints. This is particularly true of some of the old chair rungs. The reason for this is that, in the days before glue was used for joints, a chair rung may have been shaped or turned out of dry wood, with a bulb on the end. This was fitted closely into the hole of a green or unseasoned leg. As the wood in the leg dried, it shrank and the joint became tight around the bulb. Such a joint may become loose with wear, but it cannot be taken apart without damage. Many fine old pieces were put together with wooden pins or wedges and can't be taken apart without damage to the pin, wedge, or to the surrounding wood.

Shaky and rickety joints in such furniture may be reglued, if clean, without taking the piece apart. When joints fit fairly closely, apply glue with a toothpick and work or rock the piece to and fro, to get the glue well into the joint. Whenever possible, turn the piece so the joint opening is in a vertical position, so the glue can flow downward into the joint.

Glue may also be introduced into these joints by using a small oil can, plastic squeeze bottle, or a special tool called a *glue injector*. Drill a small hole (1/16 inch) in an inconspicuous spot at an angle to, or alongside, one part of the loose joint. Insert the tip of the injector into the hole and force glue into the joint. Glue should be forced out around the joint. When this "squeeze-out" appears, clamp the joint, wipe off the excess glue, and let it dry.

For satisfactory results in furniture repair work, follow these general rules for gluing:

1. It is impossible to glue loose or rickety furniture properly if the joints are filled with old glue and dirt. In such cases, if possible, dismantle the piece and clean all the joints thoroughly. To do this, pull all the loose joints apart. Use a hammer or mallet to loosen the joints that don't pull apart easily. Protect the furniture from dents with a block of wood or a thick pad of folded newspaper. Be careful that you don't break parts if you have to force them out of position during this operation.

2. Joints that are firm and tight should be left undisturbed. If such a joint *must* be loosened, soak it with warm vinegar to soften the glue.

3. Scrape, or otherwise remove from surfaces to be glued, all old glue, paint, dust, oil, wax, grease, old finish, etc. Materials to be glued must be thoroughly clean and dry.

4. When scraping or chipping off the old glue, be careful not to remove any wood. If you can't remove the glue by chipping or scraping, or if there is danger of damaging the wood, soften the old glue with warm vinegar. This is a very sticky process that saturates the wood, so you must wait for the wood to

dry before you can continue. Where possible, scrub with an old toothbrush.

5. You need *not* remove all the glue from the end grain of the joint; simply chip off the thickest lumps. Joints are usually constructed with clearance between the end of the dowel, or round, and the bottom of the hole so that the joint will fit snugly at the shoulder.

6. Uneven surfaces must be planed, sanded, or scraped to make perfect, well-fitted contact surfaces. Glue alone will not hold.

7. When possible, slightly roughen or slash the surfaces to be glued to increase the holding power of the glue. This forms a "tooth" for holding power.

8. When dismantling, it is best to take out, clean, and replace one piece at a time, unless it is obvious how to assemble and there are no similar parts. Otherwise, mark the ends of the parts as they come out and the inside of the joints from which they were removed, so you may reassemble properly. This is particularly important, since in many cases a joint would not be loose unless there has been wear, and these worn parts must be returned to the place from which they were taken.

9. When marking dismantled pieces, it is well to make small grooves with a three-cornered file or a chisel on such similar pieces as chair rungs, back slats, etc., because pencil marks may be obliterated in removing dirt, old glue, or paint. However, it is usually sufficient to mark the side wall of the hole with a pencil, as these marks are not apt to be lost in cleaning.

10. Open the pores of the wood to allow the glue to enter freely, either by dipping the parts to be glued in warm water and letting them dry thoroughly, or by laying them on top of a warm radiator or stove, or in the sunshine, until they are warm.

11. When the parts are clean and thoroughly dry, put all of them together again to test them for proper fit. If they fit closely, they're ready to be glued. If an end that goes into a hole fits a little loosely, then follow one of the methods described for *Tightening Round or Square Furniture Joints,* page 53.

12. Before gluing, be sure that all materials, tools, and glue are ready to be used. Have the furniture and the glue at room temperature, since cold glue and cold wood won't bond properly. No type of glue will function properly if it or the piece to be glued is too cold. For best results, gluing and drying of glue should be done in room temperatures of 70 to 75 degrees. Forcing a glue to dry too rapidly will also bring bad results.

13. Glue is used to hold contacting surfaces together. These may be outside surfaces that touch one another or joints, where the end of one piece fits into another. In either case, the surfaces to be glued should fit correctly against each other or the glue will not hold. A thin layer of glue, correctly applied, will hold better than a thick layer, poorly applied.

14. Apply glue to both surfaces of the joints and assemble the parts, checking the marks you made earlier to be sure of getting each part in the right place.

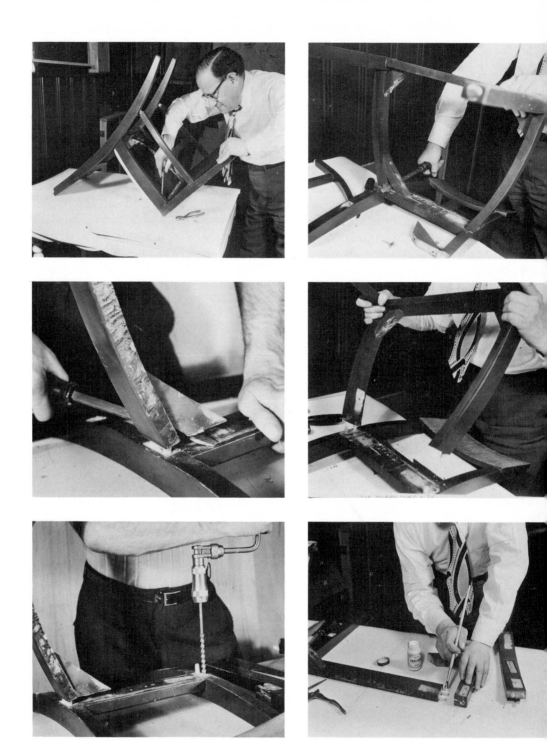

Figure 2-8. Steps in regluing chair legs: (1) Remove the chair seat by loosening the screws that hold the seat to stretchers from the underside. (2) After removing the loose rungs, remove the corner blocks, using a heavy screwdriver as a pry. (3) Remove the stretchers (on which the seat rests) from legs or posts, prying up to break the glue. (4) Pull the sections of the chair apart after the glue seal is broken, letting the tight joints remain. (5) Where dowels or rung ends are broken, use an auger to remove the broken parts from the holes. (6) Apply glue liberally to the new dowels, insert, and apply glue to the open ends for reassembly. (7) Begin reassembly by setting the stretcher back in place, forcing joints together with a mallet. Pipe clamps will draw the chair tightly together and hold it rigid while the glue dries.

Place the piece to be glued on old newspapers to catch any glue that might drop.

15. Apply pressure with clamps or tourniquet, placing thin pieces of wood or folded pads of newspaper under the jaws of the clamps or contact points of the tourniquet, so as not to injure the surfaces. Use waxed paper under the wood pieces or pads when it is likely that glue will run out under them from the pressure applied, as this type of paper will not stick to the glue.

16. Immediately after all of the parts have been glued and clamped, and while the glue is still soft, wipe the glue from the finish. Use a stick cut to a smooth chisel-edge to clean around the joints and small places, and then wipe the rest of the surface with a clean, damp cloth. Let the piece remain until the glue is dry (about 24 hours unless a fast-setting glue has been used).

17. To prevent the glue from running out of a newly glued joint when the piece is to be turned to a different position to glue another joint, wipe off the excess glue and wind a piece of string around the joint several times and knot it. A few hours later, before the glue becomes hard, remove the string. Any excess glue remaining may be removed later after the glue has become crystal hard, with a knife, without damage to the surface.

18. Test on a flat surface all pieces that have many glued joints (chairs, tables, etc.) for perfect alignment. Should this not be done and the piece be out of alignment, it would be impossible to rectify the trouble after the glue has dried.

19. Allow to dry for at least 24 hours in a warm room before releasing clamps or tourniquet and 48 hours before working on further or using a piece thus glued.

20. When the clamps or tourniquets have been released, clean off all glue that was squeezed out from joints and not reached previously. Often the glue may not be crystal hard. Remove carefully with a knife blade, taking care not to injure the surface. Any glue remaining on a surface will cause spots to show through a clear finish.

Gluing Procedures

The following procedures should be followed when gluing furniture pieces:

INSPECTION. Before applying glue to an assembled piece of furniture, examine it carefully to see whether any parts should be replaced or if, perhaps, instead of relying on glued joints for strength, screws, hidden nails, dowels, or braces might not be used to better advantage. (See *Inspecting Furniture,* page 13.)

ALIGNMENT. Before gluing, place the piece on a level surface and see that it is in correct and natural alignment. Clamps or tourniquets are used to hold freshly glued joints firmly and properly together. They should not, however, be used to force an alignment.

When possible, use clamps in pairs on both ends of the work. This will prevent one from separating while the other is being joined. For large surfaces, additional clamps are needed.

Apply even pressure on all clamps. Tighten as far as possible by hand. After a few minutes, take a few extra turns on the clamp handle, if possible. However, avoid pressing in the sides of the work.

CLAMPING. Because some glues set rather quickly, the parts of the furniture to be glued should be in place and braced before the glue sets. Have the furniture and the glue at room temperature if the room is warm, because cold wood and cold glue, except casein glue, may not hold well. Rub the glue well into the pores of the wood with a stiff brush, covering all surfaces to be joined, and press the pieces in place. Freshly glued pieces should be held tightly together until the glue has set hard. Of the various types and sizes of clamps, select the ones that force the parts together the best. If clamps cannot be had, use a rope or a stout cord and with a spike or round stick make a tourniquet to draw and hold the parts closely together. Always protect the wood and finish from damage by using soft wood pieces or thick pads of paper under the clamps or ropes where they touch the furniture.

Find in which direction pressure is needed before putting on the clamps or rope. Always put the greatest pressure right on or near the parts being glued together. Have the clamps or tied ropes directly over or near the joint or break, to draw the pieces close together and to hold them there until the glue has dried.

Sometimes it is necessary to use two clamps or to tie two pieces of rope, one on either side of the part being glued, to get enough pressure to draw the parts together. To hold a chair rung tight, place the clamp on the legs directly over the place where the rung enters; or if rope is used, pass it around the two legs at the point where the rung enters. If a rung is being glued on the other side of the chair at the same time, place a second clamp or rope in the same way.

When a loose chair back or the top of a chair is being glued, pass one end of the rope down the front and under the seat and tie it to the other end that comes over and down the back. Make the tourniquet at the front of the chair. Two ropes, one at each side of the back and tied in the same way, are better than one. If the two ropes slip off the top of the back after they are tied, hold them together with a cord.

BROKEN PARTS. Simple breaks on legs, rungs, spindles, and arms that are diagonal or lengthwise of the piece may be glued; those broken straight across the short way or across the grain, and tabletops, need special tools and skill to repair them.

A new break may be ready to glue and brace together immediately. An old break that has been glued before must first be washed out to remove the glue and then reglued as directed. Because there is likely to be great strain where the back legs are fastened to a chair seat, those places may need to be made more secure. After the glue has dried, put a long slim screw through the leg and the seat. Countersink this screw, cover the head with matching wood or water putty, and paint it, or apply matching shellac stick, so that the place will not show.

GLUING CRACKS. A large percentage of cracks in wood furniture may be glued and clamped together, resulting in a permanent repair. In every case, the accumulated dirt, old glue, and paint must be removed or the new glue will not hold. Usually, this may be done with the point of a narrow-bladed knife, a pin, or any other thin tool. If the crack is straight, it may often be well cleaned by dragging an old hacksaw blade through the crack, with the teeth down and pointing toward the worker. The loose material can then be dumped or blown out.

The procedures for this work are as follows:

For a *crack near an edge,* when possible or necessary, widen the crack with several small and thin softwood wedges. Gently drive in one wedge at a time until the crack is wide enough to insert glue. Remove the wedges and apply clamps. Place over waxed paper and put flat sticks under the jaws of the clamps, so as not to injure the wood surface. A tourniquet may often be used on wide surfaces, should you not own bar clamps.

Brads may be used, if preferred, to draw the crack together after gluing. With care and using a small hammer, drive the brad into the board edge, sink the head below the surface with a nailset, and fill the hole left with stick shellac or wood putty or dough of the same color as the finish. Smooth off carefully with a knife or fine abrasive paper.

For a *crack a distance from an edge,* after the crack has been thoroughly cleaned, test with a strong bar clamp (with blocks of wood under the jaws so as not to injure the surface) to see if it is possible to draw the crack together. If this can be done, apply glue and clamp.

If the crack runs to the end of thick

boards, in crude pieces, it is sometimes well to give added strength on the end by toenailing with finishing nails. (See *Repairs with Small-Headed Nails,* page 48.) The head of the nail may be driven below the wood surface and filled, in the way described for a crack near an edge.

If the crack is wide and long, it may be well to reinforce it on the underside of the board with "mending plates," provided such a repair cannot be seen.

When it is not possible to draw the crack together with clamps, it will have to be filled. (See *Stick Shellac,* page 37.) Remember: don't confuse a space between two boards, caused by shrinkage, with a crack. (See *Repairing Cracks Due to Shrinkage,* page 39.)

USING WOOD SCREWS

When using screws to hold together two pieces of *hardwood,* drill holes of two sizes, the larger in the upper piece of wood and the smaller in the lower. A screw driven in hardwood without proper-sized holes is apt to crack or split the wood, and the screw may refuse to enter it or may break off.

The upper or clearance hole (also called a *pilot hole*) should be sufficiently large so that the screw can be inserted with the fingers, while the lower or anchor hole, drilled for the threaded part of the screw, must be small enough to give adequate holding power. In using a flat-headed screw, countersink the mouth of the upper hole to accommo-

date the screw head, so it will be flush with or below the surface.

When working with *softwood,* holes of different sizes are not necessary unless near an edge. However, it will help to drill a small hole in both pieces of wood, smaller in size than the diameter of the screw thread, to serve as a guide for the screw.

The selection of a screw of correct length is very important, particularly for use in hardwood. The shank or smooth part of the screw should be the same length as the thickness of the upper board, to permit free passage of the screw and leave the entire threaded part for holding power in the lower board.

Use of Tables

Table 1 gives the various lengths (column 1) in which wood screws are made and the number of the screw in both *steel* and *brass* (columns 2 and 3). (The screw number will be explained below under Table 2.

Example 1: Screws 1/4 inch long are made of steel or brass in numbers from 0 to 4 inclusive.

Example 2: Screws 1 inch long are made of steel in numbers from 3 to 16 and of brass in numbers from 4 to 14.

Example 3: Screws 4 inches long are made of steel only, in numbers from 12 to 24, 3 1/2 inches being the longest brass screw made.

Table 2 gives the screw number (column 1) followed by the diameter of the shaft in inches, just below the head.

TABLES OF WOOD SCREW SIZES

1. Length of Screws

Screw Length Inches	Made in Screw Nos. Steel (Nos. inclusive)	Brass
1/4	0 to 4	0 to 4
3/8	0 to 8	0 to 6
1/2	1 to 10	1 to 8
5/8	2 to 12	2 to 10
3/4	2 to 14	2 to 12
7/8	3 to 14	4 to 12
1	3 to 16	4 to 14
1 1/4	4 to 18	6 to 14
1 1/2	4 to 20	6 to 14
1 3/4	6 to 20	8 to 14
2	6 to 20	8 to 18
2 1/4	6 to 20	10 to 18
2 1/2	6 to 20	10 to 18
2 3/4	8 to 20	None
3	8 to 24	12 to 18
3 1/2	10 to 24	12 to 18
4	12 to 24	None
4 1/2	14 to 24	None
5	14 to 24	None

2. Sizes for Screw Numbers

Screw No.	Diam. of Shaft Inch	Size Drill Clearance Hole (For hardwoods) Inch	Size Drill Anchor Hole Inch
0	1/16	1/16	1/32
1	5/64	3/32	1/32
2	3/32	3/32	1/32
3	7/64	1/8	1/16
4	1/8	1/8	1/16
5	1/8	1/8	1/16
6	9/64	5/32	3/32
7	5/32	5/32	3/32
8	11/64	3/16	3/32
9	3/16	3/16	3/32
10	13/64	7/32	1/8
11	13/64	7/32	1/8
12	7/32	7/32	1/8
14	1/4	1/4	1/8
16	9/32	5/16	5/32
18	5/16	5/16	3/16
20	21/64	3/8	3/16
24	3/8	3/8	7/32

The screw number designates the size of the screw, according to the Standard Screw Gauge. Column 2 gives the size (diameter) of the drill to use in hardwoods for both clearance holes (column 3) and anchor holes (column 4).

Example 1: No. 0 screws (column 1) are 1/16 inch in diameter of shaft, so you should use a 1/16-inch drill for the clearance hole and 1/32-inch drill for the anchor hole.

Note: Should an anchor hole be desired for softwoods, use a size smaller than designated. Example: For no. 10 screw, use a 3/32-inch drill in place of a 1/8-inch drill.

Example 2: No. 8 screws (column 1) have a shaft 11/16 inch in diameter, so you should use a 3/16-inch drill for the clearance hole and 3/32-inch drill for the anchor hole.

Driving Screws

When driving a screw, keep the following tips in mind:

1. Before drilling a hole or using a screw, mark a small *x* with a pencil at the exact spot where the hole or screw is to be located, using for this purpose, if possible, a try square. At the intersection of the diagonals of the *x*, make a small dent by hitting a center punch lightly.

2. If the boards are not already fastened together, remove the upper one and place a flat piece of scrap wood under the board where you wish to drill, to prevent the lower side of the board from tearing or splintering as the drill comes through. Drill the clearance hole, using the proper size twist drill. Power hand drills are excellent for drilling screw holes in hardwoods, providing they are handled with care.

3. Replace the upper board in the proper position over the lower, change the twist drill to the size for the anchor hole, and drill, through the clearance hole into the lower board, the full length of the screw.

4. Insert the screw and turn it down to its full length, taking care that the screwdriver does not slip from the slot and injure the wood. A small amount of soap or beeswax applied to the thread of the screw will make it go in more easily.

5. The tip of the screwdriver should fit closely into the screw slot and be as wide as the screw head. This prevents slipping and tearing the slot. It is best to use an ordinary screwdriver for furniture, particularly on fine woods. An automatic screwdriver is apt to slip from the slot and mar the wood.

6. When using steel screws, a screwdriver bit in a brace is good for the final tightening of the screws. Use it for the full drive with large screws, but never use a bit with a brace for brass screws. This metal is weak and will break off easily, usually in the threaded section, causing much trouble.

7. When there are a number of screws in a surface, leave the slots of the screws in a line with the grain of the wood for better appearance. If the screws are on a vertical surface, have the slots parallel with the floor.

REMOVING WOOD SCREWS

A wood screw is often difficult to remove, particularly a steel one that has become rusted in wood or a deeply buried flat-headed screw with a damaged slot. Methods for removing stubborn screws follow:

1. Use a screwdriver whose blade tip is as wide as the screw head and fits snugly into the slot. If the tip is too narrow and the screw is stubborn, you are apt to tear and damage the slot, and make your work more difficult.

2. If unable to remove the screw with a hand screwdriver, try a brace with a screwdriver bit. Press down firmly on the

brace, so as not to injure the slot by slippage of the bit, and give a quick turn to the left (counterclockwise) to unthread the screw. If the screw will not move, follow with a quick thrust to the right (tightening the screw) and quickly reverse the motion, to the left, again. This action will often start the screw.

3. Finally, try to jar the screw loose from its hole in the wood (particularly if the screw is rusted) by pounding it sharply on the head. To do this, place the tip of the screwdriver in the slot and strike a fairly heavy blow with a hammer. (For a flat-headed screw, a round, short steel bar not larger than the screw head may be used in place of the screwdriver.) Then try to move the screw with a hand screwdriver. If not successful, use a brace with a screwdriver bit.

A Round-Headed Screw
With a Damaged Slot

The slot can often be widened or deepened with a hacksaw, since the screw head is above the surface. If necessary, remove the saw blade from the frame. Then follow the above general rules.

A Flat-Headed Screw
With a Damaged Slot

A flat-headed screw with a damaged slot is difficult to remove, since the head is flush with, or buried below, the wood surface. Use the following procedures *in the order given:*

1. Place the point of a nail-set in the extreme right-hand end of the screw slot and at right angles to the slot. Slant it as nearly as possible toward the surface of the board (with the point still in the slot) and strike the nail-set with a hammer. If this will start the screw unthreading, repeat until the screw can be removed with a screwdriver, or until the head is raised enough to grip it in the jaws of diagonal cutters. It may then be worked out with that tool.

2. When the above method fails, try this one. Drill a shallow hole (with a twist drill about one-half the diameter of the screw head) down through the center of the head (taking care not to let the drill go so deep that it will go through the head. Select a screwdriver with a point that is *slightly wider* than the width of the hole and pound it down into the hole, thus cutting slots on each side of the hole. Continue pounding, to loosen the grip of the screw threads in the wood. Press down firmly on the screwdriver and apply a quick, jerky motion to turn it toward the left (counterclockwise). Should greater leverage be required, tighten a monkey wrench over the flattened lower part of the screwdriver blade and push the wrench as you would a brace, while pressing down firmly on the screwdriver so it will not be torn from the screw top.

3. If both of the above methods fail, drill the hole deeper until the head of the screw is cut off from its stem. The upper board may then be lifted off from the lower, the head of the screw picked out from the upper board (or driven out from the underside with a nail-set), and the protruding shaft of the screw may be unscrewed from the lower board with

a pair of pliers. A little kerosene put on the screw head and allowed to soak well into the wood will often help loosen a rusted screw. However, since this may darken the wood, particularly softwood, it should be avoided unless the wood is to be painted or stained with a dark stain.

REMOVING NAILS

Many old pieces of crude furniture were fastened with nails. It is often difficult to extract such nails, particularly the old iron cut nails, if rusted. Before attempting to remove a nail having a large head, especially if embedded, attempt to break its bind against the side of the hole. To do this, strike the head a sharp blow, but take care that the force is not such that the nail is driven deeper into the wood. For this, hold a spike with the point sawed off, or a blunt tool of the proper size, against the head and strike one sharp blow with a hammer. Then use the following procedures *in the order given.* The first is less drastic.

1. If the nail is situated where it can be raised by pounding from the underside of the board, as in the case of a nail holding a tabletop to the frame, place a block of wood 6 to 8 inches in length under the top, as nearly as possible below the nail, strike against the block with a hammer, and then pound the board back.

If this raises the nail sufficiently, draw it out a short way with a claw hammer, having first placed a thin piece of metal —a flat scraper is good—under the hammerhead to prevent injury to the wood surface. Next, place a block of wood, about an inch thick, under the head of the hammer and continue to draw the nail upward. The block under the hammer head gives a more nearly perpendicular pull.

If it is possible to raise the nail only slightly by the blow, insert a hacksaw blade (removed from the frame) between the two pieces nailed together, saw the nail through, and punch it out from the underside of the top board with a nail-set.

2. As a last resort, remove the nail with diagonal cutters. The points of the jaws will leave a slightly larger hole in the wood surface, but this can be filled with stick shellac, wood dough, or wood putty. To remove a nail by this method, force the jaw points under the nail head, squeeze the handles firmly and push down. As the jaws are set at a slight angle from the handles, this downward push will exert a leverage that will lift the nail straight up. When the nail has been raised a little, release the grip, take a lower hold on the nail and repeat until the nail has been entirely withdrawn. (It is well to place a thin piece of metal under the jaws to prevent injury to the wood surface.) Once you have mastered this method of extracting a stubborn nail you will marvel at the ease with which it is done.

WOOD DOUGH OR PLASTIC

Wood dough is often called *plastic wood.* The name is incorrect, as that is a registered trade name of a popular brand of wood dough, just as Duratite is the registered trade name of another brand. In recent years, wood plastic has been used interchangeably with wood dough.

Wood dough dries quickly and may be sanded, planed, drilled, or carved. It will hold nails or screws and can be used to fill cracks, such holes as nail or knot holes, and even for building up broken-off wooden parts. It is one of the cheapest and quickest materials for repairing. If properly applied it will make a strong and permanent repair, but it has one limitation. No matter how carefully it is smoothed, stained, and finished, it will seldom be entirely unnoticeable in a surface. The main reason for this is that, like stick shellac, it has no grain, in contrast to the wood in which it has been used.

Wood plastic has a definite use, and can't be replaced by other materials. Use it preferably in inconspicuous places, or in those places where a part must be built up, then shaped or carved, stained, and finished. Use it also in places where the repair requires strength, the ability to withstand moderate shock without chipping, or where nails or screws must be employed.

Wood dough can't replace stick shellac, which is hard and brittle, for spot repairing, filling small holes, and matching to an exact shade of color to make a repair in a surface inconspicuous. Stick shellac is composed of finely ground wood, mixed with a binder and softened with quickly evaporating mate-

rials. Most of it comes in "natural" color (something like light oak), to be later stained, if desired, but it is also available in colors to match various woods.

Wood plastic comes in tubes and cans of various sizes. Immediately after using any, close the container tightly, as the solvent evaporates very rapidly, causing the contents to harden. Additional solvent may often be purchased for softening wood dough that has thickened beyond practical use, but that which has dried too far can never be again softened for use. When a prepared thinner is not available, a high-grade lacquer thinner is recommended by many stores as a substitute.

How To Use Wood Dough or Plastic

While the instructions on the container should be followed to the letter, here are some tips that you should keep in mind:

1. See that the place where the wood dough is to be applied is thoroughly dry and free from dust and dirt. However, it will stick to old paint if the surface has been roughened.

2. Apply to the spot to be filled or added to, taking extra precaution to keep it from the surrounding surface. Pack it deeply into holes. Wet the tip of your finger and press firmly in place. Allow to dry thoroughly.

3. Strip off the surplus with a sharp knife or chisel and, if on a finished surface, sand smooth with 7/0 or 8/0 abrasive paper, taking care to sand only where applied. Wood dough shrinks slightly in drying. Should the place to be

filled or added to be large, use several applications, one over the other, but only after the previous one has dried thoroughly. Finally, build up the surface to a height slightly higher than the desired final level. This coat is to be cut and smoothed down.

4. When it is necessary to build up a part and there is sufficient depth, drive screws partly into the surface to be repaired, leaving the heads exposed but beneath the surface of the repair, when cut down to the proper level or finished by carving. The wood dough should be packed tightly around the screws. This gives added hidden strength to the repair when finally completed.

5. If when applying wood plastic, it should get on the surface surrounding the repair, it embeds deeply into the pores of the wood and is difficult to remove, especially from a wood with open pores or from a rough surface. It can be removed by sanding, but it is better to use lacquer thinner (*not* to be used on a lacquer finish). The material should not be harmful to other finishes.

If wood plastic must be stained, it would be well to place a coat of wood dough on a piece of scrap wood. Allow it to dry, smooth and sand, and then apply a coat of stain. After the stain has dried, compare the color with that of the place in the piece where the repair is to be effected. Stain usually lightens somewhat in drying and, if too dark, can't be removed. (A single coat of about one-quarter white shellac and three-quarters denatured alcohol, applied carefully to the smoothed surface of the wood-dough repair, will greatly lessen the absorption of stain.)

WOOD PUTTY

Many handymen prefer wood putty to wood plastic. Each has its advantages and are of equal importance in a shop. Wood putty, which can be purchased at paint and hardware stores, is a ready-mixed powder to which water is added when used. Its advantages over wood plastic are that the best types harden more quickly and with less shrinkage, result in a smooth finish, are preferable for use under nontransparent finishes, and can be colored with dry powder color to match wood surfaces.

The disadvantages are that wood putty, also known as *rock hard putty*, does dry to a flat surface and, even though stained, does not look like wood. Consequently, it is a poor material to use on a surface that will be conspicuous, such as in building up a broken-off part. That can be done better with wood plastic. Furthermore, neither wood putty nor wood plastic should be used for filling small holes in wood surfaces, where they will be conspicuous. Stick shellac is the perfect material for such work.

How to Use Wood Putty

Here are some pointers to remember when using wood putty:

1. Put as much as you believe you will use immediately in a waxed-paper cup or small tin can, add only a very small amount of cold water at a time, and stir to a heavy dough. It can't be retempered,

that is, used again by adding more water.

2. Dampen slightly the hole or crack to be filled and the immediate surrounding surface, apply the dough, pack it down with a dampened finger to slightly above the desired level, to allow for possible shrinkage, and take care to keep it off the surrounding surface.

3. Wipe the surrounding surface with a dampened cloth over a finger and allow to dry. Then shave off any surplus with a knife.

4. If the wood putty is to be stained with a dry powder color, add the color to the dry putty powder, but make the mixture slightly darker than the wood to be matched, as it lightens in drying. If necessary to stain a patched spot or crack after the wood putty has dried, paint it first with white shellac thinned with denatured alcohol (about 6 to 1), in order to prevent the stain from soaking in and darkening too much. Test the color before applying it to the repair.

Vinyl patching material is used by some woodworkers, and it is very easy to use. However, it is rather difficult to spot-stain, since there is very little penetration. This material is applied as directed on its container.

STICK SHELLAC

Stick shellac is used for filling cracks, small holes, dents, or gouges in either solid or veneered wood surfaces. It is more often used in hardwood furniture, such as maple and mahogany, where, since such pieces require a fine finish, every small hole or depression should be filled smoothly. It is used extensively by professionals in restoring fine antiques and for repairing high-grade and highly finished new furniture that may have received surface damage in shipment or from handling.

The end of a shellac stick is softened with heat and applied with a flexible spatula where needed. This is called *burning it in*. When such a repair is properly finished, it is unnoticeable in surfaces having no grain, but stick shellac should not be used in surfaces with a distinct grain, except for small areas, since the repair would show distinctly. This shellac is brittle, like sealing wax, which it resembles in texture, and it, too, comes in sticks. It is produced in a great variety of colors and shades, from light buff through brown and into deep red, to match different woods and finishes. Some manufacturers produce these colored sticks in two types: transparent or opaque. Sealing wax may be used for a repair; if it is the proper shade or color.

Stick shellac is sometimes difficult to find. It can usually be purchased in the larger paint stores. If not, an inquiry to a cabinetmaker or one of the better woodworking shops will disclose their source of supply. A set of about ten shades will be found sufficient for most work. However, if it is easily available, it would be a good plan to purchase various shades as needed. One stick should last a long time. It would be well, too, to own a color chart. Many manufacturers furnish them, and they are for sale by their dealers.

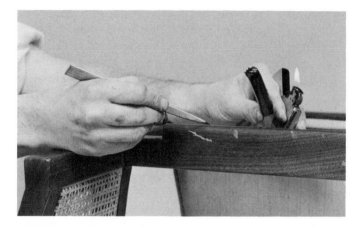

Figure 2-9. Melt stick shellac with a flame and apply with a knife or similar pointed object to the nick in the wood. Apply in small quantities and build up carefully.

How To Use Stick Shellac

Stick shellac is fairly easy to use, especially if you remember the following tips:

1. A place to be repaired with stick shellac should be cleaned thoroughly of dirt and old finsh. Scratching or pricking holes in the bottom of the repair area will give better holding power.

2. Select a stick shellac of the correct color and shade to match the finish of the wood to which it is to be applied.

3. Melt the end of the stick with an electric soldering iron, holding the stick against the iron and directly over the place to be repaired, and permit the molten shellac to fall upon that spot. Excessive heat will burn the shellac, destroy the color, and create bubbles. By the way, the point of a medium-sized screwdriver or the large blade of a pocketknife may be used to heat and melt the stick shellac, if you do not have a soldering iron. Heat will destroy the temper of the metal, so the tool should be an old one.

4. Before the shellac hardens, flatten it out in the depression with a dampened finger or with the blade of a small spatula. The depression should be filled slightly higher than the surface. If necessary, melt and add more shellac. Finally, heat the blade of the spatula over an alcohol spirit lamp and smooth the surface. Allow it to stand until thoroughly hard. Incidentally, a tool for smoothing the shellac can be made from an old round-ended table knife, by heating and bending its blade at a 45-degree angle about an inch from the end. Also remember that a spirit lamp that burns alcohol or canned heat (a jelly substance bought in cans) must be used for heating tools. An inexpensive one can be purchased or made from the base of a small oil can, with wadded string in the top for a wick. Since gas or wood flames leave a deposit of carbon (soot) on the metal, they shouldn't be used, as this will discolor the shellac.

5. Cut the raised shellac down flush with the wood surface with a sharp knife or razor blade, or, better still, with

a sharp chisel, laid flat on the surface with the beveled edge of the blade up.

6. Finish the surface of the shellac with either a worn piece of wet or dry finishing abrasive paper, with pumice stone, or with rottenstone and oil.

7. If you wish to repair with stick shellac a surface that is to be stained later, the stain should be applied and allowed to dry thoroughly before the repair is made. Stains change color slightly as they dry, and it would be impossible to select the proper shellac color for the repair until the resin has dried.

8. The use of opaque stick shellac for deep cracks or depressions, and the transparent type for those that are shallow, results in a more professional-like job.

In recent years, stick lacquer has become available, and many woodworkers prefer it to stick shellac. Stick lacquer is applied in the same manner as stick shellac.

TO REPAIR A BROKEN CORNER OR EDGE. Stick lacquer or stick shellac may be used to repair a broken corner or edge on veneer or solid wood. With tongue depressors and masking tape, build a form in which to mold stick lacquer or shellac. Fill the form with lacquer or shellac. When hard, cut the form away gently with a razor blade and remove carefully. Apply the finish coat.

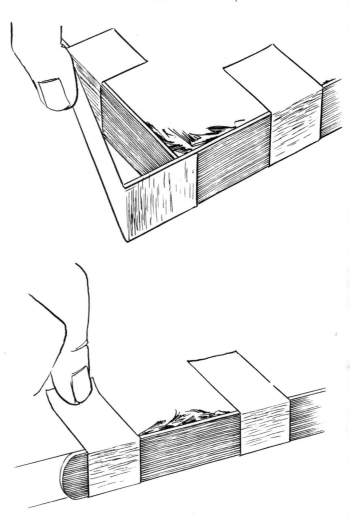

Figure 2-10. Repairing a broken corner or edge with stick lacquer or stick shellac

REPAIRING CRACKS DUE TO SHRINKAGE

When two boards that are placed edge to edge in furniture shrink cross grain, there will be a crack between them. This condition is often found in the tops of tables, dressers, cabinets, etc. The directions given for the repair of these cracks when they run the full length of the boards are intended to apply to such cases. They may also be used for cracks occurring in other parts and types of furniture. The procedure is as follows:

On Tops That Can't Be Removed

Remove from the crack any accumulation of dirt, old glue, or paint. Usually this may be accomplished with a thin knife blade, although it sometimes is easier to scrape out with the teeth of a worn hacksaw blade. Either must be handled with care.

Fill the crack with stick shellac of the right shade of color. In the case of a wide crack, this filling will be a slow and tedious job, but it is the only true method to use on high-grade furniture. If the work is done properly, the crack will not be visible, except that it will show no grain.

Wood dough may be used for the repair, but it is almost impossible to stain it to the proper color and not have it conspicuous, no matter how carefully it is smoothed, stained, and finished.

On Tops That Can Be Removed

Remove the boards and clear dirt, old paint, or glue from the edges. Roughen or scratch the cleaned edges to give the new glue a "tooth" to hold onto. Place the boards together again and test for close contact. If necessary, plane the edges at high spots. If the boards were held in place with screws, fill the screw holes with wood dough, packed in firmly, since the boards, when replaced, won't assume their exact original position. Apply waterproof glue to the edges of the boards and place them together on a level surface, over waxed paper, with their ends evenly in line. Draw them firmly together with two bar clamps or a wedge clamp. Wipe off squeezed-out surplus glue with a damp cloth. Don't release the pressure for 24 hours or handle roughly for 48 hours.

Replace the boards in their former position and refasten by the same means as originally used. Where convenient, use small angle irons and mending plates for additional strength and holding power. Strength may also often be added to the ends of boards by toenailing them in a manner that cannot be seen.

REMOVING DENTS AND BRUISES

Dents and depressions in furniture surfaces may usually be removed in softwoods, and most hardwoods, by the use of water or water and heat. (However, this method will seldom work satisfactorily with hard maple: this must be sanded to remove dents.) Various procedures are as follows:

For Softwoods—Without Heat

In this method water only is used. Apply the water to the depression with a fingertip until the water level is above the surrounding surface. Allow the water to absorb into the wood, adding more until the surface of the depression has lifted higher than that around it. The wood will shrink back a little as it dries. To hasten water absorption, prick a few minute holes in the surface of the de-

Figure 2-11. Removing dents and bruises by using a wool cloth and electric iron

pression with a very fine needle. Such holes will close up and be invisible.

For Hardwoods—with Heat

Fill the depression with water as described for softwoods. Then heat the tip of a spike (a worthless screwdriver or blade of an old pocketknife is also good), and place it in the water until it steams, taking care not to burn the wood with the heated tool. Repeat until the wood fibers are raised to or above the surrounding surface.

Using a Marble or Thimble—with Heat

This is a good technique for a depression *near* a glued joint. First, fill the depression with water as described for softwoods. Then place a clean ink blotter carefully over the water. Press the blotter into the depression with a child's marble or the rounded end of a sewing thimble. Hold a moderately heated flatiron against the top of the marble or thimble, causing the water to steam and the wood fibers to swell. It is important to remember that water will soften the

old-type animal glue, causing joints to loosen or give way.

Using a Woolen Cloth—with Heat

This method is fine for large or obstinate depressions *away* from glued joints. Lay a damp cloth on the depression and place over it a moderately heated flatiron. The warm moisture will cause the wood to swell and raise back to the normal level.

When any of these techniques are applied to a wood surface without a finish, smooth it later with fine abrasive papers of grades from 6/0 to 8/0. Of course, water applied to a nonwaterproofed final finish will turn it white. For methods of reviving the color and finish, see *Removing White Spots or Rings*, page 79.

WOODEN DOWELS

Dowels are cylindrical pieces of hardwood (usually birch), from which are cut short sections, called *dowel pins*, that are used in fastening furniture. When glued into holes directly opposite each other, they hold two members of the furniture piece together. Dowel pins give a hidden strength in flush joints, since they pass through the joint into matching holes and are invisible from the outside. For example, in the construction of tables, the top is usually made of several boards, doweled and glued together, edge to edge, to appear as a single board. The upper frames and stretchers are usually doweled into the legs. The arms of chairs, if butted against the back, and seat members, are doweled. The spare leaves of extension dining tables are doweled to make them match and fit together, but here these pins are glued into the holes on one board only.

Dowels may be purchased from hardware stores and lumber yards. They ordinarily come in three-foot lengths and are from 1/8 to 1 inch in diameter. The type of doweling having a spirally grooved surface is the best.

When making doweled joints, plan your work in advance. There are two factors to consider:

1. The thickness and length of dowel pins should be in direct proportion to the strain to which the joint is to be subjected. Thick, wide, heavy boards exert more strain on the joint and require heavier dowel pins. Dowel pins are seldom used more than 4 inches long and, where possible, not less than 2 inches. (One-half the length goes into each board.) The length is often limited by the thickness of one or both boards.

2. When it is possible to use two or more dowel pins at a joint, it will be better and stronger than if only one were used. Two small pins are stronger than one large one, and two pins provide a more widely distributed holding power. Keep in mind that a joint may often be reinforced from the underside or inside surface with angle irons or mending plates.

Marking for Dowel Holes

Marking for dowel holes may seem difficult to the beginner. The holes must be bored directly opposite each other, on an exact mark, so that when the dowel pins are placed in the holes, the surfaces of the boards thus doweled will come together properly, as had been planned. Marking for the holes is a relatively simple matter but must be carefully followed. The two procedures, according to where the dowels are to be used, are as follows:

EDGE JOINTS. Used when two boards of *equal thickness* are to be doweled together, edge to edge. (*Example:* table-tops.)

1. With a pencil, mark the sides of the boards that form the undersurface, unless it is obvious from the finish on one of the surfaces.

2. Clamp the boards together with the *ends flush* and the edge surfaces to be marked for the holes *upward* and *level* with each other. Have the undersurfaces of the boards outward, as the finish side might be damaged by the clamps or vise, if used.

3. Measure from the ends of the boards the spots you wish to mark for dowel holes. Hold a try square firmly

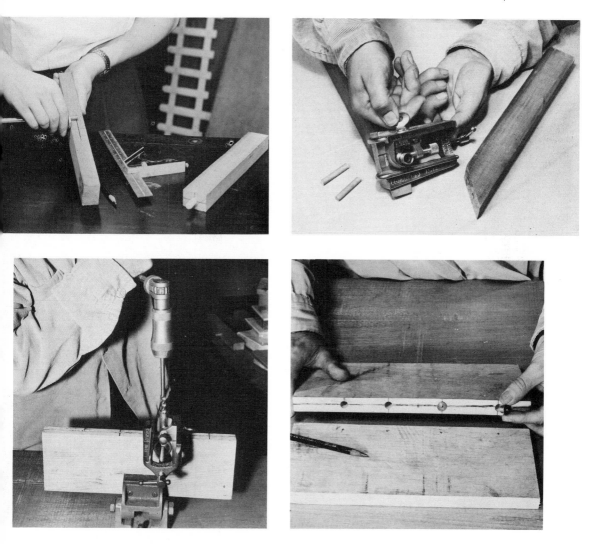

Figure 2-12. How to use dowels in furniture work: (1) Mark the exact position of each hole to be drilled with scriber and square. This enables you to center the dowel in the piece of lumber. (2) Use a doweling jig, where possible, to obtain a perfectly aligned hole. Different-size tubes are used to match the drill size. (3) Hold the piece to be drilled rigidly; use an auger or drill through the jig and the resultant hole will match with the companion piece, to take the dowel. (4) Place the dowel pins in the drilled holes to align two narrow boards when making a wide one out of them. The pins mark the center of the holes.

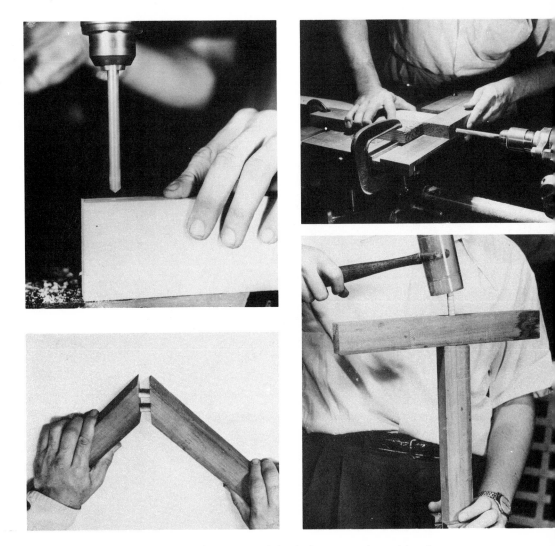

Figure 2-12 *continued*. (5) Mark the center of the hole accurately and let the drill press do the rest of the job. If the board is held properly, the hole will be perfectly vertical. (6) Guide the work into the drill, using a built-up wood-block jig whenever you convert your lathe into a drill press. The woodblock jig assures positioning. (7) Make miter joints strong by using two dowels at each corner. Use the blind method, as shown in photo 4; the dowels fit the inside of the miter. (8) The open-doweling method requires a hole drilled completely through one piece into the next, the glued dowel then being driven into both holes.

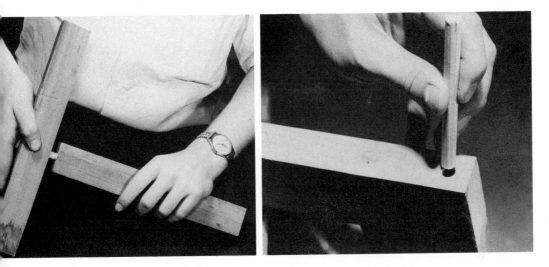

Figure 2-12 *concluded.* (9) Eliminate drilling through wood surface by using the blind-dowel method. It protects the surface of the wood and assures a good finish. (10) Force the dowel and glue into the drilled hole. Some dowels have grooves to hold glue for tight joining. Wipe excess glue off after the dowels are in.

against the side of one board, at those spots, and draw lines across the edge surface of both boards with a knife blade or the point of an ice pick or awl. A pencil line will be too coarse.

4. With a rule (a steel-type rule is best), locate the exact middle of each board edge. Measure from the *outside* surface on each board. Make a small hole on the line at those points, with the point of an ice pick or awl. Enlarge the hole slightly with a center punch. These holes indicate the exact center of the hole you are to bore for the dowel pins.

When there are more than two boards to be doweled together, as in a tabletop, the center boards will have to be marked and bored on both sides, to match the holes in the adjacent boards. Therefore, the boards should be marked (1, 2, 3, etc.) on the underside, to designate the order in which boards and edges go together. The adjoining boards must be treated as pairs.

BUTT JOINTS. These are furniture joints in which the end of a board or other member butts against the side of another. In most cases the dimensions of these boards or members differ at the joint, a smaller one butting against a larger. Here, the exact place where the smaller member butts against the larger must be determined and both members marked for dowel holes, directly opposite each other. For instance, in table construction, the ends of the upper side members of the frame (thin boards) butt against the sides of the legs (wider, thicker, and usually square).

The procedure for marking butt joints is as follows:

1. From heavy paper, make a template that is the exact size and shape of the end of the smaller board by placing the end of the board on the paper and drawing around it with a sharp pencil. Cut the paper on this line and, if necessary, trim it so that it will be the exact size of the board end. Write "top" on one side of the template.

2. Measure and locate the spot on the template where you wish the center of the dowel holes to come. (Wherever possible, use more than one dowel pin.)

3. Place the template back on the end of the piece from which it was drawn with the "top" mark *outward,* and prick through the dots into the wood.

4. Place the template in the proper position on the surface of the piece to be butted against, with the "top" mark *inward,* and prick through the holes in the template into the wood. The reason for this is that, should you have the mark for the hole or holes *off* the center line in the template and were it placed on the second surface with the "top" mark outward, the holes marked would be on the opposite side of the center line.

5. Enlarge the holes in both pieces with a center punch. These indicate the center of the holes to be bored for the dowel pins.

6. It must be remembered that the holes don't go all of the way through the board or member butted into, and that the dowel pins are hidden in the joint. Therefore, it is impossible to locate the spot for the holes except on the faces into which they are to be bored. Follow the steps carefully.

The procedure for marking two boards of equal thickness and width that are to butt against each other is the same as that given above.

Drilling Holes for Dowels

It is assumed that you have already planned on the thickness and number of dowel pins to be used at each joint. Proceed as follows:

1. Use a drill or auger bit of the same diameter as that of the dowel pin selected. It is advisable to use twist drills for holes of small diameter. With only a limited tool equipment, you will have to use auger bits for larger holes. Either may be used in a bit brace.

2. Drill the holes, where marked, to a depth of about 1/4 inch deeper than *one-half* the length of the dowel pin, if the hole is to be small in diameter. When the hole is of larger diameter (5/8 to 1 inch), the added depth should be about 1/2 inch. The extra depth is to allow space for excess glue in the bottom of the hole. (One-half the length of the dowel pin goes into each hole.) It is essential that the holes be drilled exactly perpendicular to the face of the board. A dowel pin will not slip freely into the holes in both members to be fastened if one hole is at an angle to the other. To aid in drilling a perpendicular hole in the face of a board, stand a try square upright on it, the steel-rule part up, next

to the bit. If the hole is being drilled in the end of the board, tack small sticks of wood on two sides of the board and extending above it a few inches, to serve as a guide. By these means you can tell with considerable accuracy whether you are drilling in a truly perpendicular position.

Holes may be drilled to an even depth by the use of a bit depth gauge or, as it is more commonly called, a doweling jig. A gauge may also be made for twist drills by drilling a hole through a cork and leaving the cork on the bit at the depth desired. For auger bits, use a small block of wood in the same manner.

Preparing Dowel Pins

It is important that dowel pins do not bind in the side of the holes, that their sides be grooved or roughened to give a "tooth" to which the glue can hold, and the pins be of the proper length. Prepare them as follows:

1. If the dowel material is not of the kind that comes with a spiral groove, roughen its side surface with a wood rasp. This should be done on the dowel material before the pins are cut to length. The pins should not be a "sloppy" fit but should slide into the holes with use of the fingers alone. A proper fit permits air to escape and excess glue to be forced up the sides when the dowel is put into the hole. Since the holes were drilled with a diameter the same as that of the dowels, even the spirally grooved dowels may have to be eased a little, with abrasive paper or a file.

2. Saw the pins from the piece of doweling to a proper length to fit the hole depths. Take these depth measurements with a small piece of doweling or a nail. Make allowance for the extra depth in the hole to take care of excess glue. When a dowel pin is to be used in a hole that has been drilled from the outside of a surface, where later it will be seen, cut it a little longer. After the glue has set and dried, carefully trim it as close as possible and later sand it to the surface level.

3. Bevel the edges at the ends of the pins slightly, to permit easy entrance of the pin into the hole, and to allow the glue to pass up along the sides of the pin.

When there are a number of pins to be cut and installed, mark the holes and pins with a corresponding number, to tell you where each pin is to go. (In doing handwork, it is impossible to drill holes to the same length.)

Gluing Dowel Pins

Before gluing dowel pins in place, first test to see if the pins will go into both holes without binding. If they won't, the holes may not be directly opposite each other, or they may not have been drilled perpendicular. In either case, it is best to plug up the holes and redrill them, or start again and drill new holes, depending upon the circumstances and conditions found. Sometimes the hole may be slightly enlarged or the pin made a little smaller in diameter. However, don't do anything that will weaken ease of movement; they should not be the cause of any binding. When everything is in proper order, the pins and the contacting surfaces may be glued as follows:

1. Apply synthetic waterproof glue mixed fairly thick to the sides of the holes with a matchstick or nail. Apply glue to the contacting surfaces. Don't use too much glue, particularly in the holes.

2. Insert the pins in the holes of one member and put the other member in place. Wipe off any glue squeezed out with a damp cloth. The two members should go together firmly with hand pressure only. If too much pressure is used (as when clamped) and the pieces are forced together, the result will be disastrous cracks, often caused by too much glue. The bottom of the hole fills and the glue is unable to force itself up along the sides of the pin.

3. Bind the parts firmly together with clamps or a tourniquet, being sure the parts are properly aligned. Keep in a warm room to dry. The clamps may be removed in 24 hours, but no strain should be put on the joint for 48 hours.

Dowel Pin Repairs

A dowel pin that holds a furniture leg in place sometimes breaks, leaving one or both ends in the holes. Bore the dowel out of the hole with a brace and bit, or a hand drill with straight-shank drills slightly smaller than the diameter of the dowel. Never bore beyond the depth of the dowel because the hole may become too deep or the bit in some cases may go through to the other side. Usually you can tell when to stop because boring through the hardwood dowel is slower than boring through the softwood of the furniture. With a small chisel or penknife, chip and force out what remains of the dowel, but don't cut the hole any larger. Wash out the glue with vinegar. Then select a new dowel that fits the hole snugly. Dowels with spiral or straight grooves are best because they let the air and excess glue come out as the dowel is put in place. If the parts of the joint don't come close together, the dowel may be too long. Cut a piece off the end of the pin, round the cut with a sharp knife or sandpaper, then follow the directions for gluing.

REPAIRS WITH SMALL-HEADED NAILS

Repairing with thin, small-headed nails has been a common practice for years. Here is a method for using brads (thin nails for light repairs) and finishing nails or casing nails (thicker nails for stronger repairs) that is not commonly known.

The new step in this method lies in drilling a hole for the nail to be used with a *nail* of the same size and from which the head has been cut. The beheaded nail is held in the chuck of a hand drill for drilling the hole. Should the head not have been cut off, the jaws of the chuck would bind on the bulging head only, instead of on the side of the nail.

When using nails in hardwood or before driving them into a narrow softwood surface, holes should be drilled for the nails. Otherwise, the nails may bend or split the wood.

The use of a beheaded nail as a drill, of the same thickness and length as the one to be used, results in fine holding power. The reason is that, when a hole is drilled with a nail and another one of the same thickness is driven into the hole, the final nail used binds on its *side* the full length of the hole. Furthermore, the hole drilled is not as long as the nail to be finally used, since the nail for drilling has been beheaded and is held in the chuck. Consequently, the nail driven in the hole has holding power in the wood *beyond* the depth of the hole.

The hole can be more easily drilled with a twist drill, especially in extremely hard wood. But this would require the purchase of a variety of sizes (thicknesses) of drills, and it would be difficult to match the drills to the exact size of the nail, without the use of a mechanic's calipers. If the drill was smaller than the thickness of the nail, the latter might bend or split the wood when driven in. If the hole was larger than the nail, it would be a "sloppy" fit with no binding power.

The only difficulty you may have in drilling a hole with a beheaded nail is when using very thin brads. Since they are made of soft steel, they must be properly centered in the chuck, and care taken against bending the brad while drilling.

Many joints—for example, spindles, slats, rungs, stretchers, arm posts, and legs—may often be given added strength by using this method of repair, after the parts have been glued and assembled and if the joint is near an edge.

Such repairs may be accomplished by drilling a hole in the side of the part with or into which the other part fits, at an angle and depth, so that the hole passes through the center of the part that fits into or with the other part. A full-length, small-headed nail is then driven into the hole. Should the nail head be in an exposed position, it may be driven under the surface with a nail-set and the hole filled with stick shellac, of a color to match the surface, or with wood dough or wood putty, which may be stained.

Practically every joint shown may be strengthened with nails used in this way, if they can be driven in from an outside surface. Even splits near an edge of wood 1/8 inch thick may be repaired by this method. The procedure is as follows:

1. Choose a small-headed nail of the thickness and length deemed best for the work. Cut the head off close, center in the chuck of a hand drill with a short bite, and secure firmly.

2. Drill the hole without allowing the face of the chuck to touch the wood surface, thus marring it. When using thin nails, hold the drill steady and straight so there will be no undue strain on the nail. When drilling into the edge of a very thin board, be sure the hole is centered and parallel to the sides.

3. Using a tack hammer, drive a *whole* nail (of the same length and thickness as the one used for drilling) cautiously, until the head is flush with the wood surface.

Toenailing is a method of driving a

nail at an angle, through one wooden member into another, to secure them tightly together. (*Examples:* a vertical upright being nailed into a horizontal member; two boards matched against one another in a flat position and toe-nailed together at the ends.)

The work is done, as outlined previously, by drilling the hole for the small-headed nail at an angle, while the boards are held or clamped together. The nail is then driven in place. Should the repair be located where it may be seen, the nail is driven below the surface with a nail-set and the hole filled. Use as large a nail as possible for the greatest strength.

FURNITURE JOINTS AND FASTENINGS

Many beginners, and perhaps some experienced amateur workers, have little knowledge of the various types of joints used in furniture construction. Among those most commonly used are butt, miter, dowel, mortise and tenon, dovetail, tongue and groove, and plain edge. Each type of joint may be cut by a variety of methods, especially the dovetail type, and each of these is called by a special name.

In restoration work, it is best that all wood joints be put together with glue. Where greater strength is required, it is advisable to give added support by mechanical means.

Below are listed the various types of joints, preceded by letters keying each joint to the appropriate illustration, with comments about them as to their uses and the kinds of mechanical support that may be used with some of them. These are as follows:

A. BUTT—END TO END. Should have mechanical support, unless otherwise held. If the boards are thick enough, doweling is best, as shown on pages 44–45. Can be supported with mending plates.

B. SCARF. A simple method of repairing broken boards by cutting them at an angle. Can be strengthened with screws, with the heads sunk beneath the surface, the holes later filled.

C. SERRATE OR FINGER. More complicated method of repairing broken boards. Best supported on edges with mending plates.

D. BUTT—END TO SIDE. Best reinforced with dowels, as in F. May be supported with a corner angle or flat corner iron.

E. MITER. May be supported with screws, as in B, or hardware, as in D.

F. DOWEL. Best reinforcement to use wherever possible. This drawing shows the corner of the upright piece cut away, for purpose of better illustration. See also P. This joint may be strengthened with mending plates.

G. MORTISE AND TENON. A joint commonly found in high-grade furniture. This drawing also shows the corner of the upright piece cut away. The tenon (as illustrated) is an integral part of the horizontal piece (above the letter G), and is shaped to fit closely into the mortise, a rectangular hole, in the upright piece. A modification of this joint is cutting the mortise all the way through the upright piece, the tenon extending the full depth of the hole. The best mechani-

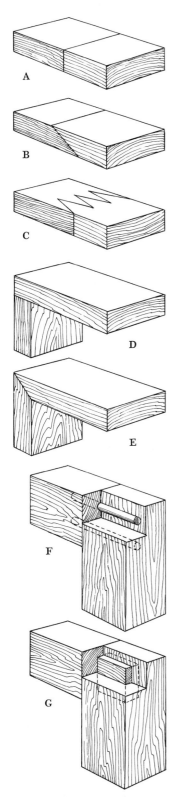

A

B

C

D

E

F

G

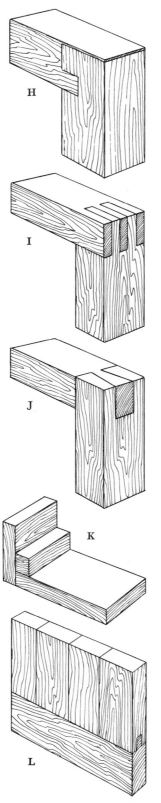

H

I

J

K

L

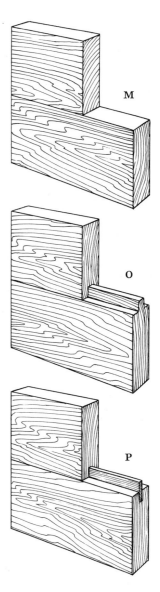

M

O

P

Figure 2-13. Wood joints
you should know. Technique
for joint P is shown
on pages 44-45.

cal means for additional support at the joint is with one or more dowels, to be installed crosswise through the tenon; mending plates may also be used.

H. DADO TONGUE AND RABBET. There are many modifications of this type of joint. It may be reinforced with corner angles and flat corner irons.

I. SLIP OR LOCK CORNER. A modification of the dovetail joint (see *J*). Found often in the back joints of drawers and other places in cheaply built furniture.

J. DOVETAIL. This is a *true dovetail,* also called a *cistern dovetail.* There are various other types and modifications, required in complicated cabinet work. These joints are found mostly in well-made furniture and, if they are tight fitting and properly glued, should require no added support by mechanical means. When the joints are worn and support is needed, it may be supplied by building up each dovetail with small shims or with corner angles.

K. BLOCK. The most common place a block is used is for securing tops to frames, as an added strength to screws that pass from the frame into the top. Not only should the blocks be glued in place but, for additional strength, holes should be drilled through them in two directions, which will permit screws to go through the blocks into both the frame and the top. Thus applied, they will give more strength and have more holding power than corner angles.

L. TONGUE AND GROOVE. Not often used in furniture construction, except in the cheaper and newer type. Typical joint for flooring. (See also illustration N.) The joint may be strengthened with mending plates.

M. PLAIN EDGE. The joint most commonly used in furniture construction (new and old) for tops, etc., made of several boards. When the boards are thick enough, the best mechanical strength (in addition to gluing) is with dowels. The boards may be held to the frame with blocks and corner angles, as directed in *K,* and the boards held together with mending plates.

O. SPLINE. A joint found mostly in finely constructed old furniture. May be strenghtened with mending plates.

P. DOWLING. See joint *A.*

One or more of the types are recommended for use in various procedures throughout this chapter, including securing tops to frames, repairing loose joints or cracks, and holding formerly warped boards in place. Some examples follow:

Corner irons (also called *angle irons*) may be used to join a top more securely to a frame, as on the underside of a table. At least two should be used for each side.

Flat corner irons (also called *L-plates*) may be used on a flat undersurface near a corner, when a joint is mitered, with or without the joint being glued.

Mending plates (also called *cleats*) will reinforce, from the underside, two boards glued together. It is well to install plates a foot to two feet apart, according to circumstances and conditions.

T-plates may often be used to advantage when a vertical member of furniture contacts a horizontal piece, such as reinforcing a leg to a frame member, or on a table.

TIGHTENING ROUND OR SQUARE FURNITURE JOINTS

More loose joints will be found in chairs and sofas than in any other type of furniture. Next comes stands and tables. Most of these loose joints occur where one member joins another and the joint is either round or rectangular (here called *square joints*). Examples of such joints in chairs are the fitting of the back slat or splat into the back post, and the fitting of the spindles into the back slat and seat. Examples in both chairs and tables are the fitting of the stretchers into the legs. Most of the square (or rectangular) joints are of the mortise and tenon type, while the round joint may be either a solid member, shaped round at the end, or a doweled joint that fits into a round hole in another member.

Joints become loose through hard usage and abuse, from lack of moisture in the place in which the furniture is kept, and from shrinkage in the wood. Joints must be tightened properly to effect a permanent repair. It is sometimes advisable to reinforce a tightened joint with added mechanical means, depending upon prevailing conditions and the type of joint. The most simple of methods for tightening round and square furniture joints are as follows:

Tightening a Joint with a Wedge

Thin, hardwood wedges (maple is good) may be used to widen a round piece (rung, stretcher, spindle, chair leg, etc.) or a square or rectangular piece (tenon, slat, etc.) so it will fit against the sides of the hole into which it goes.

To make this repair, cut a slot in the end of the piece with a saw having a very thin blade (a hacksaw blade is good) and apply glue to the slot and hole into which the piece is to fit. Start the wedge in the slot, put the piece into the hole, and drive into place with a mallet. The thickness and length of the wedge must be judged in advance. If the wedge is correct, it will hit at the base of the hole and widen the slot as the piece is driven into place.

When the piece to be widened with the wedge (chair leg, tenon, etc.), is to fit into a hole that goes all the way through the piece, cut the slot, apply the glue, and put the pieces together. Then drive in the wedge. Allow the glue to dry, trim off the wedge, and sand to a smooth surface.

Tightening a Square Joint with a Shim

A very effective means of tightening square-sided joints, such as mortise and tenon, shims are best made of hardwood. They may be of even thickness or slightly tapered, but should be as wide as the hole. Apply glue to the hole and drive the shim into place.

Strengthening a Joint with a Screw

Should the joint be one in which the hole doesn't go all the way through the member into which another is placed, as stretchers or some mortise and tenon joints, it may be strengthened by inserting a screw through the base of the hole into which the second part is placed, and into the end of that part. In such cases, a hole for the screw head should be drilled from the outside of the larger piece, and a smaller hole for the screw shank and thread should be continued through, so that, when the screw is inserted, its head will be beneath the wood surface. This can be plugged later with a small piece of dowel, glued in place, smoothed, and finished.

Plugging a Round Hole with a Dowel

When a rounded end of a furniture part has a loose fit in a round hole in another part, glue a piece of dowel of the same size as the hole into the hole and, when dry, drill a new hole for the part to be inserted. (*Example:* To fit a chair rung into a leg when there is a "sloppy" joint.)

Tightening a Joint with Cloth

This method may be used on either a round or square joint. Cut some cloth strips narrower than the end of the part to be inserted into the hole. Put these cloth strips over the end of the piece in the form of a cross. Trim off the cloth on the sides from one-half to three-quarters the depth of the joint, since the cloth stretches when going into the hole. Apply glue and put the joint together. Should the cloth protrude out of the joint, trim it off closely with a razor blade immediately after the joint is assembled, and wipe off any excess glue with a damp cloth.

SECURING FURNITURE TOPS TO FRAMES

Furniture tops must often be removed to make repairs, and must usually be taken off when warps are to be removed from the boards. Obviously, the removed tops must be put back in such a way that they will be held securely in place. For example, when warps in boards have been corrected by application of moisture or steam, the tops must be secured to the frame immediately, or the warp may return.

The method of securing tops to frames is as follows:

1. Should a top consist of two or more boards, scrape any old glue from the board edges and roughen them slightly (a knife blade is good), so the new glue will have a "tooth" to hold on to.

2. Fill any screw holes with wood dough. Pack in well with a matchstick and allow to dry thoroughly.

3. Turn the boards upside down and place them together, properly matched, over waxed paper on a flat surface. Glue the contacting edges and, if necessary, draw the boards together with a wedge clamp (see page 22). On small tops, this may sometimes be done better with bar clamps, with wood blocks under their jaws.

4. Turn the frame upside down and place it on the top. Locate its exact former position from the marks left at the edge of the frame.

5. Replace any screws that held the top to the frame and tighten securely

(best done with a brace and screwdriver bit). The screws usually go through slanting holes in the frame.

6. Install glue blocks at the joint between the top and the frame, at each end of the frame side, and also along the sides. The blocks should be of hardwood (or semi-hardwood), glued in place and also held with screws, one screw going into the frame and the other into the top. Prior to installation, drill clearance holes through the blocks so that the screws will not bind in them, then countersink the holes. Use flatheaded screws, to take advantage of the pull against the head when the screw is tightened.

7. It is advantageous to use small corner irons at the corners, and, on small pieces where there is but little strain, they may be substituted for the blocks. And if the boards have been warped, it would also be well to install flat mending plates across the contacting edges of the boards of the top, about a foot apart.

REPAIRING DRAWERS

Furniture drawers get hard usage, and as a result they often become shaky and loosened in the joints more quickly than other parts of the piece. Usually, they must be taken apart completely in order to effect a repair. To accomplish this, use the following procedure:

1. Remove the drawer bottom. It slides into a groove from the back of the drawer and is usually held in place with a small nail driven through the bottom and into the end piece.

2. Care must be used in removing the sides if they are connected with each other by dovetail joints. To release the strain, pound on a small, flat board held against the side and next to the joint.

3. Clean any old glue thoroughly from the joints; apply heavy glue to both members and reassemble. A small brad driven into the joints will hold them in place. The drawer bottom acts as a square when reassembling, but be certain that the drawer will fit properly. Try it in the opening before the glue sets.

4. If the drawer drags along its sides, it may have to be planed or sanded. A slight drag may be relieved by rubbing on talcum powder, soap, or soapstone. If the drawer drags on its slides (bottom), the slides must be planed or sanded. If the drawer is too loose vertically, build the slide up by gluing thin strips of wood to it. (An effective but incorrect method of doing this is to put a few thumbtacks on the slide.) If a drawer does not slide easily, it may often be made to do so by applying furniture wax to the slides.

5. Many chests and drawers have wooden knobs or handles that have developed "play" from repeated use. Usually they are fastened from behind with blunt screws or bolts threaded into the wood itself. In many instances, the threads in the wood are stripped. This condition is easily remedied. Dip a piece of string into shellac and wind it around the threads of the screw or bolt, working the material into the grooves. This done,

insert the bolt or screw, screw on the knobs or handles, and let the work dry out.

MAKING AND INSTALLING NEW CHAIR PARTS

Whenever it becomes necessary to replace a part of a chair that is difficult to make or install, have the work done in a professional shop, unless you are fully qualified to do this work and have the necessary equipment and tools. Such work includes the shaping of arms or carvings, or bows and combs for chair backs, and the turning of rungs, spindles, banisters, finials, etc.

The only instructions given here are for the type of work that should be within the ability of those with limited experience. Simple methods of work are given as follows:

Round Chair Rungs

Rungs that are rather large in diameter may be made from an old rake or hoe handle. Those of smaller diameter are best made from a proper hardwood to match that used in the piece.

It is not usually well to taper replacement rungs for any length toward the ends. It is better to reduce the size of the new rung at the ends only to fit the hole, leaving a slight slope or shoulder on the rung at the edge of the hole. The joint must have a tight, or drive fit. Therefore, the end beyond the taper should be round and straight. This may be done with a sharp jackknife. Test for size by first whittling to the proper diameter at the end of the new rung. When it will fit tightly in the hole, twist the rung, thus marking it for continued reduction in size. Then glue and clamp in place or use a tourniquet.

If an ornamental turned rung is missing, sometimes a similar one of the right length can be purchased at a secondhand shop.

Spindles for Chairs

When complicated, turned chair spindles must be replaced, it is best to have them made. The type of round spindle with a bulb and taper toward both ends, such as are found on many Windsor chairs, are rather easily made with a drawknife and a spokeshave, or a short block plane. Shape the spindle roughly with the drawknife and, with the wood held in a vise, finish it with the spokeshave.

When the block plane is to be used for the finish, hold one end of the shaped spindle in one hand, place the other end against a very thin block nailed to a workbench, and force the spindle to bend, while using the plane with the other hand. By bending the spindle outwardly, the bulge of a bend may be shaved off, and in this manner it may be shaped inwardly on both sides of a center bulb. Be sure to shape the ends of the spindle to fit closely in the holes in the top back rail and the chair seat. Test before installation.

A spindle of this type may be installed by bending it. A turned or thick spindle that will not bend may be installed by drilling the hole in the top back rail a little deeper. The spindle is first pushed up into the back rail and then let down into the hole in the seat. Apply glue to the holes before installation.

Odd-Shaped Back Pieces

Many of these pieces which are not turned may be easily shaped with the same tools used for making spindles, by a worker handy with tools. Such parts include arrowhead slats and splats (sometimes also called *slats*), which can often be made from the rim of a large spinning wheel. However, such pieces as a banister back slat, which is turned and then sawed in half lengthwise, should be made and installed by a professional.

Corner Blocks for Added Strength

Such chairs as occasional and dining room chairs, which have a padded cloth-covered seat, are subjected to much greater strain than chairs with solid wood seats. They must depend almost entirely upon the strength of the joint in the frame of the seat to hold them together. To give support to the seat frame, the padded seat should always be held in place in the frame with screws. Screws often do not give sufficient support, and the front legs become loose or the side members of the seat frame loosen at their juncture with the back posts. The same condition may often be found in the frames of overstuffed chairs, sofas, and other types of furniture as well.

The best means of repairing and strengthening such loosened joints is with hardwood corner blocks (birch is

good), glued in place and held with screws. The procedure is as follows:

1. Take out the padded seat by removing the screws (on the underside) that hold it to the frame. Working with overstuffed furniture is difficult, since the padding and sometimes the springs must be removed, so if you are not qualified to do this work, it is best left to a professional. Simple upholstery repairs are discussed in Chapter Eight.

2. Cut triangular-shaped blocks to fit into the four inside corners of the seat

Figure 2-14. Using dowels to repair the leg of an upholstered furniture piece

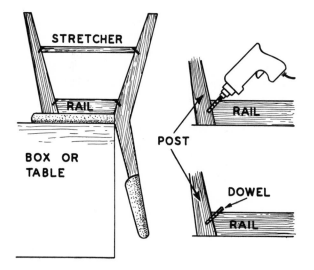

Figure 2-15. When your straight chairs turn into rocking chairs, you can tighten up those loose joints quickly without taking them apart for regluing. Use a ¼-inch drill to sink holes at 45-degree angles ½ inch from the end of each rail into the posts, taking care not to penetrate too deeply. Cut ¼-inch dowels to fit the holes, shaping the ends with a pocket-knife. Cover these with glue and drive them into the holes. The stretchers can be tightened the same way.

frame. They must fit into the corner, and the edge surfaces must contact the seat frame evenly. When possible, the blocks should be at least 1 1/2 inches thick and the side edges over 3 inches long.

3. Drill clearance holes through the hypotenuse edge of the triangular block, at an angle, for the screws to go through into the seat frame, and countersink for the screw heads. The holes must be larger than the screw-shank diameter so they will not bind.

4. Apply glue and screw the blocks in place.

LENGTHENING LEGS

You may sometimes wish to lengthen the legs of antique furniture, when the lower ends have been rotted away due to a damp floor, as happens with tables and chairs, or when legs have become shortened by years of hard usage. Also, the bottom of a leg may have been split or damaged beyond repair, or it may have broken off. A repair can be made by adding a piece to the bottom of the leg. Two methods of doing this follow:

1. If the bottom of the leg is straight (round or square), the easiest method is to dowel a new piece to the bottom, after the leg has been cut off squarely. The new piece should be a little thicker and longer than the original. When the glue has dried, the added section may be shaped by filling and sanding and then cut off to the proper length.

2. If the bottom of the leg is turned, a new turning should be made to match an existing one. This turning can be shaped at the top, with a straight shaft, to fit into a hole to be drilled in the leg bottom after it has been sawed off even. This eliminates the need for a dowel pin.

It is best to have the turning made a

bit larger at the top than the leg into which it is to fit, so that, after it is installed and the glue is dry, it can be shaped down to size. This is a precautionary measure, for, should the hole in the bottom of the leg not be drilled in the exact center, and should the turning to be added be of exact size, the two pieces would not match.

The repair should be made with hardwood and, if possible, of the same kind of wood. After it is shaped it may be stained and finished.

CORRECTING UNBALANCED FURNITURE

Often a piece of furniture may wobble or be unsteady because one or more of the legs is longer or shorter than the others. There are two rather simple procedures for correcting this condition.

Adding to the Legs

If the variance in the legs is slight, a felt chair tip (screwed in place), or metal chair guides (in the shape of a dome with claws, to be pounded in place), may be added to the bottom of the short leg or legs. The former may be available only in furniture stores, but the latter are commonly found in hardware stores.

Cutting off the Legs

This method of correction is a little more difficult. The problem is not only to cut off the correct amount from the leg bottoms, but also to have the cut parallel to the floor, so that the cut end touches the floor evenly at all points. Proceed as follows:

1. To correct the balance, put a small block of wood of the proper thickness under the short leg. This must be done on a level surface.

2. Place another block of wood, of the same thickness as the first, on the level surface, close up against each of the longer legs. Move it around the circumference of each leg, in turn, marking the leg with a sharp pencil, so that there is a circular line on the leg at the exact level of the top of the block.

3. Saw off the leg (or legs) along this mark, on its lower side (leave the line), and if the marks and saw cuts are true, all legs will touch evenly at all points.

4. Bevel off the edges of the saw cuts slightly with a file, and put a small amount of stain on the bottoms of the newly cut leg bottoms. If you find that you still do not have a perfect balance, because of an error in drawing the line or in cutting, this may be corrected by filing the bottom of the leg a little.

If the furniture to be corrected has a flat top, it would be well to place a spirit level on it before doing any of the work, to make certain the top is level. The line around the leg for the saw cut may sometimes be made better with a sharp chisel, provided the block used as a gauge is large and thick enough. (Place the back of the chisel on the block and move it around the leg.)

When it is desired to cut a considerable length off the legs and balance them, first mark each leg with a pencil (measured with a rule) at the desired point where the legs are to be cut off.

Choose a block to be used as a gauge, and measure its thickness. Then saw off all the legs at a distance below the pencil marks of the thickness of the block, and at an angle you believe to be correct, so the leg bottoms will fit flat on the floor. Then proceed with the steps, as related above, marking the block as a gauge, sawing off the legs at the mark, correcting any error in balance, tapering the edges with a file, and staining.

USING OLD WOODS FOR REPLACEMENT

Whenever possible in restoring old furniture, use old wood for patching or for replacement of a part. A surface patch must match the rest of the piece in texture and color or it will be conspicuous.

New wood used for replacement is

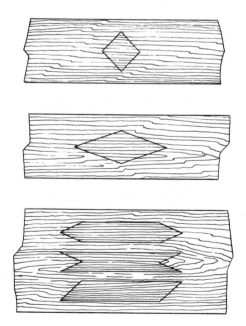

difficult to treat so it will resemble the old wood exactly. Even when stained and finished to agree in color and feeling with the old wood, there will nearly always be a difference in its appearance, due to the variation in grain and texture that age alone can give it.

Old wood will often take color merely from the finish applied to it. The natural oils in woods dry out with age and leave them more porous than new woods. A porous surface of old wood has a different texture from that of a new wood of the same species and grain. When a clear liquid finish (such as varnish or shellac) is applied to old wood, it results in a much darker color than on the new wood. (See *Wet Test for Color,* page 126.)

A proper wood for a replacement part (particularly for a surface patch) may sometimes be gotten by using a piece from the furniture to be repaired. In well-made furniture, such a piece may often be found in the frame, or in such places as the parting rail between drawers, or other places normally out of sight. Before removing such a part, make certain it is of the same species and grain of wood.

It is a good plan to accumulate old woods and keep all scraps, if large enough. Old pine boards, maple bed sides or ends, tables (or just tops and leaves) of walnut, cherry, oak, mahogany, and other woods may often be

Figure 2-16. The five recommended shapes for patches (*top to bottom*): square, diamond, double arrow, reverse arm, parallelogram patches

picked up at reasonable prices from Salvation Army, Goodwill, and secondhand furniture stores, as well as from cabinet shops. It is worthwhile having a supply on hand, whether or not it is needed for immediate use. Keep the old wood in a place away from new wood, and guard it carefully.

PATCHING SURFACES

A small dent or hole in a wood surface can often be repaired with stick shellac of the correct shade and color, or with stained wood dough, so that the repair will not be noticeable. However, when the grain of the wood shows through the surface finish, neither of these materials is practical for a surface patch.

Such surface damage should be repaired by a wooden patch. In order to secure satisfactory results, the wood used for the patch must be correct as to species, texture, grain, and age, and must take a finish that will blend it into the surrounding wood and thus be invisible. If such wood is not available, use a wood of similar grain which you can stain to match the color of the adjoining wood.

Any wood used for a patch must be thoroughly seasoned or the color will lighten greatly while seasoning, unless deeply stained. It should also be cleaned thoroughly to remove any former finish or accumulated dirt, and should then be smoothed with a fine abrasive paper.

Shallow Patches and Plug Patches

A shallow patch fits into a "grave."

This grave is a hollowed-out space with vertical edges and level bottom, cut to size and excavated with a chisel. This kind of patch is used to repair deep bruises, partly rotted surfaces, broken-away surfaces, etc. The depth and size of the grave depends upon how much of the injured surface must be cut away to get into sound wood and true it up to receive the patch.

A plug patch is used when it is necessary to cut a hole all the way through the board, to remove dry rot and injuries that extend through the wood.

The Shape of the Patch

The shape of the patch is very important. Its grain should match as nearly and as exactly as possible that of the surface into which it is to be placed. For this reason, the grain in a patch must run in the same direction as the grain in the surface. If it does, the side edges of a patch will scarely be noticeable when they run with the surface grain. The ends, however, should be cut at an angle of 45 degrees with the surface grain. An end edge, if left at right angles to the surface grain, would be very evident.

The following are the recommended shapes for patches, either long or short. The drawings depict five shapes that will be adequate for most properly designed patches, and show how they should be placed in the surface to be repaired. You will note that, where the end edges of the patch cross the grain in the surface, they do so at an angle of 45 degrees (except for the diamond patch) and the side edges run with the grain in the long patches.

To make a template for the patch, follow a procedure such as this:

1. Measure, with a rule, the length (with the grain) and the width (across the grain) of the place to be patched. Be sure to include all of the damaged or rotted area so that the patch, when in place, will be entirely in sound wood.

2. Choose the type of patch you believe will be best suited for the size and shape of the hole and the circumstances of its position.

3. Make a cardboard template, following the measurements taken of the type of patch chosen. Draw to size, using a straightedge and a 45-degree angle (except for a diamond patch). Cut straight, clean edges with a sharp knife or razor blade.

4. Lay the template (lengthwise with the grain) on the surface and over the place to be patched. Mark closely around the edges of the template on the surface with the point of a sharp knife.

Digging the Grave for a Shallow Patch

The work sounds a bit tricky, but it's not too difficult if care is used.

1. Cut down with a sharp chisel, then, with a mallet, hit the chisel lightly into the surface along the lines marked from the template. Hold the chisel with the beveled cutting edge inward and perpendicular to the surface. Cut square corners.

2. The surface included within your lines is to be cut down to the correct depth. Start about 1/2 inch back from the far end. Place the chisel blade at right angles to the grain of the wood and at an angle of about 45 degrees with the surface. Pound the chisel lightly with a mallet to raise chips. Move the chisel back about 1/4 inch toward you and continue until you reach the near end. Chisel out these chips until you have reached the proper depth. Be sure the bottom is level and the depth uniform.

The depth of the grave is important. When a shallow patch is to be glued in place, its upper surface should be slightly higher than that of the surrounding area. This can later be sanded down to make both areas equal. Disregard the chisel marks on the bottom of the grave. They increase the holding power of the glue. A chisel with deep-beveled sides, as well as a deep bevel on the blade, is best for this work. The beveled sides aid in cutting clean corners, and the deep bevel in the blade makes it easier to cut chips and to smooth the bottom of the hole. The cutting edge of the chisel should be straight and very sharp. The work is more difficult with a chisel having square sides and only a shallow bevel on the blade, even when equally sharp.

Cutting a Hole for a Plug Patch

For this type of patch, a hole of the correct dimensions and with smooth, perpendicular sides is cut *through* the thickness of the board. Proceed as follows:

1. Bore holes (about 3/4 inch in diameter) with a brace and a bit through the board and in each corner within the

lines you drew around your template with a knife point. The holes should be close to the lines, but not touching, at the corners of your outline. (For a smaller patch use a correspondingly smaller bit.) A sharp auger bit is necessary to produce a clean hole. When possible, a piece of wood should be held firmly against the under surface where the point is to come through. This will prevent the undersurface from being torn or splintered. If this is not possible, reduce your pressure on the brace as the bit comes through the undersurface.

2. With a keyhole saw, cut off the hole for the patch. Keep your saw cuts straight and a little inside of the lines for the patch.

3. Remove the wood remaining to the lines with a wood file. The sides of the hole should be properly squared at the corners and at right angles to the surface.

Making a Patch

The following procedure applies equally to a shallow patch or plug patch:

1. Lay the template on the wood you are to use for the patch, being sure that the long dimension is lengthwise with the grain. Mark around the template with a *sharp pencil.*

2. Saw or cut the patch to approximate size, leaving the lines. Test the size by matching it with the hole into which it is to fit.

3. Finish the patch to nearly exact fit. This may be done on thin patches with a sharp knife or with a file or small plane on thick patches. Follow by rub-bing the edges with a piece of moderately fine abrasive paper placed over a flat block of wood. The edges must be clean cut and square.

Make the patch after the hole has been prepared. You may experience difficulties in cutting and trimming the hole to the lines of the template or you may find further rot in the wood that could not be seen from the surface. In such cases, a new template must be made, since the patch cut from the original template will no longer fit.

The patch should fit the hole exactly. It can be made to do so with careful workmanship, a particularly important point when the patch is in a conspicuous place or when installed in furniture with a distinctive grain.

Gluing a Shallow Patch

Mix some powdered waterproof glue reasonably thin. Apply this glue sparingly to the sides and bottom of both the grave and the patch, then press the patch in place.

Gluing a Plug Patch

The first two steps in the following procedures are for gluing a plug patch, while 3, 4, and 5 apply to both kinds of patches.

1. Mix some powdered waterproof glue, fairly thick, and apply it to the edges of the patch and the sides of the hole. Press the patch in place, leaving its surface slightly above that of the surrounding wood.

2. Hold the patch in place by inserting a small brad or pin in the cracks on two

opposite sides so that it will not slip too far into the hole. Remove these fastenings when the glue has begun to harden.

3. Wipe off excess glue and allow the patch to dry for 24 hours.

4. Sand the patch down to the level of the surrounding surface. Sand with the grain, using 8/0 abrasive paper. Take plenty of time, as a careless rush job will show up under a finish in the completed work. You cannot avoid rubbing the edges of the surrounding surface.

5. If glue is permitted to remain in the cracks at the surface level it will show through the finish. When the glue has thickened, but before it has hardened, scrape it out with a pin for a short distance down into the crack. This can be filled later with wood dough (which will take a stain) or with stick shellac of the proper color. This is important if the patch doesn't fit the hole exactly.

Staining Patches

To stain any type of patch, follow this procedure:

1. Stain is usually necessary to match the color of the patch surface with that of the old surface surrounding it. This will require a little experimenting. It should be done on a surplus piece of the wood used for the patch.

2. A paste filler may be needed on the patch to secure the correct surface texture.

3. If the patch was made of old wood, the proper color may often be obtained by using linseed oil without a stain.

Often this may be determined by making a "wet test" (page 126).

4. It is almost impossible to match the color of the patch exactly to that of the surface. If the match is not exact, it may be necessary to stain the entire surface.

If the patch material has been taken from a part of the furniture being repaired, it may match exactly in color by the application of the correct finish alone, providing the woods are of the same species. A sealer coat should be applied before and after a paste filler.

Finishing Patches

When the patch alone is to be given a final finish, it is best to use the same materials that were used for the original finish of the piece. The two finishes will then match more exactly. Usually when you have to patch furniture, you intend to refinish the entire piece. In such cases, you can use different materials for the new finish from those which were originally used, especially when you plan to stain the entire surface.

VENEER

Veneer is a very thin layer of wood, usually cut from the more expensive species of hardwood, and chosen for its beauty of wood patterns or grain. The veneer may be glued to a thicker board base of another species (usually less expensive), which does not have the cherished patterns or grain. In considerable early American furniture, pine was used for the base.

The wood patterns in veneer often match, as on table and dresser tops, or as on old Victorian drawer fronts, where two pieces have been cut out of the same grain pattern (often a crotch), and butted together in reverse position. The effect, as you may have seen, is one of beauty.

Veneered furniture is more apt to be damaged by hard usage, age, and dampness, than solid wood. You may often find marks resulting from flowerpots or hot utensils having been placed upon them. Any of these may break or mar the veneer, or cause the glue to loosen, resulting in defects such as raised edges, cracks, blisters, or waves. Often sections of the veneer lift from the base.

The furniture you are to repair will, most likely, be veneered with mahogany, walnut, or rosewood, as these are the woods most commonly used for veneer. They show beautiful figures when the veneer has been cut from the proper angles of the grain and from such selected sections of the tree trunk as limb crotches, stumps, or abnormal growths in the trunk.

Repairing Veneer

General information on this special type of repair and the methods used are as follows:

1. Where there is a choice, use that method of repair which will permit you to glue the old veneer back in place without cracking it. Such cracks will leave lines in the surface that will show through the finish.

2. If any lines do show, fill them. Use stick shellac of the proper color and shade.

3. When it is necessary to replace a part of the veneer, use material of the same color, grain, and thickness as the old. If you do not have any on hand, take a small sample from the furniture to be repaired to a cabinetmaker. You will usually find them most obliging. Use an old piece of veneer whenever possible.

4. When a piece of veneer is cut to the size of the patch, it is best that the edges be trimmed on a bevel slanting inward, so that it fits tightly when clamped. This makes a closer fit when sanded.

5. Veneer darkens with age. Therefore, since new material will be lighter in color, it will have to be stained. This should be done before it is trimmed as the stain may expand or warp the veneer. After the patch has been trimmed its edges must be stained, but, before staining, sand the edges lightly to get them smooth.

6. New glue will not stick over dirt or old glue. Both should be removed with a knife blade that is sharp, thin, and pointed.

7. Powdered waterproof glue is the best kind to use for this type of repair. Apply the glue thinly to the hole or patch, insert the patch, and cover the area with waxed paper. Clamp a flat block of wood over this place or place a weight on it. Allow the glue to dry for 24 hours; then sand with an 8/0 grade of abrasive paper to level the patch to the adjoining surface.

8. Small veneer repairs are not difficult. If the surface affected is large, it might be best to take the work to a cabinet shop, where they have special equipment. You may be able to hold a newly glued piece of veneer in place on a small curved surface by using a sandbag, but a larger curved area will require a special mold. Also, an extensive flat surface may require a large press.

SMALL DEFECTS. A great variety of small defects are often found in a veneered surface. Among these are bruises, dents, and chips. Stick shellac should be used for the repair of such a defect whenever it is away from the edge of a surface, but, since it is quite brittle and may be broken off easily, it should not be used on corners or edges. Should the defect be at the edge, use wood dough. When hard, sand smooth, stain, and apply a finish.

Small, shallow depressions from bruises may often be repaired by the same method as that given later for plywood. This involves raising the surface with moisture. It may not be successful with very thin veneer, but is worth trying. If it fails, use stick shellac.

LOOSE EDGES. There are two methods for this work, their selection depending on the conditions you find. They are as follows:

Method 1: If there is no dirt under the loosened veneer and there is life left in the old glue, this method should work. At least it is worth trying because of its simplicity. Proceed as follows:

1. Lift the veneer slightly with the blade of a small spatula, being careful not to break or injure the veneer. (The same spatula used for applying stick shellac will do.)

2. Work a little water under the veneer or spray it under with an atomizer.

3. Heat the spatula blade over a spirit lamp (wipe off any carbon deposits if you use some other method of heating) and run the spatula back and forth under the loosened veneer to heat the water and soften the glue.

4. Cover the veneer with waxed paper, a block of wood, and a clamp, or use a weight in place of the clamp.

Method 2: If there is any dirt under the veneer, proceed as follows:

1. Scrape out the dirt and old glue carefully.

2. Spread fresh glue on the end of the spatula blade. Lift up the loosened veneer slightly, insert the blade under the veneer, and press down the veneer. Withdraw the spatula, leaving a thin deposit of glue under the veneer.

3. Squeeze out the excess glue, wiping it off with a damp cloth, or the veneer may bulge. For this you can also use a roller similar to that used in photographic work, rolling it toward the edge. Clamp the veneer or hold it with a weight.

The tool used for this work should have no sharp corners on the blade, as they might tear the veneer. The type of spatula recommended has a rounded end. If you do not own this type of spatula, a piece of heavy paper cut with rounded corners may be used for inserting the glue.

BLISTERS AND WAVES. These are

raised places on the surface of veneer, much like blisters on the skin, as from a burn, that are caused by an excess of moisture, either from the air or because a liquid has been spilled on the surface and allowed to remain until it has penetrated through the veneer to the glue beneath. This results in the glue softening and the veneer swelling. The proper method to use for repair depends upon the circumstances in each case.

Method 1 (unbroken surface): This method is simple. Whether it will work depends upon the condition of the old glue and whether there is enough moisture in the wood below the veneer. If this method fails, use Method 4. Proceed as follows with Method 1:

Place a moderately heated flatiron on the raised veneer surface gently enough so that it will not cause a crack. The iron should not be so hot that it will ruin the finish. The heat should draw out sufficient moisture from the base wood to soften the old glue and make it stick. Leave the iron in place for 24 hours, reheating the iron occasionally.

Method 2 (broken surface): When the raised veneer is broken and a piece is missing, it is usually best to cut out that section and repair with a patch, as follows:

If you have the broken piece or pieces and they still are in good shape, a very satisfactory job can often be done by flattening the edges that are intact with a moderately hot flatiron over a damp blotter. Next, glue in place the loose piece or pieces, being careful that the edge lines do not show. Clamp or hold with a weight for 24 hours (over waxed paper).

Method 3 (cracked surface): If there is *no* dirt under the surface, use this method. If it does not work because the old glue will no longer hold, use Method 5. Proceed as follows with Method 3:

1. Fill the air pocket with hot vinegar and keep the piece in a position which will prevent the vinegar from running out. Let it stand from 8 to 12 hours and then drain off any vinegar that hasn't been absorbed. The vinegar is not to remove the glue but merely to soften it.

2. Dry the area with a moderately heated flatiron over dry blotting paper. The heat will shrink the veneer back to a flattened position and the blotting paper will absorb the moisture.

3. Lift the edge of the crack with a knife blade and, using an eyedropper, insert glue through the crack under both sides. Rub the surface, away from the crack, to spread the glue. Then rub it toward the crack and wipe off excess glue with a damp cloth. Clamp or hold with a weight for 24 hours (over waxed paper).

Method 4 (cracked surface): When there *is* dirt under the veneer and this dirt *can* be easily removed, use the following method:

1. Make a cut with a razor blade, directly *across* the crack, down to the flat surface on both sides. If necessary, cut the *crack* down to the surface through the center in both directions, thus leaving four attached flaps.

2. Scrape the old glue off the bottom surface and from the underside of the flaps. Scrape any glue from the edges of

the cut or flaps to permit the edges to return to their original positions without interference. If necessary, dampen with a wet cloth to make the veneer pliable.

3. Insert glue under the veneer and press the flaps down in place. Wipe off any excess glue with a damp cloth and clamp or hold with a weight for 24 hours (over waxed paper).

Method 5 (*cracked surface*): When there *is* dirt under the veneer and it is *difficult* to remove, use the following method:

1. Make a cut along three edges of the raised veneer with a razor blade. Two of the cuts should be with the grain and the third across the grain. This makes a flap.

2. Raise the flap and scrape away the dirt and old glue from the bottom surface and the underside of the flap. Glue, clamp, or hold with a weight for 24 hours (over waxed paper).

MISSING VENEER. If any of the veneer is missing it will have to be replaced with an inlay that should be of the same thickness and grain pattern as the surface into which it is to be placed. Proceed as follows:

1. Trim the place in the veneer to be repaired so that it will have straight and vertical edges. Two sides of this grave should run with the grain and the other two sides directly across the grain, or at an angle to it, depending upon how conspicuous the patterns in the veneer are and how closely the inlay pattern should match the sound veneer. For this purpose use a straightedge and razor blade.

2. Make a template from a piece of paper. To do so, lay the paper over the "grave" and rub a finger around the edges, producing lines on the paper. Cut on those lines to fit the hole.

3. Place the template over the veneer to be used as the inlay and mark along the edges with a sharp pointed pencil. Trim the inlay with scissors to size and check it for correct fit into the "grave."

4. Glue and clamp or hold with weight for 24 hours (over waxed paper).

Veneer may be purchased from some lumber dealers who specialize in cabinetmaker's supplies, as well as from mail-order houses that cater to craftsmen. If only a small piece is needed, or if it is impossible to locate a matching piece of veneer, you may be able to "borrow" a piece from the back of the furniture unit or from some inconspicuous corner where a missing piece would be much less noticeable. To do this, lift up a small piece of the veneer with a sharp chisel, then cut it out with the point of a sharp knife. With careful cutting and fitting, a surprisingly good job of patching can often be done —particularly if you make the patch irregular in shape rather than a square or rectangle.

Sometimes wood plastic of a matching color may be substituted for a missing piece of veneer.

REMOVING BOARD WARPS

In furniture, the most severe warps are often found in the hinged drop-leaves of tables and hinged chest or stand tops, since they are not secured in a flat position from the underside. To a lesser extent, warps often occur in the tops of tables, dressers, chests, or stands. This warping is found most frequently in tops that are not fastened securely enough to the frames from the underside or when there are not a sufficient number of properly placed glue blocks or screws to hold the top securely in place.

One important cause of warping is the failure on the part of the cabinetmaker to apply a proper finish (linseed oil, shellac, varnish, etc.) to the lower surface when finishing the top, a point to be remembered when you are finishing furniture. This neglect allows a greater amount of moisture from the air to penetrate the wood from the undersurface than from the top, causing the board to warp.

A board may twist lengthwise with the grain, but it warps across the grain only. Furthermore, the board edges of furniture always tend to warp up toward the finished side. This is the concave (inwardly curved) side of the warp. The reverse side of the board is the convex (outwardly curved) side.

If the top or leaves of furniture are badly warped, you will want to correct this condition. A slight warp is permissible by the standards of the collector. In fact, such slight warpage often adds a note of charm to the piece.

If a wide, one-piece board used as a top for furniture is not too badly warped, it may often be clamped back and properly secured in place. However, this work should be done with great care, the clamps being tightened only a little at a time. A narrow or badly warped board should never be forced to flatten out. Disastrous cracks will result.

It is important that an examination be made of the frame, to see if it is sound and rigid. Any work to tighten a frame should be done before attempting to remove a warp. Next, examine the warped surfaces and select a method for removing the warp. This will be determined by conditions and circumstances, such as the degree of the warp, the thickness of the warped boards, and their location in the piece. Various methods are used for tops, table leaves, and other such parts, as related in the procedures to follow.

All of the procedures call for careful planning of the work, and care and prompt action is required to obtain satisfactory results. When using methods employing moisture or steam, the materials for holding a board in place after the warp has been removed should be on hand before any work is started. There are four methods for removing board warps, as follows:

Method 1. Removing Warp with Moisture

This is the most simple method of all. It rarely results in a permanent correction and it is impossible to tell in advance whether it will work or not. That depends upon the ability of the wood pores to absorb moisture or the angle or grain when the board was cut from the log. Therefore, correcting a warp by this method should be followed immediately by securing the board flat by mechanical means, before the moisture dries out and the warp has a chance to return. This method is best for boards that may be secured in place, especially from the underside. (*Examples:* Furniture tops or table drop-leaves held flat with cleats.)

1. Fill any screw holes on the underside of the board with wood dough. Pack the wood dough deeply and allow it to dry thoroughly.

2. Lay the board on damp grass in the sunlight or over wet burlap before a heated stove, with the concave side up. It usually takes from one to several hours for the board to flatten out, the time depending upon the degree of the heat applied, the thickness, width, or density of the wood, and the presence or not of open pores. It may be necessary to remove paint or finish to permit a board to absorb moisture. Usually the back of a board used in furniture has little or no finish, so that is the side to be placed downward to absorb moisture. It is important to recognize that wide tops and wide table drop-leaves are usually made of more than one board, glued together, side by side. When warped, such pieces usually give way where glued and each board warps independently. Because waterproof glue was unknown when old pieces were made, any glue still holding at such joints may give way when moisture is applied.

3. If and when a board has flattened, secure it immediately, before it dries, to the place from which it came. If it was held with screws, replace them. It is advisable to give additional reinforcement by holding the board in place with corner irons and mending plates whenever it is possible to use them. When cleats are to be fixed to a board to hold it in a flattened position, the work should be done immediately after the warp has been removed. (See page 72 for more information on cleats.)

4. If it is necessary to secure a board temporarily in a flat position, do so by clamping rigid strips of wood on both sides near the ends and at the center. Otherwise, the warp may return.

There are many modifications of the above method, mostly complicated and to be avoided. A brief example would be when several boards are involved, as in removable table leaves. They are stacked with wet sawdust between and around them for days, removed, restacked with cleats between them, gradually flattened with clamps across the boards about a foot apart, and allowed to dry. The clamps are made of heavy wood, wider than the boards, with long bolts through holes near both ends. The bolts are tightened in rotation, little by little, so that the pressure won't crack the boards.

Method 2.   Removing Warps with Steam

Warps that are stubborn and cannot be removed by Method 1 will usually submit to this method. With it there is a far better chance that the warp correction will be permanent than if the warp is removed by Method 1, as the penetration goes all the way through the board.

1. Remove all paint and surface finish to permit penetration of moisture.

(Various methods are given in Chapter Four.)

2. Have the board steam-treated in a steam box. Such boxes are not too common, but you should be able to learn where such work is done by inquiry at a cabinet shop or lumber yard.

3. Follow steps 1, 3, and 4 under Method 1.

If the warped board is extremely dried out or of the type that has open pores, it is sometimes advisable to apply a single even coat of half pure white shellac and half denatured alcohol, so that the moisture will not be absorbed too rapidly. However, inquire at the shop to do the steaming before applying it.

Method 3. Removing Warps with Grooves

This method, which may be new to some workers, is a very satisfactory way to remove warps. It is done with a power saw. Since the grooves are cut on the reverse side of the boards only, it leaves the face undamaged, a point in its favor. This method can be used only on parts of furniture that can be removed to be sawed, such as a tabletop, and should never be used on a part where the grooves may later be seen, such as table drop-leaves.

1. On the reverse side of a flat wood surface, the side that swells outward, saw slots (grooves) lengthwise where the warp occurs about 3 inches apart and to a depth of about three-quarters the thickness of the board, with a power saw. The grooves should run lengthwise with the grain of the wood for the full length of the board, but should stop just short of the ends, so they won't be visible on the end surfaces.

2. Replace the board (or top) and secure to the frame by the means previously used (usually screws). Reinforce with corner irons and glue blocks.

In cases of extreme warpage or with thick boards, it is well to straighten the warp from the grooved board (or top) before attempting to secure it to the frame, to avoid cracks. This may usually be done by Method 1 or by laying the board over wet burlap before a heated stove with the grooved side down. This method is similar to that used by carpenters in building construction, when a flat molding is placed around a curved wall surface by sawing cross-grain slots close together on the reverse side of the molding.

Method 4. Removing Warps by Sawing Boards in Strips

This method of removing a warp must be done in a professional shop equipped with the large power tools required for boards wide enough to warp. The work cannot be attempted on boards too thin to plane level, as is necessary in the final operation. Usually boards should be in excess of one inch in thickness for this method to be used, but it may be used on boards of lesser thickness, if the warp is not too great. This method is best for such items as table leaves that are hinged to hang down and the reverse side of which can be seen, as the operation results in a smooth finish on both sides.

For your information, the work is done as follows: The board is cut lengthwise with a ripsaw into strips about 3 to 4 inches wide. The cut edges are smoothed on a joiner, alternate strips turned *upside down* and glued together under pressure. When dried, the board is put through a planer and then sanded on both sides. This eliminates the alternating convex and concave curves that were on both surfaces, due to every other board having been turned over. This procedure for removing a warp destroys all evidence of age and wear, and the board is thinner. The new surface, when finished, will seldom match the rest of the furniture in color or tone, which is why many workers object to this method. When it is possible to use cleats on the reverse side of the board, that method of straightening a warp is preferred by many.

Cleats on Hinged Table Leaves

The best method for keeping a hinged table leaf flat, after a warp has been removed by moisture or steam, is to install cleats. The method is relatively simple and is acceptable to most collectors. The work should be done immediately after the warp has been removed and before the leaf has had a chance to dry out. The cleats should have been prepared previously; the glue, screws, and clamps should be at hand.

Cleats are installed on the underside and across the grain of the leaf. They should be set in from the ends of the leaf, in a position from which they will not interfere with the frame or legs when the leaf is hanging in a vertical position. Usually, two cleats only are used, one near each end of the leaf. However, if it is possible to install a third cleat near the center of the leaf and still not have it interfere with the frame-arm or brace (which swings out from the frame to hold the leaf in a horizontal position), the additional support furnished by this third cleat is desirable.

The procedure employed is as follows:

1. The cleats should be of hardwood (oak is good) to be effective. On medium-width table leaves the cleats should be 3/4 inch thick and from 1 to 1 1/2 inches wide. Their length should be to within an inch of the width of the leaf. When a cleat is installed, its narrow edge is placed against the board, its width dimension standing vertical to the board surface.

2. To make cleats, saw them lengthwise from a board of proper thickness for the *narrow edge* and of a determined width dimension. When a cleat is made in this manner and installed on its edge, it gives the greatest resistance to bend.

3. Use flat-headed steel screws of the proper length to go through the cleats and take a good hold in the table leaf. (Since brass screws are made of soft metal, they are apt to break off if the leaf is hardwood.) Drill holes through the narrow width of the cleats, not more than 6 inches apart and large enough to give free clearance for the shank of the screw through the cleat, and countersink with a rose drill so that the screw head will be flush with the surface. Round off or taper the upper ends of the

cleats so they will have a neat appearance, then sand off the upper edges.

4. Take an accurate measurement of all four corners from the edge of the leaf to the leg or frame. If the table isn't too large, it would be well to turn it upside down over cloth or paper while doing the measuring. Draw lines from these measurements, representing both side edges of the cleats. Leave enough clearance so the cleats will not interfere with the leg or frame when the leaf is in a hanging position. The lines must be parallel to the board ends. Recheck your measurements and marks. It is most important that they be correct.

5. Remove the finish from the surface where the cleats are to be installed to assure the glue holding. Mix some powdered waterproof glue fairly thick. Apply the glue to the contact side of the cleats. Secure the cleats to the leaves with screws, driven in tight with a screw bit and brace, being careful to place the cleats in the exact position between the drawn lines. Wipe off the excess glue with a damp cloth.

6. Apply clamps over the cleats to hold them firmly to the leaves. Place in a warm room and permit the glue to dry for at least 48 hours. Should the cleats be installed immediately after the warp is removed, the leaves will contain moisture.

7. Stain the cleats to match the underside of the leaves.

8. After the leaves are thoroughly dry, seal the underside of the leaves with a coat of 75 percent commercially boiled linseed oil and 25 percent pure turpentine or with a coat of varnish or shellac. This prevents absorption of moisture from the air, which was the cause of the warp.

Cleats are often applied by this method to the undersides of the hinged tops of chests, stands, etc., after a warp has been removed. In these cases, when space will permit, they are most frequently installed under the extreme ends of the top.

Another method of keeping a board flat, after a warp has been removed, is with hardwood dowels. Holes are drilled from side to side through the board edge, and dowels are inserted and glued. The drilling requires accurate workmanship, and is best done with a power tool. The boards must not be too wide nor too thin. This method is rarely used, but it is well to know about it.

FURNITURE CASTERS

Casters used for furniture are usually the stem-and-socket type. The stem is the round shaft on the top of the caster. Near the top of this shaft is a slight groove. The socket, called the *ferrule*, is the hollow tube made with a beveled top and a plate, with upturned jagged teeth, at its base.

To install casters, proceed as follows:

1. Measure the outside diameter of the socket tube. This is usually 3/8 inch for smaller casters and 1/2 inch for larger ones.

2. Drill holes in the center of the bottom of the furniture legs, about 1/2 inch deeper than the length of the socket

tube, to allow the stem to protrude through the tube. If the furniture legs are small in diameter, wrap friction tape around their base to give added strength to the wood while drilling. If this isn't done, the legs may split, especially if the bit is not sharp or the wood is very dry. The bit should be the same size as the diameter of the socket tube.

3. Pound the socket gently into the holes until the jagged teeth engage firmly in the wood of the leg bottom.

4. Insert the stem in the socket and hit sharply with the palm of the hand. This forces the stem through the beveled top of the socket, where it is held by the groove. Finally, remove any friction tape.

Here are three methods of tightening loose caster sockets:

1. Shred steel wool, twist it, and work it into a string. Wrap it tightly around the socket, cover it with plastic-type glue, insert it in the socket hole, and drive it into place.

2. Wrap the socket with tough paper or cloth, glue, and insert, or wrap it with friction tape or rubber bands and insert.

3. Fill the hole into which the caster fits with wood dough that has been thinned by additional solvent. Assemble the caster with the stem in the socket and drive it to its full depth in the hole before the wood dough has a chance to harden. Twist the stem around several times and work it up and down a bit to make a space at the end of the stem so it won't bind when the wood dough hardens.

CHAPTER THREE

Reviving Old Finishes

When restoring old furniture, as was stated in Chapter One, don't attempt to make the piece look new. Part of the charm of old furniture lies in the sign of age and use that remind you of the people and social customs of earlier days. Overrestoration can ruin a fine old piece.

If the piece isn't disfigured, for instance, leave some indications of age— the marks of the cabinetmaker, some signs of wear. The proof that a piece is an antique, and its commercial value as well, often rests on these marks.

Many old pieces of furniture *need only to be cleaned*. If the original finish is smooth, adhering well, and isn't chipped, do not remove it. Removing the original finish of a valuable piece, if it is in good condition, would destroy much of its value and character. That is, amateur refinishers often assume that an old finish must be completely removed and a new one applied. The condemnation of the old finish often results from jumping to conclusions too quickly after a casual inspection, but such condemnation results more often from inexperience and not knowing that the existing finish can be revived.

Old finishes often become dull and drab in appearance merely from an accumulation of dirt and grime from long usage. Both shellac and varnish finishes will take on a milky effect from dampness, while varnish will check or alligator when the atmosphere is too dry. Under normal conditions, this could have been avoided if the furniture had had the proper care (see Chapter Nine).

The finish on furniture is subject to scratches and marks from carelessness or accident. It may become stained by acid and ink, or it may have white spots or rings left by hot dishes, water, or alcohol.

Methods and materials to be used for reviving the entire finish, or for spot work, are described in this chapter. The effort to revive an old finish is well worth a trial. Should it not be a success, little time and material will have been wasted. The old finish may then be removed and a new one applied.

TEST BEFORE CONDEMNING AN OLD FINISH

It is always possible to test these simple methods of restoring an old finish by trying them on a small area. If the results are not satisfactory, the old finish can then be removed and a new one put on without any harm having been done. Some old furniture, such as the Hitchcock chair and the Boston rocker, were constructed of wood that was intended to be painted, and these should be restored by painting, although those still carrying their original paint can often be revived.

Generally speaking, checking and white on an old finish are signs of bad adhesion. A simple test of brittleness and adhesion is scratching an old finish with the edge of a coin. Make the test in an inconspicuous place, because the scratches will probably whiten. (The test scratches may be removed as described later in this chapter.) If you can't scrape through to the wood with relative ease, you probably can get away with rejuvenation instead of removal.

You will sometimes find the varnish

Figure 3-1. Identify the wood. It is nearly always possible to identify the wood in a piece of furniture by inspecting its underside, where bare wood is usually exposed. Often, too, the manufacturer stamps the species name here. Some of the things to consider are: Is it plywood, veneered, soft or hard wood, open- or close-grained? What is the age of the wood (antique or modern) and design (inlay, carved, etc.)? Now form a mental picture of the finished product—type of finish desired, upholstery, grain, color, and general appearance. Let this serve as your guide and the refinishing chore will seem much easier.

on furniture made of hardwood such as mahogany, maple, or walnut in bad condition due to age or abuse. Such a finish may have been marred, dented or scratched. If its condition isn't too bad, it can usually be satisfactorily revived, but, when it is very badly checked or alligatored, there is no alternative but to remove the old finish and replace it with a new one, suitable to the type of furniture and its use.

It is often difficult for the amateur to determine what kind of an old clear finish was used on a piece of furniture. It may be shellac, varnish, or lacquer, with no definite characteristic to indicate the finish that was used.

A test to show whether the material was shellac can be made by applying denatured alcohol with a rag to a small area (free from wax) to see whether the finish will soften or rub off, since shellac is always thinned with alcohol.

To distinguish between varnish and lacquer, treat a small area (free from wax) in the same manner, but with lacquer thinner. Lacquer will soften or rub off with this material, which will not be harmful to varnish. Very often a heavy lacquer finish may be distinguished from one of varnish by the mere fact that lacquer is almost crystal hard as compared to varnish.

CLEANING MAY RESTORE FURNITURE

If the finish is smooth, use a furniture cleanser-conditioner to:

1. Clean wood and restore the natural grain and color.

2. Disguise scratches and retard checking.

3. Remove cloudiness and dullness caused by smoke, grease, and dust.

4. "Winterize" furniture to withstand the dryness and heat of rooms in fall and winter.

There are a number of products made for reviving old finishes. These are often sold in grocery, hardware, and paint stores, but it may be best to inquire at a furniture store for special types of products. Most of the commercial products are for general cleaning of dulled surfaces. When this work is completed, as directed on the container, the piece should be finished with a good furniture polish or waxed. Some products will do a much better job than others in the complete elimination of foggy, cloudy, milky, or faded conditions, while others will usually remove white spots, rings, or other blemishes.

No harm will be done to a finish that is basically in good condition by the use of a good commercial product made for the purpose, providing it is used correctly. It should be tried on a small space to see how it works. The balance of this chapter gives treatments for various ailments on finished surfaces, and in some cases special products are recommended.

REVIVING A CLEAR FINISH

The condition of an old clear finish may often be such that it can be revived satisfactorily with a single coat of the same kind of finishing material that was originally used.

Wax should be removed before attempting to revive a surface. This may be done with a cloth dampened with turpentine or a product especially made for the purpose.

After the wax is removed or if none was used, the piece should be washed with a solution in the proportions of two heaping tablespoons of sal soda to one gallon of hot water to remove traces of grease, etc. Rinse with clear water, wipe with clean dry cloths, and allow to dry thoroughly. On veneered pieces, use the solution sparingly, washing, rinsing, and drying each surface independently and quickly, so as not to loosen the veneer.

When the piece is dry, sand it lightly (to give the new material a "tooth"), apply the finish material, and allow it to dry. Then complete the finish to the smoothness desired (as directed in Chapter 6) for the type of finishing material used.

Another *very* good cleaner-conditioner can be made by mixing three quarters boiled linseed oil (buy commercially prepared—don't attempt to boil linseed oil at home) and one quarter gum turpentine in a glass container with tight-fitting lid. Shake well before using. You can store the mixture indefinitely in a tightly closed container.

To apply this cleanser-conditioner, dip a cloth into the oily mixture floating on the surface of hot water. Apply the solution to a small area at a time. Keep excess moisture away from joints to prevent the glue from softening. Rub the surface with the mixture, using a toothbrush on carvings and grooves. Dip a

3/0 steel wool pad into the solution and rub lightly with the grain to remove dirt, if needed. Dip a clean cloth in clear, warm water, wring, and wipe the surface. Wring dry for shellac surfaces. Wipe the surface with a dry cloth. Discard the mixture when cold. Do *not* reheat—it is flammable and it will become gummy.

After cleaning, use furniture polish or wax, if desired.

WASHING SOILED FURNITURE

There are three basic methods of washing soiled furniture, as follows:

Method 1 is commonly used for mild cleaning. Wash the piece thoroughly with a soft, clean rag and warm water to which a small amount of pure white soap has been added. Wipe dry with clean cloths.

Method 2 is used for badly soiled pieces, and is especially suitable for varnish finishes. Wash the piece with a mixture of 1 quart of hot water, 3 tablespoons of boiled linseed oil, and 1 tablespoon of turpentine. (Turpentine aids in cutting dirt; oil lubricates, feeds, and polishes.) Use an old double boiler to keep the mixture hot, since it is flammable. Rub the wood with a soft cloth that has been wet with the solution, then polish with a soft, dry cloth. Repeat if necessary.

Method 3 is used for removing butter, finger marks, syrup, etc. Use green soap, available in drugstores. Soak a soft cloth with warm water, put a teaspoon or more of the soap on the cloth, fold it into a pad, and rub the surface of furniture with a circular motion until it is covered by a lather. Then remove the soap with a cloth dampened in tepid water, and finally dry and polish with a dry, soft cloth, rubbing with the wood grain.

Great care must be taken when washing veneered surfaces to prevent the water from getting into the glue and loosening the veneer. When the veneer is not broken or cracked, wash only a small area at a time and quickly wipe it dry. Should the veneer be in poor condition, the surface is best cleaned with a commercial product made for the purpose. Remember that water damages shellac too, so be sure to use care when employing a cleanser-conditioner containing it.

REVIVING WAXED SURFACES

A scratched or spotted waxed surface may often be revived by rubbing it with a little turpentine on a soft cloth and then rewaxing it.

REVIVING FOGGY, CLOUDY, MILKY, OR FADED FINISHES

It is difficult to state just what materials and methods to use to revive extensively overcast or faded finishes. It may at times require a bit of experimenting. Any wax on the surface should be removed. Sometimes this itself will remove an overcast, especially when turpentine is used as the medium.

1. *Shellac finishes* may often be revived with a mixture of 2 parts paraffin oil and 1 part white shellac. Apply and rub with a cloth for mild cases, but with a pad of 3/0 steel wool for severe cases, rubbing with the grain. Wipe dry with a clean cloth.

2. *Varnish finishes* can generally be revived with a mixture of half raw linseed oil and half turpentine. Apply as in Method 1, above.

3. A *foggy appearance* should be treated with a mixture of 1 quart of clear water to which has been added 1 to 2 tablespoons of vinegar. Dampen a clean cloth and rub with the grain.

4. A *milky effect* on varnished surfaces, particularly in damp climates, is probably due to an inferior grade of varnish. A good rub with a mixture of half raw linseed oil and half turpentine will sometimes improve or entirely remove the defect. Use a closely woven cloth of hard texture. If the piece is not improved, it will need to be refinished.

5. Commercial materials are made for the purpose of reviving old finishes. Apply as directed by the manufacturer.

When applying any of these materials to carvings and other raised or depressed surfaces, use a small hand brush, dipped in the mixture. Then dry with a cloth. Use a pointed stick under the cloth for depressions.

In àll cases, after cleaning use furniture polish or wax, if desired.

REMOVING WHITE SPOTS OR RINGS

Most white spots or rings on a furniture finish may be removed. The method employed depends more upon the depth of the damage than upon using a particular method for various types of finishes. However, finishes that are very thin must be treated by a less severe method than that used on those which are thick.

It is best to attempt to remove the white spot first by simple methods, using mild abrasives. If not successful, it will then be necessary to use more drastic means. The methods listed run from the mildest to those requiring special materials or coarser abrasives.

1. Dust cigarette or cigar ashes over the spot or ring; dip a 3/0 steel wool pad or cloth into a lightweight oil—sewing machine oil, lemon oil, paraffin oil, olive oil, or raw linseed oil. Then rub lightly *with* the grain of the wood. Apply lightly to the entire surface to prevent spotting; wipe surface with a soft cloth.

2. Dip your finger into lightweight oil, then common table salt, and rub the spot with the mixture. If the white spot is old or very deep, much rubbing may be needed.

3. Dip a cloth in clear water, wring it, then hold it up to the mouth of a bottle of household ammonia to moisten. Whisk the damp cloth over the spot lightly and quickly. Rub with a dry cloth. This method is especially good for a varnished surface.

4. Rub with rottenstone and some lightweight oil on a cloth as described in Method 1, above.

5. Rub with a thick paste made of grade 3/F pumice powder and lightweight oil, using a cloth as described in Method 1, above. This method is also especially good for a varnished surface.

6. Use a commercial product for removing white spots from furniture, following the manufacturer's directions.

If the white on a surface is successfully removed, follow with an application of furniture polish, after a slight interval to permit the cleaning materials to evaporate or harden. If the white cannot be removed, it will be necessary to refinish the surface or the entire piece.

REMOVING SCRATCHES

On woods with a *natural finish,* use a furniture cleanser-conditioner (see page 77) to clean and blend the color of the scratched area with the natural finish. To disguise minor scratches, use broken pieces of the meat of nuts, such as pecan, English or black walnut, Brazil, or butternut. Rub diagonally along the scratch until it darkens.

On woods with an *oil finish,* use a 3/0 steel wool pad dipped in lightweight mineral oil, *boiled* linseed oil, or paraffin oil. Rub carefully with the wood grain. Wipe the entire surface with a cloth slightly moistened with oil, then with a dry cloth. In badly scarred instances use boiled linseed oil.

On woods with a *lacquer finish,* use a shellac thinner or denatured alcohol solvent to soften the shellac around the scratch.

On woods with a *varnish finish,* use gum turpentine to soften the varnish and cover a small scratch. You may also employ a commercial scratch remover; use as the label directs.

On *stained* woods with a *natural finish,* use a stain to blend with the old stain, of the color and type originally used on the piece, if possible. For example, on wood stained yellowish-brown, use a base of walnut stain and a small amount of yellowish maple over the base. (See page 134 for colors.) Dry, and apply the type of finish used originally.

To color a scratch, apply colors in oil (such as burnt umber), thinned with turpentine, or varnish stain, ready mixed in wood colors. If too concentrated, add the stain to a clear varnish of the same brand; or commercial scratch remover; or clear varnish tinted with colors in oil; or colored varnish. The latter may be added to clear varnish of the same brand. Set the container in a pan of hot water before applying.

To apply a stain or solvent to a scratch, proceed as follows: With your finger or a small pointed brush, apply the stain or solvent diagonally along the scratch, feathering it out toward the edges. When dry, rub the surface with a lintless cloth. It may be necessary to repeat the process after 24 hours. When dry, rub varnish or shellac finishes with pumice and oil, lacquered surfaces with rottenstone and oil (see pages 153–57).

Deep scratches may be filled with a stick lacquer or shellac of a color shade that matches the finish most closely (see pages 37–39).

When scratches have been removed, revive the finish with furniture polish or wax.

REMOVING PAPER ADHERING TO A SURFACE

To remove paper that has adhered to a wood surface, pour enough *warm* lightweight oil on the surface to saturate the paper. Let stand. Rub lightly with a 3/0 steel wool pad. Apply more warm oil, rub again. Wipe the surface with the oil, then with a dry cloth.

REPAIRING GOUGES, HOLES, AND BURNS

When wood finishes are gouged or burned, repairs may be made on the existing finish. Or, during refinishing, burns, holes, and gouges may be filled after several coats of the new finish have been applied and are dry.

To remove the discoloration or char, scrape the charred spot or darkened edges of the holes with a knife blade or a 3/0 steel wool pad wrapped around an orange stick or pencil. Brush out the scrapings with an old toothbrush. To bleach the area, sponge it with denatured alcohol. Repeat the process, if necessary.

If the damaged area is *shallow,* fill it with several coats of colored sealer or varnish, if stained. Or use a clear sealer or varnish.

If the hole is deep and *no larger than a thumbnail,* fill it with stick lacquer or shellac (see pages 37–39).

If the hole goes clear through, use wood putty or wood dough underneath (see pages 34–37). Fill the top with stick lacquer or shellac.

REMOVING INK OR DARK SPOTS

Ink spots are difficult to remove. Ink penetrates deeply into wood, especially when the surface is not finished, as is often the case with old desks. The stain may usually be minimized and sometimes removed by the application of pure household ammonia, or a saturated solution of oxalic acid. It is often necessary to use repeated applications (see page 107).

When an ink stain is only on the surface of a finish, it may usually be removed with a mixture of pumice stone and light oil made into a paste. Rub with the grain of the wood, using a soft cloth. Clean off with turpentine on a clean cloth.

When ink spots are on top of a finish and do not completely bleach out with treatment, they may often be completely removed by scraping the finish. However, this is useless to attempt for stains on bare wood.

Dark spots may often be bleached out with ammonia or the oxalic acid solution, as outlined above. If not, they may have to be scraped.

CORRECTING CHECKED AND ALLIGATORED FINISHES

Many different terms are applied to those finishes that have dried out, leaving shallow or deep grooves that look like the skin of a snake or alligator. Those with very fine lines are here termed *checked* while those with deep lines are called *alligatored*. The fine lines (or grooves) may usually be corrected so well with a product known as an amalgamator that they will scarcely be noticeable.

It is usually considered a hopeless task to correct an alligatored finish satisfactorily. However, methods are given here that have sometimes been satisfactory to professional finishers. It is advisable to take the time to try and remove an alligatored condition. If it is unsuccessful, no harm will be done. It may aid in the removal of the old finish, prepatory to applying a new one.

To correct a *checked finish,* proceed as follows:

1. Fold into a pad a piece of closely woven, smooth-textured, clean cloth 12 to 15 inches square. Wet this pad with benzol or a commercial product that may be used as an amalgamator. Gently rub, a limited area at a time, to soften the finish and to smooth it out. Rubbing is done best with the wood grain. These liquids evaporate rapidly, so keep the rag wet at all times. When a finish begins to smooth, complete the area by extremely light rubbing, to avoid rolling up the finish.

2. Allow a smoothed finish to dry overnight and then polish with wax or furniture polish.

An *alligatored finish* can sometimes be corrected by the following methods:

Method 1 is especially adapted to varnished surfaces. Apply either benzol or a commercial amalgamator to an alligatored surface in a liberal quantity with a paintbrush. Keep the surface wet with the material until the finish softens and flows. Then allow the finish to dry completely and smooth by rubbing with a pad and grade 3/F pumice powder. Use water as a lubricant with the powder for a varnish finish and oil for a shellac finish, as directed in the procedures for those finishes (on pages 153 and 163).

Method 2 may be successful with shallow grooves. Apply a very limited amount of a commercial paint and varnish remover to a small area at a time with a dauber made of a soft, lintless cloth. Rub lightly to soften slightly and spread the finish, thus filling the cracks. The action of the remover may be stopped by wiping the surface with a lintless, soft rag, saturated with turpentine. This method is slow in action and hard to complete. It is used best on that part of furniture which has been alligatored from heat or sun.

It's very important to remember that paint and varnish removers are extremely flammable, while benzol or commercial products capable of use as an amalgamator are extremely volatile. They should be used with care, in a well-ventilated room in which there is no flame or spark.

REPAIRING A SPOT WORN THROUGH THE FINISH

This work is the bane of refinishers. There is nothing difficult in the procedure, except that it takes time and much care in selecting or mixing a stain that will ultimately match perfectly the surrounding color. Applying a finish over the stain and rubbing down is the simplest part of the work.

There are mixtures, sold in small bottles and in many colors, that are made especially for this work. However, some of the products that have been put on the market have not been successful. Make inquiry at a paint store for a good product. Should an improper product be used, it might cause damage to the spot applied, especially if it is the wrong color when dried out.

The following method is for the use of standard products:

1. Prepare the spot and feather the edges by rubbing lightly and carefully with no. 400 wet or dry finishing paper. Use water as a lubricant on the paper for a varnish finish and a light rubbing oil (paraffin is good) for a shellac finish. Clean off and allow to dry completely.

2. Apply a thin wash coat to the spot, using the same material that was used for the original finish. This is to keep the stain from penetrating into the wood pores, so that it may be removed if not the proper shade. (See *Preliminary Wash Coats,* page 128.)

3. The spot is then stained. It is wise to check for the exact shade of color before the stain is used by applying it (if possible) to an unexposed part of the piece. When satisfied with the color, thin the stain considerably and apply coat after coat until you have obtained an exact match, allowing each coat to dry thoroughly. Each coat of stain adds color. Sand lightly with used 7/0 or 8/0 finishing paper between coats.

4. Apply enough coats of the same

kind of finishing material as was used for the original finish to produce a smooth and high gloss. Allow each coat to dry completely. Sand lightly between coats with worn, fine paper, as used for the stain.

5. The last coat of finishing material on the spot must then be rubbed down to match the surrounding finish in texture. For an ordinary *semigloss* finish, use 2/0 or 3/0 steel wool, rubbing carefully with the grain. For a smoother grade of this finish, use no. 400 wet or dry finishing paper. Follow the directions in step 1, above.

For a *polish rubbed* finish, smooth the spot with grade 3/F pumice powder and a rubbing pad, using water on varnish and light rubbing oil on shellac.

6. Complete the finish by waxing or using furniture polish over the entire piece.

It is advisable to use an oil stain for this work, as it may be more readily removed than any other type of stain material should the color not match properly. (See *Oil Stains*, page 132.)

RESTORING BRASS HARDWARE

Brass hardware—handles, keyhole plates, handle plates, escutcheons, hinges—is favored for its durability and appearance. If the original brass hardware remains, it adds to the value of an old piece, so restore it if possible.

To polish *solid* or *pressed brass,* apply a commercial brass cleaner or household ammonia. Or remove the brass hardware gently, if you can, and soak in household ammonia briefly. Then rub with 3/0 steel wool, and clean in warm, soapy water. Rinse and dry. Rub hard-to-remove spots with hot vinegar and salt or lemon rind and salt.

To polish *antique-finish brass,* use pure lemon oil (not lemon oil polish).

To polish *brass finishes,* apply a commercial brass cleaner or a thin paste of rottenstone and commercially boiled linseed oil. Wipe off paste with a cloth moistened in boiled linseed oil. Polish with a dry cloth. Or use a paste of whiting and denatured alcohol solvent. Allow it to dry on the brass before polishing. Wash, rinse, and dry.

When the brass finish on hardware has peeled, you cannot restore it. You may paint the hardware off-black to cover discoloration, if you wish.

REVIVING PLASTIC SURFACES

While laminated plastic surfaces cannot be classified as old or antique material, it's used a great deal in furniture making.

Laminated plastic surfaces can become dull and shabby in spots from excessive wear or when abused by the use of harsh abrasives. To bring back the new look, clean occasionally with a low-luster cream polish or a silicone-base wash—the wax will protect against wear and make daily maintenance easier because spilled things will not stick. On badly worn areas a single-step auto cleaner-polish will provide great improvement. Pour a little on a thick pad of clean, soft cloth and rub on the worn area, using long, even strokes and rubbing with the "grain"—that is, the length of the pattern. Do not use a circular motion, as this might cause swirl marks. Rub until an even gloss develops, then wipe with a clean cloth. Then apply a cream polish or a silicone-base wax.

To remove spots from laminated plastic surfaces, do not try to remove with abrasive cleaners, which damage the surface of the plastic. A treatment with an automotive cleaner, as just described, will remove most spots and will not scratch the plastic.

If a laminated plastic surface should become loose from its base, scrape away the old adhesive as best you can. Make certain both surfaces are dry. Then, with a spatula, spread a waterproof counter-top adhesive (but not contact cement) in the crack according to the manufacturer's instructions. Then clamp or weight the plastic in place. If the plastic is under tension at a nearby point —for example, if a faucet escutcheon is bearing on it—release the tension before clamping the laminated plastic in place.

CLEANING MARBLE

Small scratches on marble surfaces can usually be eliminated by rubbing them with a very fine abrasive paper, such as no. 10/0. Then wet the surface with water, sprinkle on a little polishing putty or tin oxide (available at most drugstores), dampen a cloth, and rub briskly until a shine appears.

While large scratches and pit marks can be removed by rubbing evenly with abrasive materials of successively finer grit sizes and polished as above, the job is rather difficult and is best done by a professional marble dealer.

Stains can be removed from marble surfaces. After soaking the stains in very hot water, you can start the cleaning with a stiff brush and one of the more powerful detergents. If you apply pressure during the scrubbing and then rinse with clear water, most of the stains will disappear. If any are left, you can make use of cleansers with a lye or other *alkaline* base (plain lye soap, for instance, or cleansers with a lye content), since marble is basically limestone and won't be damaged by this type. Avoid acid cleansers of all kinds, as they destroy marble. Be sure to rinse well, for marble is quite porous and dirty water can sink in deeply and stain it.

Oily stains made by butter, salad dressing, cream, etc., should be removed before waxing. Place a white blotter soaked in lighter fluid over the spot and let dry. Repeat several times if necessary. If this does not remove all the stain, bleach with an application of hydrogen peroxide to which a drop or two of ammonia has been added.

To remove marks that have been etched into the polished surface by alcohol or acids in fruit juices, sand gently with finest sandpaper. Then rub with polishing putty or tin oxide on a damp, soft cloth. Tobacco stains may be bleached out with an application of hydrogen peroxide.

To clean marble safely and apply protection at the same time, use a cream polish or a silicone-base spray wax. These waxes are especially recommended for white, rose, and beige marbles. For additional protection on black and porous travertines, follow cleaning with a light coat of paste wax and polish thoroughly while the wax is moist.

If a marble item should break, wash the edges if dirty and let them dry thoroughly. Then apply an epoxy glue to one edge, press together, and clamp securely. Allow at least 24 hours before removing the pressure.

CLEANING LEATHER

Leather on tables, chairs, and other furnishings may be renewed and maintained by washing with saddle or castile soap and water. Avoid using furniture polishes, oils, and varnishes on leather. These often contain solvents that will make leather sticky.

To clean leather on furniture, use lukewarm water with mild soap flakes and a teaspoonful of vinegar. Dip a clean, soft cloth into the water and rub it over the leather. Then, to wash off any suds, go over it with the cloth wrung out in clear, lukewarm water. When it is thoroughly dry, polish the leather with a lamb's-wool shoe brush or a dry, soft cloth onto which you have squeezed a dab of neutral leather dressing from a tube. This cream also comes in liquid form in a bottle, and may be obtained at any notion counter or shoe repair shop. Never use polish on leather; it will weaken the surface.

CHAPTER FOUR

Removing the Old Finish

There are no shortcuts to good refinishing, and each step, from removing the old finish to the final rubdown, must be followed in order and each properly completed before proceeding to the next one. With most finishes, the work is not too difficult—if you are willing to follow directions carefully, have the necessary patience and take sufficient time to do the work well. Experience is necessary to develop the proper technique when working on a highly finished piece.

When it is obvious that the old finish must be removed or when you have determined, from the test described in Chapter Three, that its removal is necessary, the question then arises as to the proper procedure to follow to secure the best results and cause the least amount of damage to the wood surface.

There are three techniques you can use for removing an old finish. They are:

1. *Using paint and varnish remover.* In liquid, paste, or semipaste form, these are combinations of several chemicals that soften the old finish so it can be lifted off with gentle scraping or washed off with water.

2. *Mechanical removal.* This means that the job can be done by hand scraping and hand or power sanding.

3. *Heat.* This method accomplishes the removal by using a portable blowtorch or an electric heating tool to burn the old finish off.

Of the three, the best and most harmless method of removing an old finish is with the use of a commercial paint and varnish remover. Before using this material, estimate the time it will take to complete the entire job of removal. It is poor practice to allow the remover to dry on the surface of your work. When you see that cracks and crevices are filled with old paint, or that there are

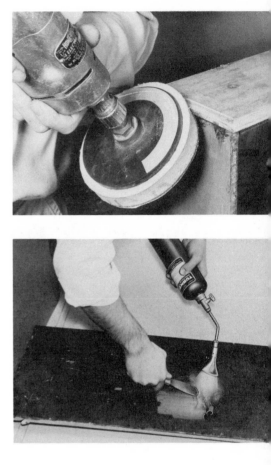

Figure 4-1. Three techniques for removing an old finish: *upper left,* paint and varnish remover; *upper right,* mechanical removal; *lower right,* heat removal.

places where the finish is thicker than on the surface, it is well to apply the remover to those spots first, to allow extra time for softening. Incidentally, there is no difference between a paint remover and a varnish remover, and the industry usually refers to the material simply as *paint remover.*

Both the mechanical and heat methods of finish removal are not recommended for the home handyman. The original wood surface may be destroyed by scraping with sharp tools or glass, by planing, or even by butting too deeply with abrasives. Also, a beginner may risk gouging the surface when using a scraper or sanding machine for the first time. The mellowness and texture (patina) in the old wood are built up by age, years of use, and repeated rubbings. Once removed, patina cannot be restored.

With the heat method of removing a finish there is not only a danger of fire, but it is also difficult to do without scorching the wood. In addition, the heat technique is often slower than either one of the other methods, therefore it is foolish to take the extra risks involved.

You should not use lye to remove wood finishes. Lye burns and pulps the wood. It is difficult to remove and counteract the action of lye, so the new finish often remains sticky and does not dry. It may even come off in a short time.

In the present chapter will be found, under titled procedures, various methods for removing old finishes and complete instruction for their use, preceded by detailed information as to their value, use, and abuse.

Do not let yourself get discouraged. The piece on which you are working may appear to have been ruined by your efforts, and the task of getting off all the smeared mess of old finish may seem impossible. But time and patience will produce results worthy of your effort.

EQUIPMENT YOU WILL NEED

No job should ever be started without proper tools. The same rule applies for stripping old finishes. Rigid paint scrapers are not advisable, as their sharp edges have a way of gouging the wood, in spite of the greatest care. For removing finishes that have been softened by a good paint remover, you'll find a broad, round-cornered putty knife useful for shoveling away thick layers of old paint. In most cases 2/0 steel wool

pads will remove the sludge. The basic equipment is:

a good paint and varnish remover
denatured alcohol solvent
gum turpentine (if the remover
   contains wax)
a putty knife
a wide-wall spatula
an old or cheap paintbrush
   (about 2 1/2 inches wide)
orange or lollipop sticks
burlap ravelings or twine
an old toothbrush
burlap squares
2/0 steel wool pads
clean old cloths
newspapers
covered containers for remover
   and alcohol
covered metal container for used
   rags and papers
waterless hand cleaner

Old clothes or a washable coverall are recommended.

Paint removers, cleaning solvents, and finishing materials in general must be handled with care and certain precautions must be followed. For instance, the FLAMMABLE or KEEP AWAY FROM FLAME on containers mean that the products give off flammable vapors at room temperatures. When you open the container, flammable vapors come out of the opening. As soon as you spread one of these substances on a surface, the vapors circulate much faster. And as these vapors mix with the air, they will burn or explode if a spark or flame ignites them. The striking of a match, the operation of a light switch, or even the flame in a gas-range pilot light can ignite such fumes.

To prevent any problems, take the following precautions when using finishing materials or cleaning solvents:

1. Read the manufacturers' labels and heed their warnings.

2. Provide good cross-ventilation to carry vapors away quickly, to prevent toxic effects from breathing fumes, and to reduce the danger of fire.

3. Don't smoke in the area where you use flammables.

4. Replace caps immediately after pouring finishing liquids.

5. Do not let containers of flammable liquids stand uncovered. Place the cover on the container while you work.

6. Place rags or papers used in finishing in metal-covered cans after use, or destroy them at once. Don't leave them crumpled in open containers. Under certain conditions they are subject to spontaneous heating, and can start fires in your home.

GENERAL RULES FOR REMOVING OLD FINISH

When removing an old finish or paint from the wooden furniture surfaces, it would be well to abide by the following rules:

1. Do nothing that will harm the patina or the original surface, unless it is in such bad condition that drastic methods are called for or unless the piece is to be painted.

2. If you plan to replace the old finish with a new one of a clear type, all old finish must be removed so that the new one will hold properly.

3. When removing old paint, it is not only permissible but acceptable to most collectors that the marks of wear through the years be allowed to remain, as well as traces of color from the old paint, so that they will show through the new finish. Traces of old paint add interest to the piece by their variations of color, and are evidence of age. However, old paint should not be left on in thick patches or blotches.

4. Usually stubborn paint can be removed down to a satisfactory level, but it is often impossible to remove it all, particularly from cherry, mahogany, and walnut.

5. Before attempting to remove an old finish or paint, it is a good plan to scrape off a small area, in an inconspicuous spot, to determine the condition of the finish and the number of coats that have been used, and to inspect the undercoat. If this undercoat is found to be of the refractory type, the necessary materials for its removal should be at hand before the paint and varnish remover, if used, has had a chance to dry.

6. For the final cleaning, after using a remover, use a cabinet scraper or knife blade on joints, corners, and angles on flat surfaces and steel wool to clean out carvings, turnings, moldings, cracks, and crevices. Some workers make scrapers of hardwood, with a beveled edge and handle, instead of using a metal scraper, as wood is safer and cannot injure the surface. Orange sticks, wooden meat skewers, and sharpened hardwood

dowels make good tools for use in small places. The points of such tools should be covered with a piece of cloth. Doweling, of various diameters, that has been cut on the end of an angle of 45 degrees, makes a fine tool for removing softened finishes from grooves or moldings.

7. If the old finish is shellac, you don't need a paint and varnish remover. It can be taken off with denatured alcohol solvent and 2/0 medium steel wood. To test for a shellac finish, see page 76.

8. After using any kind of material as a remover, the piece must be allowed sufficient time to dry out thoroughly. This usually takes 24 hours or longer. If shellac is to be used as a sealer or for the finish and the wood is not completely dry or traces of remover have not been properly cleaned from the surface, the finish may turn white or discolored. Moreover, many materials (other than shellac) used for a final finish may not dry hard over some of the old finishes, if any has been left on a surface.

9. Remove all hardware, table leaves, and doors from the piece before applying the paint remover. You can save yourself some work by keeping remover off any surface that doesn't need to be stripped. Mask off cane seat and glass, for instance. Prevent accidental spills by plugging screw holes for pulls, hinges, etc.

10. Clean the hardware carefully. Pour some paint remover in an old glass bowl and dip hinges, pulls, and other hardware in it. Varnish and paint will come off the metal fairly quickly. Wipe away residue with a cloth, then spray the hardware with clear lacquer to keep it bright.

SELECTING YOUR PAINT REMOVER

Commercial removers are solvents, rather than corrosives. They act more slowly on older paints than on new, but are the only materials that can be used with safety. They attack the vehicles only, such as linseed oils used in paint, or the resins in shellac, varnish, and lacquer. They won't injure a surface by burning it or leaving marks, they won't be harmful to glue or raise the grain of the wood. They may be used on veneered surfaces without causing the veneer to loosen, as they contain no water. When properly applied and then washed off, solvent-type paint removers leave the surface clean.

These removers are available with a thick, waterlike consistency and in semi-paste and paste forms. They are sold under many trade names and are made from various formulas. Some contain paraffin or wax. They may be purchased in containers, from one pint to a gallon, at most hardware and paint stores. Solvent-type paint removers are, of course, more expensive than other materials that might be used, such as lye, but, because of the excellent results from their use, they are usually the cheapest in the end. Always read the full directions on the container.

Some professional workers prefer the thin liquid form of remover, claiming it is best for speeding up the work. But for the average home handyman, a thicker

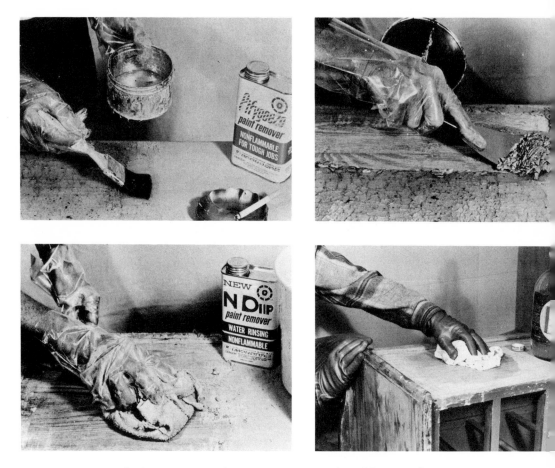

Figure 4-2. Removal of paint: (1) Apply paint remover to the tabletop with a brush. (2) Scrape the softened paint off with a scraper. (3) Apply water-rinsing paint remover with toweling. (4) If the remover used includes a waxy retarder, follow the scraping operation with a rinse of paint thinner—alcohol, solvent, or turpentine.

liquid type (more like syrup) is preferred. It will "stay put" better when applied and remain wet longer, and there is less waste. Also, those removers that are made *without* wax or parrafin are preferred. These substances are added to retard evaporation, but it is difficult to remove all traces of the wax or paraffin. If any remover is left on the surface, the new finish won't stick properly. By the way, wax-free types are required for finishes that contain residues of silicone polishes. That is, if the piece has been treated with one of the modern-day furniture polishes that contain silicone, all traces of that chemical must be removed before refinishing. Otherwise, craters and pits will form as the finish is applied.

Even with the use of wax-free paint and varnish remover, you may not be able to remove the silicone residues completely. Therefore, after the old finish has been removed, wash the surface with gum turpentine. Allow the turpentine to remain in contact with the surface for 2 or 3 minutes before wiping it off. When wiping, change to clean cloths frequently to prevent the transfer of silicone residues from the cloth back to the wood surface. Removers containing paraffin or waxes also require a "wash-down" with turpentine, alcohol, or benzine before new finishes are applied.

"Rinse-away"-type removers are not usually recommended for fine furniture wood since they have a tendency to burn or stain them, and since the water used with them may damage the bare wood. In addition, they are expensive to use.

HOW TO REMOVE OLD FINISHES

Dislodging layers of old paint or varnish isn't difficult, but patience, time, and perseverance are required. Here are the basic directions for using paint remover:

1. Place the piece to be worked on over layers of old newspapers (on a table if the piece is small), in a good strong light, and, if possible, with the top surface in a horizontal position.

2. Shake the remover thoroughly, pour a small amount into a can or jar, and apply thickly with a full brush in one direction. Do not rebrush. Limit the surface to be covered to not over 2 feet square.

3. Let the remover stand, without touching, for a period of from 10 to 20 minutes, or until the paint or finish "lifts." This is indicated by a crinkling of the surface. Do not let the remover dry. If it begins to dry, apply an additional coat and wait for it to act.

4. When the surface covering has lifted, remove it with a dull putty knife. The corners of the knife should have been rounded off to prevent gouging. To remove the accumulation of remover and finish, wipe the knife on a piece of old newspaper from time to time.

5. Wipe off as much of the remaining finish as possible, using burlap squares (best) or crumpled paper.

6. Scrub the surface with a small brush dipped in denatured alcohol.

7. Wipe off with several clean cloths.

8. Rub the surface with steel wool, dipped in denatured alcohol.

9. Wipe with cloths dipped in alcohol. This not only cleans the traces of remover from the surface but neutralizes its further action. Some professionals use gasoline (not ethyl), benzine, or turpentine for this work.

10. Allow the piece to dry thoroughly (at least 24 hours).

Figure 4-3. Liquid and semipaste paint removers may be poured onto flat surfaces, then spread with the edge of a piece of fairly stiff cardboard. This provides even distribution.

Turned and Carved Surfaces

Removing the old finish from grooves and carving requires a little more patience and work. Here is how it should be done:

1. Apply the remover, as previously instructed.

2. When the finish "lifts," wipe off as much as possible with a burlap square.

3. Scrub crevices and grooves first with a toothbrush dipped in remover, then with a larger brush dipped in denatured alcohol.

4. Clean turnings as well as possible by holding a pad of steel wool (dipped in alcohol) in the hand and using a twisting motion. Follow with the use of threads from burlap or steel wool, twisted into narrow strips, for the final cleaning of turnings. Clean crevices in carving with an instrument such as an orange stick or a meat skewer, with a piece of cloth over its end.

5. Allow at least 24 hours for complete drying.

Additional Tips on Finish Removal

Here are thirteen "lucky" tips on finish removal:

1. Circumstances may be found wherein some of the steps given here may be shortened or even omitted. Some experts add another step (after step 5). They brush the surface lightly with remover before the final cleanup.

2. If any of the old finish is still visible in spots, this must be removed by repeating the procedure or the new finish may not dry in these places.

3. If any streaks of color are left on the surface, dip a clean cloth in alcohol, wring it out, and wipe the surface with long, light strokes.

4. If the piece must be repainted, the new paint will adhere better if the surface is sanded smooth. The only reason for removing the old paint is to have an even surface upon which to apply the new.

5. After the upper coats of paint have been removed and it is discovered that the undercoat is of the refractory type, the surface should be kept moistened by applying one or more coats of the remover.

6. If there are several coats of paint and these are found to be difficult to remove, several layers of the remover should be used, one on top of the other. Cover with layers of wet burlap or cloth and allow to stand for several hours or

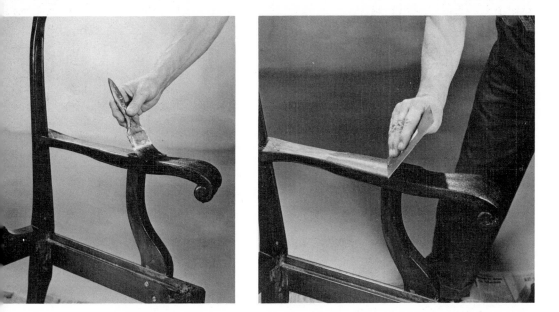

Figure 4-4. Removing varnish from a fine furniture piece: (1) Apply varnish remover with a brush, spreading in one direction as evenly as possible. The removal liquid permeates the finish while a retardant covers the surface to slow evaporation. The old finish is softened and gradually raised from the wood in blisters. The area covered on the first application should be small; increase gradually until the maximum surface area can be covered and removed before the remover and varnish begin to harden again. (2) When the chemical has done its work, the varnish is removed. For flat surfaces, or where there are scratches or burns, a metal scraper does the job very well. The depth of the cut is determined by the angle of the scraper and the pressure applied. Two-handed pressure at an almost perpendicular position will cut through to the wood, while one-handed light pressure at about a 30-degree angle will merely skim off the top varnish coat, leaving the others there.

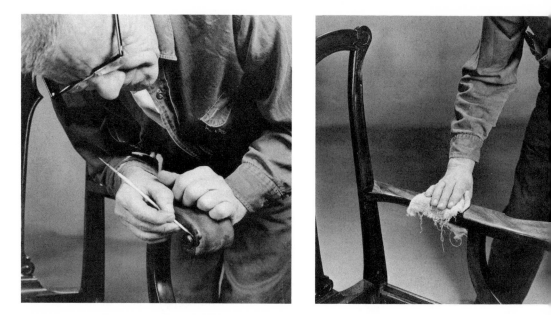

Figure 4-4 *continued*. (3) Crevices in carvings require special treatment. An additional application of removing liquid is brushed into the crevices; a sharpened orange stick and a fiber brush dipped in alcohol, wielded with care and patience, will eventually rout out the most stubborn deposits. (4) Follow the varnish-removing process with an immediate application of alcohol. A rag should be thoroughly soaked until the alcohol runs on the wood when applied. All varnish removers carry a retardant vehicle in the fluid; this is often wax, which must be removed or the finish that you apply will not dry correctly.

even overnight. If this covering is kept wet, the old paint can usually be removed with a putty knife. The action of the remover on old paints is very much the same as that involved in removing several layers of wallpaper. They both sometimes come off layer by layer.

7. The drawers and doors should be removed from the piece before using a remover.

8. Whenever possible, apply removers to flat surfaces in a horizontal position. This may be accomplished by turning the piece. Put small pieces and parts on a table or workbench, over old newspapers.

9. A large piece sometimes cannot be turned over or moved to a position, so the remover will have to be applied to a vertical surface. In such cases, tilt the top of the piece toward the surface to be worked upon by placing blocks under the opposite surface. In this way the remover will not run on to unfinished horizontal surfaces. (*Example:* When using a remover on the front surface of a

dresser or a cabinet from which drawers or doors have been removed.)

10. Any remover that has gotten on to bare wood should be wiped off with a cloth dampened with denatured alcohol. Otherwise it will leave a stain on the wood.

11. Get rid of dirty burlap pieces, cloths, and paper on which you have wiped the putty knife or placed the removed finish.

12. Spread out cloths, clean enough to be used again, so that alcohol will evaporate.

13. A paintbrush used with removers becomes unfit for other uses. Clean with denatured alcohol and then wash with hot soapy water for further use with removers.

REMOVING REFRACTORY PAINTS

You may find another disturbing factor in the removal of paint from antique furniture. This arises when the only coat of paint, or perhaps the undercoat of many layers, is a "refractory" (obstinate) type, which has penetrated deeply into the wood pores. Before the days when linseed oil was used as a vehicle in making paints, many paints were made by mixing a pigment with skim milk or buttermilk. These pigments may have been soot (lampblack) from kerosene lamps or colors from the earth, such as sienna (brown) or iron oxide (red). Refractory paints were used generally on pine, because of the desire to cover knots or other imperfections in the wood. They produced an effect that made cheap woods appear more beautiful. It is said that finely grained and finished furniture was often covered with this paint to make it appear less valuable in the eyes of the tax appraiser. However, we cannot understand why so many fine woods were thus painted.

This stubborn paint may often be successfully removed by the following method:

1. Apply a heavy coat of the remover and allow it to stand awhile in an attempt to further soften the old paint.

2. While the remover is still wet, scrub the surface with pads of grade 1 steel wool. Turn each pad to a new surface when the old one is filled with paint and remove all paint possible, repeating steps 1 and 2 as long as any paint can be removed.

3. Scrub the surface with a fresh pad of steel wool dipped in denatured alcohol and wipe with a rag.

4. With a knife, carefully remove any paint remaining in joints and corners.

5. Allow to dry for 24 hours and smooth by sanding, followed by steel wool.

When the only coat is a refractory type of paint, it usually can be removed with certain materials, but just which to use is difficult to determine in advance. You will have to learn by trial which may be successful. It is, therefore, a good plan to start with the least harmful and then try the others later.

The first suggestion is to use *denatured alcohol*. Next try *sal soda* or *trisodium phosphate*, and *lye* as the last resort. Refractory paints may be red,

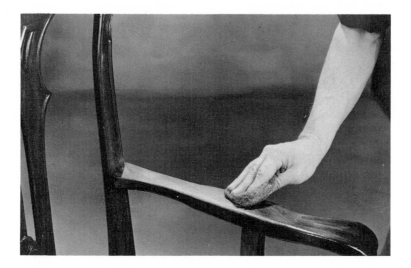

Figure 4-5. Varnish removal with steel wool. When there are only surface scratches, it is best to remove the varnish with a pad of fine steel wool. The steel wool can be used dry or wet with commercial alcohol or *alcohol-base* antifreeze. This complete process may have to be repeated. If the manufacturer wanted to hide light grain streaks or knots, he used a deep-colored filler and varnish stain. It took two applications of remover to bring up the grain on this chair.

black, green, or brown. If you find in advance that the undercoat is black, it is best to remove all coats by scraping, as a liquid remover will drive black deeper into the wood grain. This will leave a gray color that even bleaches will seldom lighten.

Denatured Alcohol

This method is the easiest because so little equipment is required and it is less messy than any of the others. Try it first. It may do the trick.

Moisten the surface with denatured alcohol and use 2/0 steel wool or 6/0 abrasive paper, rubbing with the grain of the wood. Wipe off occasionally with a clean cloth, moisten the surface again, and continue rubbing. Finally, wipe off with a clean cloth dampened in alcohol. If the paint is well into the wood grain and there is more of it left than you feel is desirable, try the procedure for using shellac (page 101).

Sal Soda or Trisodium Phosphate

A solution of sal soda should be used while the surface is still wet after an attempt to remove the paint with a commercial paint and varnish remover. Trisodium phosphate (a powerful alkali often used in water softening), may be substituted for the sal soda. Neither will harm the wood, but they should not be used on a veneered surface, since the water will soften the glue holding the veneer. You can get sal soda at your grocer's, in pound packages. Trisodium phosphate, in the form of small crystals, will be found in most paint and building supply stores.

Here is the equipment you need:
two medium-size galvanized or
    enamel pails
a cotton dish mop with long handle
a large scrubbing brush (8 or 10
    inches with handle, if possible)
hot water, both for making the
    solution and for washing it off
a supply of sal soda or trisodium
    phosphate (2 pounds is usually
    enough for a piece of moderate
    size)

Glasses or goggles should be worn while doing the work. Use rubber gloves (or canvas with leather palm, treated with waterproof oil) and old clothes with long sleeves (either solution will burn the skin). The work should be done on a cement floor with a drain, or outside in the shade. Here's how to use sal soda or trisodium phosphate to remove a refractory type of paint:

1. Dissolve 1 pound of either sal soda or trisodium phosphate in a pail containing 5 quarts of hot water. Have the other pail filled with hot water only.

2. Apply the solution sparingly to one surface, using a dish mop. This surface should be in a horizontal position, if possible.

3. Let stand less than one minute and then scrub vigorously with the scrubbing brush for a few seconds.

4. Dip the scrubbing brush in clear hot water and wash the surface.

5. Continue applications of solution and the scrubbing until you have removed enough of the paint or until you are convinced that some other method must be used.

6. Use clean cold water to flush off the surface, and then, if you are satisfied with the result, turn the piece so that one of the other surfaces will be horizontal and repeat the procedure.

7. Use a hose to flush all surfaces while *scrubbing thoroughly*, particularly in cracks and grooves.

8. Keep the piece in the shade. Direct sunlight will cause the wood to warp. Let it dry thoroughly. This will usually take several days.

Either of these solutions, in hot or cold water, is excellent for cleaning a piece following the use of paint and varnish remover, particularly where the remover has dried and left a considerable amount of paint color on the surface. Scrub with clear water and dry, as above.

Lye

Lye is a dangerous substance for anyone to handle. It is a powerful caustic and has a chemical reaction that causes even the most stubborn paints (refractory type) to powder instead of lifting (as do paint and varnish removers). Lye should never be used to remove other finishes.

Lye is inexpensive (a few cents per can at the grocer's). Its action is quick and thorough. Knowledge of its properties and great care in its use are necessary. It will burn certain woods, turning them black, and must, therefore, be washed and scrubbed off completely and thoroughly, particularly from any cracks and crevices. Unless the *utmost* care is taken in removing all residue, it will raise the wood grain and spoil any later finish you may apply.

A strong solution will destroy clothing, burn the skin, and injure the eyes. It is least harmful to hickory, maple, and pine but should never be used on open-grained woods such as butternut, chestnut, oak, or walnut. It will ruin cherry or mahogany and should not be used on veneers, because of the water in which it is mixed. These warnings should *not* prevent you from using lye when it is necessary.

In your first attempt at using lye, select a piece of furniture of little value, either intrinsic or sentimental. If you will use it only on the woods suggested and make sure that you have washed off every trace, you should be successful. Don't attempt to use lye unless you have the proper equipment and are willing to spend the time it requires.

Here's the equipment you'll need for lye work:

> two cans of lye (13-ounce size)
> a supply of white vinegar
> a 10-quart galvanized or enameled
>   pail (never use an aluminum one)
> running water with hose
>   attachment

You should have a long-handled cotton dish mop, brush, glasses or goggles, gloves, and old clothes. The work should be done on a well-drained cement floor or out of doors in the shade. The directions for lye use are as follows:

1. Fill the pail half full with *cold* water. Pour in the lye from the two cans. Dissolve by stirring with the mop and then fill the pail with more cold water. The water should never be poured onto the lye, since this will cause it to foam up out of the pail. Have water running slowly through the hose.

2. Using the long-handled cotton dish mop, apply sparingly to a horizontal surface.

3. Let it stand for about 30 seconds and then scrub vigorously with the brush.

4. Wash off with the hose and continue scrubbing.

5. Repeat until enough of the powdered paint has been removed from all of the surfaces, turning the piece so that you always work on a horizontal one.

6. Scrub well with water from hose and a brush, working deeply into cracks and crevices, until all of the slippery film of the solution has been removed.

7. To neutralize the caustic action of the lye, wash with vinegar on a clean cloth.

8. Place the piece in the shade and allow it to dry thoroughly for 24 hours or longer. Direct sunlight may warp the wood.

This solution is very strong. The secret in removing the paint without burning the wood lies in not letting the solution remain on the surface long enough to injure it. The more often and more quickly you apply the solution and wash it off, the less danger there is to the wood. It is nearly impossible to apply the solution to one horizontal surface and not have it get on an adjoining vertical one. Therefore, these other surfaces should be scrubbed off at the same time, as in step 3 in the lye procedure.

Should there be spots of paint that are stubborn, let them remain, rather than continue the use of the solution, for fear of injury to the wood. These may usually be removed easily with a cabinet scraper after the wood is thoroughly dry, as much of the life has been taken from the paint by the lye solution.

REMOVING DEEPLY BURIED PAINTS

A deeply buried paint may often be removed entirely or partially by a simple procedure. This paint is usually that which is left after you have removed the previous coats with remover or by light scraping. Because of its simplicity, this procedure is worth trying.

1. Apply a liberal coat of the shellac with a brush and let it dry for at least 24 hours.

2. Use the remover as previously directed. All or part of the buried paint may come off with the shellac.

Removing Paint Hardened by Heat and Containing Dirt

Heat from the sun or a hot stove will often soften a finish, and when it has cooled and hardened again, dirt and dust will be found imbedded in its finish. A commercial remover will often fail to remove it, particularly in those cases where another coat of paint has been added over the dirt.

This paint can often be removed by applying a mixture made of equal parts of linseed oil and turpentine. This is rubbed into the surface, allowed to stand, and then cleaned off with fine steel wool dipped in turpentine. If necessary, this process is followed by a light scraping.

Removing old Varnish with a Scraper

Very old varnish will, at times, be found to be so flaky that it can be removed easily with a cabinet scraper, or the sharp blade of a large knife, without injury to the wood surface or destruction of the patina. This should be attempted only by those familiar with the use of such tools.

REMOVING FINISH FROM STENCILED CHAIRS

You may, at some time, wish to remove old varnish from a Windsor or Hitchcock chair or a Boston rocker, without injury to the paint or the stencil design with which they are so often decorated. The stencil may have been covered with paint that you want to remove, leaving the stencil intact.

The removal of old varnish is more simple than the removal of paint. However, both require careful and delicate handling. Either may often be removed in part by light scraping and the balance by the method given below.

If you suspect that a stencil has been

painted over, first experiment at the spot where you might expect a stencil to be. There is usually one on the front side of the top back. Use a scraper with care to remove only the hard outer coat of paint so that the materials for removing (see below) can penetrate the under-coats more easily.

The decoration of furniture, by painted or stenciled designs, is a spe-cialty and hence beyond the scope of this book. Some such pieces can be re-stored if the condition of the outer sur-face is not too bad. They must then be refinished by a fresh coat of shellac and wax or with varnish and a rubdown (see Chapter Six).

Following are the methods to use in removing an outer coat of varnish or paint:

Removing Varnish

Try to soften the varnish by applying denatured alcohol on wads of cotton to small areas. If successful, wipe off the varnish. If this does not work, try a mixture of equal parts of benzine and alcohol. Finally, try a mixture of equal parts of pure turpentine and alcohol. These solutions are given in the order of their strength.

If none of these will soften the var-nish, clean off a small area and apply a light coat of a commercial remover. When the varnish starts to lift, stop the action by washing off the remover with alcohol on a wad of cotton and start again. Repeating this process may bring results. The great difficulty is in know-ing when to stop, in order to save the stencil.

Removing Paint

Use fine 3/0 steel wool dipped in alcohol and a sharp knife blade, or deli-cately use a scraper, as in the procedure for removing refractory-type paints page 97).

CHAPTER FIVE

Preparing for a New Finish

This is the turning point in the work. Thus far you have been given general instructions for repairs and the removal of old finish. Now you are ready to prepare the surface for a new finish. This requires careful workmanship and full knowledge of the necessary procedures and methods, as the quality of the final finish depends directly upon the carefulness of this preparation. Except for handling a scraper, which isn't often used, the work is not too difficult, but at times it calls for careful selection, judgment, and forethought.

Before starting the work, make a thorough inspection of the piece, especially after you have removed any old, heavy paint. You may find dents, holes, cracks, and other damage that were not previously visible in the surface and that will require repairs. This must be done before preparing for the new finish.

You may often be agreeably surprised to find a wood of beauty after old paint has been removed from a surface. When it is sanded and smoothed, you may see how the piece is going to look with a clear, new finish by making a simple wet test (page 126). Should the wood have a drab appearance, the color can often be restored, but, if it is discolored, it may require a bleach. You may find a piece made of many kinds of woods of various colors that you may wish to stain a single color, or you may wish to stain it or a "nude"—a new unpainted piece—to match other pieces, or, perhaps, you may have to stain an inserted patch to match the surface into which it is placed. Finally, if the piece is of such utility, quality of workmanship, or fineness, or if it is customary that it have a polish rubbed finish, the surface must be prepared with a paste filler.

Some of the procedures in this chapter are seldom used, but all are described to give you a full knowledge of them. The number and choice of those to be used for a single job is determined by the condition of the wood, after a former finish has been removed, and whether it must be bleached, stained, or the surface filled for a final finish of extreme smoothness. Each procedure is accompanied by information as to when and why it is used. Some are necessary, according to conditions, and some are a matter of choice.

BLEACHING

Bleaching is necessary only when the color of the wood must be lightened, or when it is necessary to remove undesirable stains. Thanks to bleaching, you may swing a room now traditional in motif to modern. Old pieces that were a part of everyone's home a generation ago are literally given away today. Yet, cut down, remodeled, and bleached, they fit into the most modern room.

BLEACHING QUALITIES OF WOODS

Wood	Bleach	Blond*
Ash	Fairly easy	Preferably not
Basswood	Difficult	Yes
Beech	Fairly easy	Yes
Birch	Easy to bleach	Possible
Chestnut	Difficult	No
Cyprus	Difficult	No
Douglas fir	No	Yes
Gum	Fairly easy	No
Mahogany	Fairly easy	No
Maple	Fairly easy	Yes
Oak	Easy to bleach	No, when the oak is old
Pine		
White	No	Yes
Yellow	No	No
Poplar	Difficult	Yes
Red cedar	Difficult	No
Redwood	Difficult	Possible; preferably not
Rosewood	Difficult	No
Southern alm	Difficult	Yes
Walnut	Fairly easy	No

*A light finish with white undersealer, without bleaching.

Knowing your wood is never more important than when it comes to bleaching it. A bleach that may work successfully on mahogany may be a total failure on birch. Easiest to bleach are the naturally light-colored woods—oak and birch. Next in line are walnut, mahogany, ash, maple, and beech. Cherry, chestnut and poplar may be bleached with much difficulty. How satisfactorily depends on the power of the bleach and the condition of the wood. Douglas fir plywood, and white and yellow pine may *not* be bleached. However, you can achieve a blond finish on these woods by another method, which will be treated later.

After the old finish has been removed from a surface, any darkened or discolored spots that may remain can be lightened or entirely removed by the proper use of a bleach. Although you may feel justified in wishing to remove all traces of old stain and marks of discoloration from antique furniture, these, in most cases, add to the charm of the finished piece and may be left when they do not show too plainly through the new finish. Some collectors prefer that a certain amount of this evidence of age and usage be left. However, when working on pine or maple, it is best to remove discoloration and freshen up the surface.

Types of Bleaches

There are four common bleaches used by home handymen to lighten wood and help remove undesirable stains. They are:

PREPARED BLEACH. The simplest method of getting a good bleach is to buy a prepared bleach, which usually comes in the form of two solutions that may be applied successively or mixed together, according to the directions on the label.

HOUSEHOLD PRODUCTS. Sometimes a laundry bleach in which sodium hypochlorite is the bleaching agent is effective for such woods as maple, walnut, and gum. Household ammonia is a good bleaching agent on all but dark woods. It is, however, best for spot work only.

OXALIC ACID. This bleach, once so popular, is losing favor because it works only when a mild bleach is needed. Under this condition, it can be used quite successfully for such open-grained woods as oak, chestnut, and ash.

HYDROGEN PEROXIDE. Probably the most satisfactory but most expensive bleaches are those based on a strong solution of hydrogen peroxide (30 or 35 percent). This concentrated commercial-grade bleach should not be confused with the 3 percent solution used as an antiseptic.

Using Prepared Bleach

Commercially prepared wood bleaches, as previously stated, are two-solution preparations that must be intermixed or applied in successive steps. All contain strong chemicals, so it is important that rubber gloves be worn to protect the hands. An apron or old clothing should also be worn, since these bleaches will attack most fabrics—and follow label directions carefully!

The bleach can be applied with a brush or a sponge, and should be al-

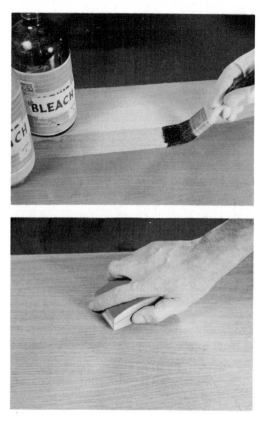

Figure 5-1. How to bleach: (1) Apply bleach according to the directions for the particular brand. Be sure to wear gloves to protect your hands. (2) When the bleach has remained on the surface for the required time, usually 5 to 15 minutes, apply neutralizer as directed. (3) Allow the wood surface to dry for at least 24 hours. A light sanding with a block will be necessary, for bleaching raises the grain.

lowed to dry on the surface until the desired effect is reached. The instructions will tell whether neutralization or rinsing is required. After bleaching and rinsing have been completed, the piece of furniture should be allowed to stand until thoroughly dry. Then stand lightly, with very fine sandpaper, to remove the raised grain. However, be careful not to sand more deeply than the bleach has penetrated.

Using Household Products

Most household products are better for spot work than they are for large areas. Here's how to use laundry bleach and ammonia as bleaching agents:

1. Apply the product full strength over the spot or surface of the wood.

2. Wash the product off with clear water after it has been on the surface about 15 minutes. Check to see if the desired color has been attained. If not, repeat the treatment again.

3. When the right color has been achieved, rinse all the surface with water.

4. Let the furniture stand to dry for at least 48 hours.

Using Oxalic Acid

Oxalic acid isn't expensive. It can be purchased at a drugstore in either crystal or powder form. It is also sold by some paint stores. The following is the procedure for using oxalic acid to bleach wood:

1. Prepare a solution of oxalic acid by dissolving 1 ounce of the powder or 2 ounces of the crystals in 1 pint of very hot water. Some woods, maple in particular, respond more readily to a solution of 1 ounce of oxalic acid crystals and 1 ounce of tartaric acid powder (available at drugstores) in 1 pint of very hot water.

2. Using a large brush, apply the solution (hot) to the entire surface, from which the finish has been removed, or to a spot with a small brush. In the case of the spot, work the solution carefully to the edges with the brush. It is recommended that you bleach an entire surface rather than remove a spot only. However, you may be very successful in spot-bleaching when the outline of the spot is clearly defined. If your efforts to remove a spot are unsuccessful, no harm is done, since the entire surface can then be bleached.

3. Let the solution remain for 10 to 20 minutes and then wipe it off with a damp cloth. If the discoloration has not been bleached sufficiently, repeat until you obtain the color you are after.

4. When the proper result has been secured, wash off the solution with 1 part ammonia in 10 parts of water. This will neutralize the bleach and stop its further action. Then wash with clear water and allow the piece to dry for at least 24 hours. Some workers recommend the use of white vinegar (full strength) as a neutralizing agent following the use of oxalic acid.

Removing Discoloration

You may find that the surface of a piece, particularly pine or maple, has a gray or faded appearance. It may be freshened and brought back to a more satisfactory color by the following procedure. This is recommended for a surface that has just been cleaned with a paint and varnish remover and before it has again dried.

1. Scrub with the soap powder in water that is just under the boiling point. Wash off with hot water and wipe with cloth.

2. While the surface is still wet, apply a hot solution of oxalic acid. Let this stay on for about 10 minutes and then wash it off and neutralize its action with the ammonia or vinegar. Let it dry thoroughly.

This treatment will raise the grain of the wood, but it usually removes the fine particles of colored pigment. The grain will settle down again when dry and can be sanded later. The surface won't have the appearance of new wood, but, if circumstances are favorable and the work has been done properly, it should have an even mellowness.

Removing Grease Stains

Frequently, oil and grease penetrate the wood of tabletops, cheese or meat boards, or salad bowls. It is necessary to remove as much grease as possible from the surface so that the new finish will adhere.

A grease stain from animal fat may usually be removed by an application of benzine or other commercial cleaners, such as those that come in small containers for removing spots from clothing. In a well-ventilated area or outdoors, scrub the surface with a dry-cleaning solvent. Scrub first with a brush, then with 3/0 steel wool. Allow to dry thoroughly. Repeat two or three times, allowing about a day for drying between treatments.

Another method of removing this type of grease stain is to make a paste of fuller's earth and a dry-cleaning solvent. Apply to the greasy surface. Leave the paste on the wood 24 hours, then brush off. Repeat the paste treatment, if necessary.

If the grease spot is of vegetable origin, it will usually respond to the use of acetone. This may be purchased at a drugstore. The remover should be applied to the spot with a small artist's brush, and then worked around with the brush and removed with a piece of absorbent tissue paper, such as are sold for use in removing cosmetics. The operation should be repeated until the spot has been removed.

If the surface feels sticky after the old finish has been removed, it's an indication that some of the old finish remains. The solution—apply another coat of remover to the entire section.

If the surface appears smoky after removing the old finish, wash the section again with denatured alcohol.

SANDING AND SMOOTHING

Any surface on which a new finish is to be applied requires smoothing, an operation that brings a surface to a fine, silky condition without destroying the patina and evidence of age and usage. Many pieces are free from any finish or paint and need no repairs. However, these must go through the smoothing operation as well.

The smoothing of a wood surface, free from a finish, is done with abrasive papers and is called *sanding*, by first working with relatively coarse papers, followed by those of finer grit. Steel wool is often used for final smoothing, and at times it is necessary to use a scraper (to be avoided if possible) to smooth a surface that is to be followed with fine abrasive papers and steel wool.

The degree of smoothness a piece requires depends greatly upon the type of the article and the wood of which it is made, as well as the type of final finish that is to be used. For example, a crude piece of pine furniture does not call for as smooth a surface as a well-designed piece made of hardwoods, nor would the final finish be smoothed to the same degree.

When smoothing a surface, all work must be done with the proper materials of the right grade of fineness and with great care, or the results will be disastrous, since scratches show through any kind of a final finish. You must remember that you are working with wood surfaces for which you must have regard and respect, regardless of whether the woods are rare or common, old or new. The following procedures give brief information about the uses of abrasive papers and emery cloth.

Abrasive Papers and Emery Cloth

The use of the term *sandpaper* to designate one of the various abrasive papers is a misnomer, since none of them any longer use sand for the abrasive coating. Sand has round edges and corners and will not smooth a surface but only scratch it. The so-called sandpaper that you buy at the store is covered, instead, with a coating of crushed flint in various degrees of fineness, which are marked on the reverse side of the paper. This flint sandpaper should not be used in the restoration of furniture if it is possible to obtain anything better, since it is not durable. In recent years, the flint has been replaced by more effective and durable abrasive materials.

MAKING ABRASIVE SHEETS. Abrasive paper or cloth is produced in large sheets. These are then cut into standard or special sizes for use in hand-sanding, smoothing or polishing, or into belts, spirals, or other necessary shapes for use with power sanders. They also come in sizes for attachment to discs and cones. The fineness of the grit varies according to the nature of the work to be done.

The abrasive materials are glued to a cloth or paper backing, differing in thickness and pliability as their specific use may require. The abrasive may be applied in a heavy, medium, or light coating, according to its suitability for any particular job.

TYPES OF ABRASIVE PAPERS AND CLOTHS. It is important that you understand the various kind and types of materials used as backing for abrasives, since only the correct type should be used in any specific step in your work. They must be of the proper grade or weight to accomplish the purpose effectively and speedily, yet without damaging the piece on which you are working. Such understanding can best be gained by here describing the various abrasive sheets, their backing and the type and grades of grit used on them, in accordance with their distinguishing numbers. Instructions are also given in the use and proper handling of the various types and grades.

Flint paper is coated with a species of quartz, off-white in color, that occurs as a mineral deposit in the ground. When crushed, for use as a coating for an abrasive, its cutting edges are not sharp and they crumble in use. It is by far, however, the most commonly sold abrasive sheet for sanding exterior paint coatings.

Garnet paper is also a mined stone, light reddish-brown in color, and is classed as one of the semiprecious gem stones. It is crushed into grains that have hard and durable edges and corners. Garnet paper is very popular, easily obtainable, and is used largely for smoothing, finishing, and polishing wood surfaces.

Silicon carbide paper is produced in

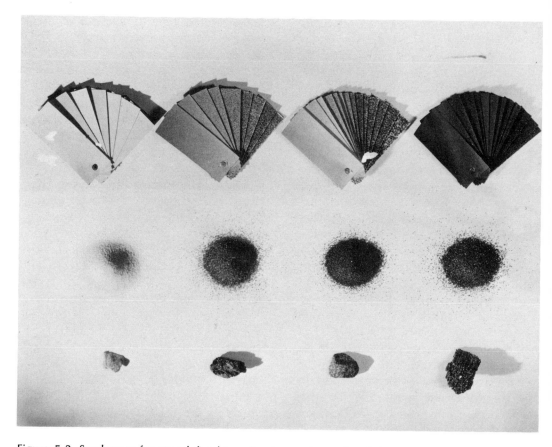

Figure 5-2. Sandpaper for wood finishing. Sandpaper is made of these four minerals: silicon carbide, aluminum oxide, garnet, and flint.

an electric furnace and ranges in color from dark gray to black. It is crystalline in form, very hard and sharp, and commonly called *carborundum*. This paper is widely used in place of garnet papers by many cabinet shops and amateur workers. It is sold under trade names rather than by its technical name.

Aluminum oxide paper, brown in color, is also produced in an electric furnace under rigid heat control and is almost pure cutting agent. It is dense, resists breakdown, and is the toughest and most durable of all abrasives. It, too, is sold by a trade name rather than by its technical designation.

Emery cloth is a dull-black, mined mineral. Since its cutting edges break down under pressure, it is, therefore, mixed with one of the harder abrasives, even though sold as emery cloth. It is glued to a cloth backing instead of paper. About the only use for emery cloth in restoration work (other than on tools) is, because of the strength in the backing, for cleaning or smoothing turnings. For this work, only fine-grade cloths should be used.

BACKING. Backing is the material to which the various types of materials are glued. This may be paper, cloth, fiber, or a combination of them. The paper and cloth types come in standard size of 9 inches by 11 inches, and we shall deal only with these.

Paper backing is tough and of a special quality. It comes in various thicknesses, called *weights*, as follows:

A weight is a soft pliable grade of paper, and is used where flexibility is required.

C- and D-weight papers are thicker, and are used for the more severe hand-sanding jobs.

E weight is the heaviest of the backing papers, and is used primarily for machine sanding.

Cloth backing comes in two grades, as follows:

Lightweight material is marked *J*, and is used for a backing on emery cloth for handwork and on some finishing and polishing cloths.

Heavyweight material is marked *X*, and is used with power tools.

Some manufacturers distinguish the weight of the backing by producing it in different colors.

CLASSIFICATIONS OF ABRASIVE PAPERS AND CLOTHS. The reverse side of all abrasive papers and cloths are printed to show the grade of density or type of abrasive and often the weight or quality of the backing.

Finishing paper is the name applied to those papers designated as *A* or lightweight and which have a fine or extra-fine grit.

Cabinet papers are the papers known as *C* or *D* (medium) weight, and have grit of medium fineness.

Closed-grain papers contain thickly applied abrasive grains, and are the papers most generally used.

Open-coat papers are papers whose abrasive covers only 50 to 70 percent of the backing surface, leaving a certain amount of space between the grains. This increases the pliability of the paper, allows faster cutting with less pressure, and is used on the softer woods, which tend to clog the surface of the paper more rapidly.

Wet or dry papers are papers whose backing is waterproofed; they are made with only the finest grades of abrasives. In restoration work, they are used for the final rubdown with water, gasoline, or oil. They are sold under various trade names. Most of them designate whether they are for wet or dry use or are merely marked *waterproof*.

GRIT NUMBERS OR GRADES. On the back of all standard abrasive sheets are printed figures indicating the grit or grade. These are as follows:

Word Description	Grit	Grade	Use
	600	—	
	500	—	
Superfine	400	10/0	
	360	9/0	Polishing and
	320	—	finishing
Extra fine	280	8/0	
	240	7/0	
Very fine	220	6/0	
Fine	180	5/0	
	150	4/0	
	120	3/0	Finishing
	100	2/0	
Medium	80	0 or 1/0	
	60	1/2	Cabinet
	50	1	
Coarse	40	1 1/2	
	36	2	Rough sanding
	30	2 1/2	
Very coarse	24	3	Coarse sanding
	20	3 1/2	

These figures are standard for both grit (number per square inch) and grade. They may vary, however, in their designation as to grit, in the naming of the classification for cabinet and finishing papers or those with a cloth backing.

MARKINGS. The form of marking on the back of the sheets may vary greatly among different manufacturers. Sometimes either the grit or grade only is given and sometimes both. Also, information may or may not be furnished as to the weight of the paper or the kind of grit used, but it will usually be given as to whether it is the wet-or-dry type by denoting that it is waterproof, either by using that word or a coined one. (*Example of marking:* "3/0–120 A" means the grade is medium fine, that it has 120 grits (per square inch) and the weight (thickness) of the paper is A (thinnest).) You may have to guess at the kind of abrasive material used, but you should know it from the color. This paper may or may not be marked *finishing paper*.

In recent years, some manufacturers have instituted a new grade-marking system that involves the following word description: very coarse, coarse, medium, fine, very fine, and superfine. A grit comparison of these word descriptions is given in the chart above.

BUYING ABRASIVE SHEETS. Standard sheets may be purchased from paint and hardware stores and are sold more cheaply in quantity than in single sheets. Most dealers will permit you to mix grades or types when buying, and, if you are doing much work, it is well to have a supply on hand, since many grades are needed and they do wear out quickly.

The flint papers are by far the cheapest, but the other papers last so much longer, and do the work so much better and more quickly, that they are the least expensive in the long run. The reason is because the latter stand up under service and have better cutting edges (when fed on to the paper or cloth, the grit is

SANDPAPER SELECTION CHART

Use	Grit	Grade	Backing	Word Description
Rough sanding and shaping	80	1/0	D	Medium
Preparatory sanding on softwoods	100 or 120	2/0 or 3/0	A	Fine
Preparatory sanding on hardwoods	120	3/0	C	Fine
Finish sanding on softwoods	220	6/0	A	Very fine
Finish sanding on hardwoods	220 to 280	6/0 to 8/0	A	Very fine Extra fine
Polishing on all woods	280 or 400	8/0 or 10/0	J or X	Extra fine Superfine

electrocontrolled, compelling the particles to stand on end with point upward, affording better cutting edges and corners).

TYPES AND GRADES. Abrasive papers are used for: (1) rough sanding and shaping, (2) preparatory sanding and smoothing, (3) finish sanding, and (4) polishing.

No. 1 paper might be used on very soft and rough wood as the first medium in smoothing, followed by grades of 1/2 and 1/0, but it is far better to make a rule *never* to start with a coarser grade than 1/0, to be followed by those of less coarse (2/0, 3/0, etc.), especially on hardwoods. It is always a good plan to take more time in smoothing with the finer grades of papers than to take chances of damage with the coarser ones.

For finishing, after smoothing, it is well to forget the intermediate grades beyond 3/0 and jump immediately to a grade from 6/0 to 8/0, for, with new paper, it is fine enough for most woods.

For polishing, use 8/0 or finer waterproof (wet or dry) papers, or cloths with water or proper oil as a lubricant, and finish up with pumice and rottenstone (should a finish call for them).

CLEANING AND USING OLD ABRASIVE PAPER. Good abrasive paper is fairly expensive, but many home handymen are prone to discard it long before it has become unfit for further service. Papers clog up with powdered wood, but this may be removed with a small, stiff hand brush. Should the material be difficult to remove, as is the case when it is gummy, and if you know the type of that material, dip the brush in the proper solvent before scrubbing. When clean, allow the paper to dry. (*Examples:* for varnish, use turpentine; for shellac, use alcohol; for lacquer, use a lacquer thinner.) By such methods, the useful life of abrasive papers may often be doubled.

Used or dulled abrasive papers are of great value, and are recommended for use in many stages of work. It is well to have a special place in which to store them.

TEARING AND FOLDING ABRASIVE PA-PERS. Great economy can be had from tearing or folding papers. A paper is torn best across the short (9-inch) dimension to form strips about 3 1/2 inches wide. It can be torn by securing an old hacksaw blade (with screws) to the side edge of a board prepared for the purpose, with the teeth of the blade slightly above the flat surface, or it may be torn over an edge of a carpenter's steel square. The surface of the board can be marked with a scale to measure the width of the tear.

Full-size sheets of thin paper may be folded in squares by first folding it in half on the 11-inch dimension, folding it again to one-quarter size; then again to one-eighth size. The folds should be creased firmly. The edges of the fold are useful for smoothing in angles o cleaning out cracks.

SANDING BLOCKS. The best size for sanding block is 3 inches wide by inches long and 1 to 1 1/4 inches thick It may be of felt, cork, or rubber. On made of hardwood (maple is good) i preferred because of its weight, and th long sides may be coved or shaped fo easy gripping. The face of any hard ma terial used for a block should have rub ber tacked or cemented over rounded edges, to avoid sharp corners.

A block of this size may be used best with a sheet of abrasive paper cut cross wise into 5 1/2-inch by 9-inch pieces. The paper is then folded into one-half that size (4 1/2 inches by 5 1/2 inches) and placed over the rubber face of the block, with the long dimension of the folded paper over the long way of the block. This leaves it slightly longer than the block, at both ends. The paper is turned up over the sides and gripped with the fingers. When worn it may be

Figure 5-3. Sanding blocks are indispensable in wood finishing.

shifted to present new edge surfaces, then turned upside down, thus using practically all of the abrasive paper surface. Never tack paper to a sanding block.

There are many types of hand-sanding blocks that may be purchased. Some are good and some poor, but most of them require special sizes of abrasive paper and do not utilize the full surface. A blackboard eraser, like the ones used in schools, may be purchased at most five-and-tens and makes an excellent sanding block. It is padded, and of approximately the right size.

Rules for Sanding

The sanding of a wood surface is the least difficult of all procedures in restoration work, yet it is one of the most important parts of refinishing and must always be done thoroughly and with great care, regardless of whether it is accomplished by hand or with a power tool. If not done correctly, the surface will be a mass of scratches. A good sanding job is essential to a good finish.

When sanding, remember these three rules:

1. Always sand with the grain of the wood—never across the grain.

2. Use straight strokes with an even pressure, avoiding a twisting or circular motion.

3. First use a paper of as coarse a grade (grit) as the wood will stand without scratching, then finer ones until the surface is as smooth as the wood will become. The results will vary with the kind of wood.

Sanding Tips

Here are some very important points about sanding:

1. Planing and scraping are not substitutes for sanding. When such tools are used, sanding should follow.

2. Moistening will often permit better sanding on old and relatively smooth wood surfaces. Wring out a wet cloth and rub the surface. When dry, the fine ends of the fibers (termed *wood whiskers*) will be raised. Sand with a very fine or extra-fine grade of paper (6/0 to 8/0).

3. To raise the fibers of new woods (and veneer) before sanding, moisten the surface with a glue water (1 ounce of liquid glue, such as LePage's, to 1 pint of hot water). Dry and finish as in rule 2 under the rules for sanding above. Be careful of wetting veneers too much.

4. The general rule is to start and finish with finer grades of papers on hardwoods than on softwoods. Also, on softwoods it is better to use the "open-grain" papers, especially when using the coarser grades, since these woods respond to sanding more readily than do hardwoods and clog up the paper.

5. Clean papers often by brushing and you will prolong their life and cutting power.

6. Sanding blocks or folded paper may be used to advantage on large surfaces.

7. The removal of paint or varnish must always be followed by sanding to get rid of any wax that may have been in the remover; otherwise a finish may not harden.

8. Inwardly curved surfaces may be sanded by wrapping the paper around wood dowels of various sizes, according to the curve. Soaking the paper with turpentine will make it more flexible.

9. Turned surfaces are best smoothed with emery cloth of a fine grade (grit) torn into narrow (1/2 to 1-inch) strips and worked back and forth in the grooves, holding the strip by its ends. Great care must be exercised in smoothing the bulge of turnings, also long cylindrical surfaces (like chairs or table legs), or harm may be done. It is best that this work be accomplished with steel wool, especially on very old antique furniture, since these parts may have been turned by hand-powered lathes, resulting in slight ridges on the long surfaces that should not be obliterated. This will happen if they are sanded.

10. Sanding the edges and ends of the tops of tables, cabinets, etc., should be done with only the finest grades of abrasive papers, regardless of whether the part is of hardwood or softwood. Unless otherwise designed, the edges must be true and the corners square. Improper treatment of board ends may spoil an otherwise beautiful finish. They should be brought to an almost glazed surface by sanding with no coarser than an 8/0 sharp paper and finished with a worn paper of that grade or finer. When working on square ends, place the paper over a sanding block to make sure such surfaces are kept flat. Should the edges or corners be too sharp when this work is completed, relieve them slightly with light strokes of the sharp paper first followed by polishing with the worn paper.

11. After sanding, and after using steel wool, all dust must be carefully removed by wiping with a tack rag. This is a cloth that is treated to attract and hold dust. It is usually available at paint dealers who handle wood finishes, or one can be made out of any piece of dry, lint-free cotton cloth. To make one, sprinkle the cloth with varnish that has been diluted with about 25 percent turpentine. Fold tightly, then wring the cloth out till almost dry.

12. Crude pine furniture will be greatly improved in its finished appearance if the top corners of the used surface as well as the corners of nicks, and dents, are rounded down considerably by sanding and smoothing along the upper edges of the used surface, to make them look as though such rounding had come from usage. The same is true of other parts or places on surfaces of crude furniture, if such work is not overdone. For example, a natural crack that runs only a short distance from a surface edge into a top will often look better if it is not filled but widened slightly along its edges and rounded on the upper corners of its outlet, by sanding and smoothing, just as though it had been worn into that condition. Also, many pieces of crude, yet most attractive early American furniture were fastened together with nails that either rusted or were used in such a manner as to leave holes around their heads. Others can be found that have narrow cracks

between small partitions or parts. The appearance of such pieces will be greatly improved if these holes and cracks are carefully filled with wood plastic or putty and then sanded, to expose the top of the nail head and to remove the surplus wood dough from the surfaces around the cracks. The remaining dried wood dough should then be stained to match the piece, with the use of a small artist's brush. This procedure ties the surface together and greatly improves the appearance of the piece; in fact, you would be surprised at the improvement in eye appeal.

Power Sanding

Sanding can be done by hand or with a wide variety of power tools. Of the various power sanders, the so-called finishing sander is the most useful for the home handyman doing finishing and refinishing of wood furniture.

There are three varieties of finishing sanders: orbital, straight line, and dual action. Orbital action means your abrasive is moving in a flat, tight oval rather than straight back and forth. Each orbit, typically, is less than 1/4 inch wide, so it's scarcely as if you were sanding against the grain; but you are doing just that, and enough to make cutting faster. This still produces a fine finish, while at the same time expanding the tool's capability for some rougher jobs.

Straight-line sanders, with the abrasive moving back and forth, can be restricted totally to sanding with the grain,

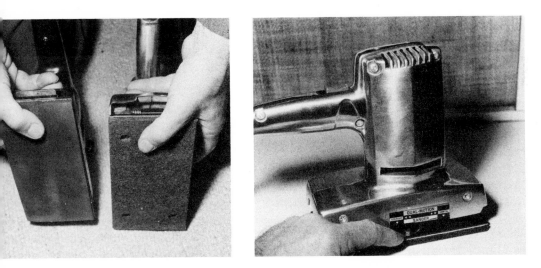

Figure 5-4. *Left:* Felt sanding pads *(right)* are better for flat surfaces, neoprene for contours. *Right:* Orbital to straight-line shift on this sander is done with a plastic wrench.

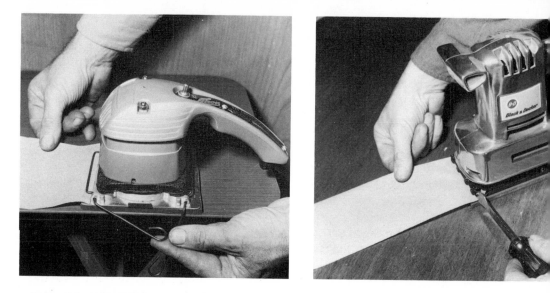

Figure 5-5. *Left:* Simple mousetrap arrangement secures the sandpaper to the pad of this model. *Right:* A holding roller turned by a screwdriver is used here to attach paper to a sander.

and are for extra-fine finishing. There are enough jobs of that kind in the average house to let it earn its keep. The straight-liner doesn't remove much material, or do it quickly, but it does it with ultimate smoothness. And it does not cut corners, but gets up into them. It can almost completely eliminate the need for hand sanding. At 9,000 strokes a minute, each 3/16 of an inch long, how can you compete?

The dual-action sander combines both orbital and straight-line action, giving you the best of both worlds. You can start out with orbital action for heavier stock removal, then at the flick of a lever or turn of a key switch to straight-line action for finish and flush sanding. A dual-action sander doesn't cost quite twice as much as a straight-line and orbital sander combined, but it approaches it.

Aside from differences in action, finishing sanders differ in the size, shape, and kind of pad they have. The bigger the pad area, the more work a sander is likely to do. The standard size of sheet abrasives is 9 inches by 11 inches. Some sanders use half a sheet, others use a third of a sheet, still others a fourth, a fifth, or less.

A small pad is at its best in tight situations and on irregular surfaces. On broad, flat surfaces, the big pad goes to town. So an in-between size is a compromise that satisfies most handymen most of the time. But it may not satisfy you, and you're the one who's going to be using it.

The pad on which the paper goes may be either felt or neoprene (synthetic rubber) sponge. The felt may have a little more firmness and bite, good especially for flat surfaces. The neoprene may

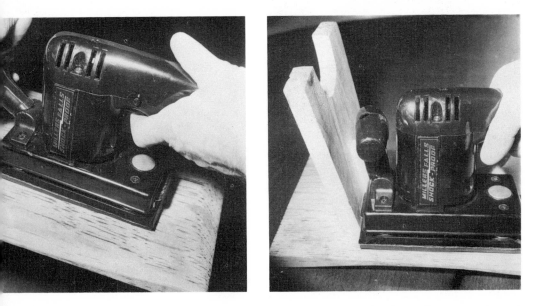

Figure 5-6. *Left:* The adjustable front handle swings down for greater control on straight-line work. *Right:* When sanding close to an obstruction, the front handle swings up out of the way.

adapt to uneven contours slightly better, and can be used for either wet or dry sanding. For some sanders, you can get either or both kinds, and use them interchangeably. Some pads extend beyond the sides of the sander, which, it is claimed, makes them better for handling corners. The way the paper attaches to the pad may be of some significance to you, too. They all add up to the same thing, but some aspects may be slightly different in appeal to different people.

Some sanders feel twice as heavy as others, either because of a difference in balance or because of an actual difference in weight. Weight is important. Pressure, which will slow the speed of the sander and cause its paper to clog, should not be applied on a sander. The weight of the sander alone, plus the natural weight of your hand, are all the pressure required in normal operation. A heavier sander usually has a more powerful motor, and will be more of a workhorse.

Sanders kick up a lot of dust. Often, a sander must be used in a living area, and occasionally you may find it necessary to sand with freshly painted surfaces nearby. You will always find it less pleasant in an atmosphere that is dust-laden. To overcome these problems, you can use a dust collector. Many sanders have vacuum attachments available as an extra. Some have their own vacuum

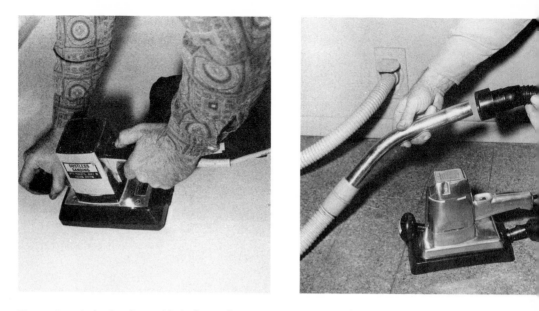

Figure 5-7. *Left:* Sanders with independent vacuum systems do dustless jobs on plaster joints. *Right:* Some sanders can be attached to any standard vacuum dust-collection system.

bag. Others have a hose that you can attach to almost any tank-type vacuum cleaner.

This will not exactly be "dustless" sanding, but most of the dust does get picked up. Removing dust as you sand enables you to sand faster—some say 25 percent faster. With no layer of dust to obscure your work, it's much easier to see what you're doing and how much more remains to be done. With a vacuum attachment it is necessary to place an enclosing skirt around the sander's pad. This skirt can be somewhat of a nuisance when you're trying to sand close to vertical surfaces and when you want to change paper. But you'll settle for these disadvantages to gain the greater benefit of getting rid of most of the dust.

The tank-type arrangement may offer a stronger vacuum than the integral back pickup. But the bag is handier to use. Just remember to empty it when it becomes about a quarter full and its efficiency will stay relatively high.

Selection of the right kind of paper is an important part of success. Don't use ordinary flint sandpaper. It's cheap to buy, but it wears out so fast it's more expensive to use. It's not made for the high-speed operation of power sanding.

The paper most commonly used for finishing sanders is aluminum oxide. You can recognize it by its brownish color. Also used is garnet, a natural abrasive that is slightly softer. It is recognizable by its reddish color, and is used exclusively for wood. Silicon carbide has limited application. It is black and very hard, and is used mostly for very fine finishing of lacquered and varnished surfaces.

Garnet and silicon carbide papers are available waterproof. You can recognize the waterproof type by its oiled-paper look. It can be used with oil, water, or other liquids as lubricants, just as long as they're not flammable.

For best results on a typical sanding job, use only open-coat paper with a grit no coarser than 1/2–60. (Some manufacturers say 1 1/2–40.) An open-coat paper works faster than closed coat, doesn't clog, and produces just as smooth a finish. Possible exceptions are high-speed vibrating sanders. They can take closed-coat paper satisfactorily because their rapid action shakes dust loose remarkably well.

For many sanders you can buy abrasive sheets, in packages of ten to twenty-five, of the exact dimensions you need for your sander. The usual run of grit, from very coarse to extra fine, is 40, 50, 60, 80, 100, 120, 150, and 220. These numbers are mesh sizes, the number of openings per square inch in each direction on sieves used in grading the grit. Formerly (and sometimes still) you'll find grit sizes indicated by old-style arbitrary numbers like 1 1/2, 0, 2/0, etc. They translate like this: 1 1/2 is 40, 1 is 50, 1/2 is 60, 0 is 80, 00 is 100, 0000 is 150.

One accessory you can get for a sander is a felt rubbing pad. This pad, usually about 1/4 inch thick, is used with finishing compounds on furniture. It can be used with loose abrasives, finer than any that come on paper. Another good accessory is a lamb's-wool polishing pad for "hand-finish" polishing of furniture and paneling.

GUIDE TO POWER ABRASIVE SELECTION

Type of Wood	Rough	Finish	Fine Finish
Birch	2 1/2–1	1/2–0	2/0–4/0
Cypress	2 1/2–1 1/2	1/2–0	2/0
Fir	1 1/2–1	1/2–0	2/0
Gum	2 1/2–1 1/2	1/2–0	2/0–3/0
Mahogany	2 1/2–1 1/2	1/2–0	2/0–3/0
Maple	2 1/2–1	1/2–0	2/0–4/0
Maple (curly)	2 1/2–1 1/2	1/2–0	2/0–4/0
Oak	2 1/2–1 1/2	1/2–0	2/0–4/0
Pine (white)	1 1/2–1	0	2/0
Pine (yellow)	2–1 1/2	1/2	0
Walnut	2 1/2–1 1/2	1/2–0	2/0–4/0

When you start sanding, and when you finish, flick the switch only when the sander is not in contact with the work. If you start up or shut down while the sanding surface is in contact, you may make marks you'll be sorry about. If you have your choice of orbital or straight-line motion, use the orbital for such jobs as removing an existing finish, cutting wood down to size, or preliminary rough sanding. Use the straight-line deal for fine finishing, and always in the same direction as the grain of the wood.

Begin with a grit coarse enough to accomplish the dirty work, then move on to a finer grit and a still finer grit until you're satisfied with the smoothness of the results. For a fine finish with a minimum amount of sanding, start with the finest grit that will remove the surface defects. On many projects you may want to round corners and edges slightly. They will look better, wear better, and hold finish better. When proceeding from coarse to fine paper, don't skip more than two grits at a time—better, no more than one. A good and perfectly legitimate progression might be from 60 to 80 to 120. For between-coat sanding of enamel and varnish, you won't want anything coarser than 220. Keep the sander moving. If you stop in one place for long you will make a rut. With a straight-line sander, if you go across the grain you'll tear the wood fibers. With an orbital sander, grain direction isn't quite so critical.

Follow the manufacturer's directions for care and maintenance. Some sanders never require lubrication, others do. On most sanders, you can replace worn carbon brushes on your own, but you may invalidate your guarantee rights if you undertake any major repairs.

Keep the tool clean. It is especially important that ventilating holes never become clogged. Overheating can affect the life of the motor. If the motor does overheat, remove the sander from the work and run it at no-load speed to cool it off.

Sanding Sealers

A sanding sealer permits you to sand wood smoother than would be possible any other way. It is possible to purchase a sanding sealer ready-mixed or you can make one by diluting 4-pound cut shellac with 3 or 4 parts of denatured alcohol. The latter is brushed on smoothly, allowed to dry, and then sanded.

When using the ready-mixed sanding sealer, stir it well before using, but do not shake. Thinning, which can be done with mineral spirits, is not required except for spray application, or when sealer is used as a wash coat or filler coat. Apply sanding sealer liberally in an even coat. When thoroughly dry, after two or three hours, sand lightly with very fine sandpaper. Two or three coats of sanding sealer are necessary when it is to be used as a complete finishing system; only one coat should be applied when used as a sealer under varnish. Remove all sanding dust before recoating or applying varnish.

Before using sanding sealers, it's well to keep in mind that they do have an effect on the penetration of stains and other finishing materials. If this could be a problem, run some tests on identical wood to determine the effect of the sealer on the materials that follow it (see pages 137–38).

USE OF STEEL WOOL

Steel wool is made of finely shredded steel and is a most important and economical material for use in many stages of restoration. Many finishers ignore steel wool and depend entirely on abrasive paper for smoothing, thereby losing the benefit of this most valuable material. It must be remembered that a poorly smoothed surface is likely to be a poorly finished one.

There are only six grades of steel wool that should be used for woodwork. They are as follows:

No. 3—the coarsest grade, rarely used in furniture work.
No. 2—should be used on rough lumber only.
No. 1—the coarsest grade that should be used on furniture.
No. 1/0—the most commonly used of all grades.
No. 2/0—used for rough smoothing.
No. 3/0—the finest grade and used for final smoothing.

Steel wool is commonly carried in paint and hardware stores. It usually comes in packages of sixteen individual pads, and it's well to have a package of each furniture type (no. 1 to 3/0) on hand. Steel wool may be purchased also in small packages of mixed grades, but it's not too economical to buy it that way. It also comes in a large one-piece roll in packages of the same size as those containing the sixteen pads. If there is a choice, avoid this type, since it is hard to tear and roll into pads, which is the best way of using it.

Steel wool uses in refinishing are as follows:

1. After paint and varnish removers, as an aid in mopping up or cleaning off the messy residue left after most of the remover has been removed with a putty knife or burlap. Use grade no. 1 for this work. It will not scratch when the surface is wet and it may be used to advantage when dipped in alcohol.

2. After sanding or scraping a surface, use the finer grades for greater smoothness. Start with grade no. 0 and finish with the finer grades in turn. Steel wool is best on hardwoods, and is particularly good for smoothing turnings and carvings. On long turned surfaces (like table or chair legs) it will work rapidly and will not disturb marks or ridges left from the old, slow-turning lathes. Steel wool will put a smoother finish on end grain surfaces after they have been sanded.

3. When stains are to be applied to a surface, it is better not to smooth the surface too much, to allow the stain to penetrate, but a light rubbing with fine steel wool will smooth the surface after the application of the stain without injury.

As steel wool is used it disintegrates into minute particles, many of which go into the air. It shouldn't be used outdoors because of the danger of its blowing into the eyes, and those with tender hands should wear gloves to keep it from working into the skin. The pads of steel wool fill with wood dust during use, and their life and cutting power may be prolonged if the dust is knocked out by striking the pad against something. New sharp surfaces may be brought to the top by turning the pads inside out, but it's not a good plan to add a new pad to an old one, for steel wool mats as it is used, especially in the finer grades.

CABINET SCRAPERS

A cabinet scraper is a difficult tool to use properly. Its sharp, hook-shaped edge removes a very thin shaving from the wood surface. Unless this edge is sharp and smooth, it won't do the work properly but will leave marks that will later show through the final finish. Watching an expert use a scraper is indeed a pleasure, in fact, it would be well for an amateur to take lessons from such a person, both in the handling and sharpening of the scraper. In the art of cabinet making, both operations are among the most difficult to perform correctly.

Scrapers are used in cabinet shops for final smoothing of surfaces after they have been planed. They are particularly well adapted for smoothing cross-grained boards, which are difficult to dress with a plane. Some experienced workers like to use the scraper for removing paint or varnish. One should be sufficiently adept in its use or great damage may result.

One cause of damage lies in a scraper not being properly sharpened (causing scratches), another in gouging the wood with the edge or corners of the scraper. There is less risk in using a scraper on hardwoods than on soft, since softwoods are more likely to rip and fuzz. Extensive sanding is then necessary to restore them to their proper condition. A scraper should not be used on old woods (such as pine), that have a beautiful patina, since some of this cherished surface is bound to be lost in the process.

Many experts warn against using a scraper on mahogany, walnut, or cherry. Scratches on the surface of these woods will show through a clear finish. It is often difficult to remove color from maple without resorting to the scraper. However, the best rule to follow is never to use a scraper except as a last resort.

A scraper is a very handy and satisfactory tool for many small jobs and as a supplement to other tools, as in removing spots from paint left by a paint remover. It is also useful for removing paint from angles and crevices or as the only means for removing flaky paint from the legs of chairs, etc. Indeed, there are many people with experience who understand the proper use of a cabinet scraper and who don't consider their work properly done without it.

There are two kinds of scrapers recommended for use. These are as follows:

Hook Scraper

This scraper consists of a shaped wooden block into which is inserted a narrow, curved steel blade. This blade is placed crosswise in a metal groove at one end of the block. The handle end usually has a compartment for storing spare blades. Several manufacturers produce this type of scraper, which is available at hardware stores and tool supply houses. It comes with extra blades, and additional ones may be purchased as needed. In the hands of an inexperienced person, this tool can be a dangerous one, since the blade corners are sharp and apt to gouge a surface if not properly handled. The edge of the blade is beveled and will retain its sharpness for a longer time, if burnished.

Blade Scraper

These blades are fabricated from flat pieces of hardened tool steel about 1/16 of an inch in thickness. They may be purchased in the stores mentioned above. The type of blade most commonly used is rectangular in shape (in sizes up to 3 inches by 6 inches), while others are available in different shapes or may be ground to any shape required. The edges are squared, then hook-turned and burnished.

It is well worthwhile to practice using a scraper (of any type) on pieces of scrap wood before undertaking work on a piece of furniture. The following general rules are, for the most part, applicable to the use of both the hook and blade scrapers.

1. Because of its construction, a hook scraper is drawn only toward the worker and should be used with one hand. The tool should be tilted at the most advantageous angle and just enough pressure applied to *shave* the surface properly.

2. Most of the work with a blade scraper is done on a plane surface, by pushing the tool away from the worker. The scraper is held with the fingers of both hands on the far side of the blade and with the thumbs on the near side. When working on a surface at a corner or adjoining a molding, etc., it is easier to pull the blade toward you. The blade can then be held in one hand. The angle at which the blade should be held is approximately 45 degrees, with the top slanting in the direction of the push or pull.

3. On plane surfaces (with either type of scraper) make the strokes as long as possible and with an even pressure, lifting the tool on the return stroke, or you will dull the edge.

4. Scraping with the grain is best, although you can scrape across it. You should avoid scraping across the grain or on an end grain. Scrape away from surface ends rather than toward them. When the scraper is held at a slight angle to the direction of the push or pull, the result is known as a "skewed cut." This type of cut is smoother and the blade stays sharp longer, but great care must be exercised to prevent a corner of the blade from gouging or scratching the surface.

5. If it is found difficult to secure a smooth surface with a scraper, a light sponging of the surface before scraping will aid in getting more satisfactory results.

6. The use of hand scrapers requires caution, since the blades are not held at a fixed angle or position, as are the blades in a plane or other types of tool scrapers. Consequently, on some kinds of woods, hand scrapers tend to follow the contour of the surface, cutting more deeply into soft areas and riding over hard ones.

7. When a scraper no longer lifts thin, curved shavings, and shows a tendency to fuzz the surface, the blade needs to be resharpened. These same conditions may arise when the scraper isn't properly handled or the cutting edge has not been correctly sharpened or hooked (turned) by burnishing.

WET TEST FOR COLOR

Make a wet test to see whether a change in the bare wood will take place if a clear finish is applied. This test can be made on wood that has had no finish, and is the next step after a surface is free from previous finish or paint and after sanding and smoothing. The test will show the approximate color the wood will take when a clear finish is put on.

Merely wet a fingertip with clean water or saliva and touch the surface. The drier and more porous the wood, the greater will be the change in color. The most pronounced difference in color from this test will be found in softwoods like pine, but the change will hardly be noticeable in green or unseasoned woods.

Woods with open pores, whether they are softwoods or hardwoods, darken more after an application of a clear finish than do those with closed pores. Neither type of wood will absorb to a great degree until the sap has dried out. Those which contain more of the natural oils and gums dry out more slowly than those containing these to a lesser degree.

The purpose of this simple test is to determine whether it will be necessary to treat the surface with a linseed oil mixture or stain.

COLORING WITH LINSEED OILS

Pure linseed oil, applied in a mixture with pure turpentine to a wood surface that has been freshly sanded, smoothed, and cleaned, may produce rich colors that are admired by some refinishers and disliked by others. These colors may range from various shades of yellow to reddish-brown, depending upon whether raw or boiled linseed oil is used, the number of applications, the condition and age of the wood, and whether the wood is open-grained or close-grained. Raw linseed oil is lighter in body than boiled oil, penetrates deeper, and usually results in a lighter color.

The degree of color, from a single application, is often affected by the wood's ability to absorb the mixture—that is, whether the wood is old and the sap and natural oils have dried out, whether it is open-grain or closed-grain, hardwood or softwood.

The colors desired from refinishing change in style from time to time. This is especially true in the case of antique pine furniture. In the past, the most popular color for pine was reddish-brown, but, now that the vogue is for modern houses and bleached, streamlined furniture, it has influenced the taste, and pine finished in natural color is the more popular.

Maple may be given a beautiful golden

tone by the application of the boiled oil mixture, while old oak and other porous woods may darken too greatly from either the boiled or raw oil mixture, even though it is applied very lightly. The shade of color may often be judged or predetermined by a wet test.

The procedure for either the raw or boiled linseed oil mixture is as follows:

1. Saturate a clean cloth about 10 inches square in a mixture of half pure linseed oil and half pure turpentine, squeeze it out or apply it as is, according to whether a light or heavy application is desired, and rub the entire surface to a uniform color.

2. Wipe off any surplus mixture completely with a clean cloth. (If not wiped off, surplus oil will become sticky.)

3. Allow to dry at least 24 hours in a warm room or in the sunlight, until the odor of turpentine, with the nose held close to the surface, is entirely gone.

4. When dry, rub surfaces with 2/0 steel wool, even though the mixture didn't raise the grain.

It is a good plan to use a mixture of (commercially) *boiled* linseed oil on any unexposed surface, regardless of desire for color from its application and also irrespective of the type of final finish to be used on the *exposed* surface, to protect the unexposed surface from moisture absorption and warpage. It's also a good idea to keep the mixture in a container (a mason jar is good) for future use. Leave the small rag for application in the mixture. Label the container and secure the lid tightly, or the turpentine will evaporate.

COLOR RESTORERS

A wood surface that has been sanded and smoothed will usually appear rather drab. It is difficult to see any grain the wood may have, and the color is usually much lighter.

If you have made the wet test for color after smoothing, you now know the approximate color that will result from the application of a transparent finish. However, at this point in the work, many workers like to use a color restorer as a guide in deciding whether the piece should be stained or not. This is especially true if a surface has been repaired with an insert patch, as the patch may be of newer wood that will not stain the same color as the surface. The color of a cleaned surface may be partially or entirely restored by either of the two methods, as follows:

1. Brush or wipe on a thin coat of 1 part pure linseed oil and 5 parts pure turpentine. Allow to dry for 24 hours, or until the odor of the turpentine has disappeared. With this treatment old pine and maple take on a very nice color. Oak, mahogany, and other open-grained woods may darken too much.

2. Brush on a thin coat of 1 part white shellac (4-pound cut—see *Shellac Finish*, page 159) and 5 parts denatured alcohol and allow to dry for several hours. This is primarily a wash coat, but is often recommended and used at this point in the work. It brightens a color, shows the wood grain, and may be used on fine or coarse grain woods without fear of overdarkening them.

PRELIMINARY WASH COATS

Some experienced wood-finishers advocate that a wash coat be used on a wood surface before a stain is applied while others do not. A wash coat is a mixture of 1 part white shellac to 6 or 8 parts denatured alcohol. It is mixed, used, and applied similarly to a color restorer.

It stands to reason that no wash coat should be applied if it is going to lessen the penetrating ability of a stain, for without penetration a stain will not last. A wash coat may be beneficially used under certain conditions and circumstances, whether softwoods or hardwoods or those with large pores (called *coarse-grained or coarse-textured*) or with small pores (called *close-grained or fine-textured*).

The deciding factor is the condition of the wood. As previously stated, some woods dry out greatly, depending on the amount of natural oils or gums they contain. Some old pine dries to the point where it powders when sanded. It sounds reasonable, and it is my contention, that when woods are considerably dried out, a wash coat is beneficial before the application of a stain. However, this must be judged by the worker according to the condition of the wood and the type of stain to be used.

When making a decision, it must be borne in mind that a wash coat of the type recommended has but a very small proportion of shellac and will be absorbed quickly and deeply into well-dried-out wood. It should never be used on woods that are not well seasoned. The purpose of the application is to seal the pores partially and to retard the absorption of a stain, but not to prevent its absorption into the pores to such an extent that it will remain upon the surface only. The rate or speed of absorption of a properly sanded and thoroughly dry, clean wood surface may be judged with much accuracy by making a wet test.

It is recommended that no wash coat be applied when water stains or spirit stains (reduced with water) are to be used, and it is not needed under a varnish stain or a penetrating sealer, for these materials both seal and finish. A wash coat is often beneficial when oil stains are used.

All brush work with very thin materials should be done with as few strokes as possible. Three strokes only should be used—one stroke each way to lay the material on the surface and one stroke to tip it off (to remove or spread excess material). For this work a full-tipped brush (2 inches wide is good) is best, but don't overload it. Proceed quickly until the surface is covered.

STAINING WOODS

Stains are employed to bring out the full beauty of the grain or to emphasize the color of woods. They are also used to harmonize the color of a patch with the surrounding surface, or to match pieces of wood of different colors to bring them to a uniform color.

Stain will add color to wood that has no natural beauty of color in itself or if the color has faded. There is a definite need for stains in refinishing, but it is well to pause for consideration and not jump to conclusions before planning for its use.

Woods with no color that must be stained or painted are:

basswood	gumwood
poplar	white pine

Light-colored woods that may be finished in their natural color or stained include:

ash	primavera
beech	chestnut
birch	Philippine
elm	mahogany
oak	korina
maple	

Stain is not usually used on veneers or woods with natural beauty and rich color, such as:

butternut	rosewood
cherry	teak
mahogany	maple
myrtle	

Such woods as mahogany, walnut, cherry, pine, and maple, which have a natural beauty of pattern and color, should be finished to bring out those characteristics and should not be stained. Any type of clear finish will darken a wood somewhat and magnify the beauty of the grain and the wood patterns.

It must be remembered that a stain is *not* a finish and that a finishing coat must be applied over it, except in the cases of varnish stains, penetrating wood-sealer finishes, and lacquer containing stain.

It takes patience and experience to learn the art of staining, but the general information to follow should be of assistance. Some portions may be repeated from the information about or use of the various types of stains.

1. A surface to be stained should not be too smooth, but should be dry and free of dust or other foreign matter, before a stain is applied. When you can rub a piece of nylon hose over the surface without catching, it is smooth enough for staining.

2. A surface having a drab appearance may need a color restorer.

3. When the wood is extremely dried out, a surface should be treated with a wash coat as a preliminary coat, before the application of some stains.

4. A stain should be tested for color, shade, or tone of color to match by applying it to an unexposed surface of a piece, or to a wood of the same kind, and allowed to dry.

5. Stains of a similar type may be intermixed for shades of color and thinned for a lighter tone.

6. One coat of stain may be applied over another for a darker color and, if a piece is of several colored woods, stain to the darkest shade.

7. A stain should be brushed or wiped on quickly in an even coat and without overlaps. It is best applied on a horizontal surface, as it may be smoothed out more evenly there. If it becomes necessary to apply it to a vertical surface, wipe out sags and runs evenly.

8. After a stain has been applied, all surplus should be wiped off with a lint-

less cloth to an even color tone. The longer the unabsorbed stain remains on the surface, the darker will be the final effect. Times vary as to when the excess stain should be wiped off, according to the types and thickness of the stain and the condition or kind of wood.

9. Care must be exercised in wiping the edges and corners of the piece, to avoid removing too much stain.

10. It often requires two coats of stain to get a uniform color. There should be at least 24 hours between coats.

11. End grain surfaces, which are porous, will soak in too much stain, which will often result in too dark a color. To overcome this, the surface should be well smoothed and, if necessary, treated with extra wash coats.

12. When insert patches are to be stained, it is usually necessary to stain the entire surface into which they are placed.

13. When applying a stain (or paint) to an article like a chair, it is always best to do all the inside of the underpart first, then the outside of the underpart, and, finally, the upper part of the piece.

14. All stains should be applied in a room or place free from excessive heat or drafts.

15. Allow stain to dry for at least 24 hours unless otherwise instructed. If a stain is not thoroughly dry, it will weep (blend) with the sealing coat to follow and won't dry.

16. A stained surface should not be smoothed with an abrasive until after a sealer coat has been applied and dried.

17. Colors don't appear true in artificial light, especially fluorescent light. Therefore, apply stain during the daytime in strong natural light.

18. Stain colors of the same type can be intermixed—oil stain with another color of oil stain, one water stain with another.

Commercial Stain Colors

Color charts, which are furnished by the manufacturers of the various types of stains, are supplied without cost to customers in those retail stores (paint, hardware, and builders' supply) where wood stains are available. These charts show the various colors available, and each manufacturer has his own version of the shade of a color. These shades vary greatly, and are often called by a coined name, rather than by the name of the wood they represent.

Those most commonly found are oak, maple, mahogany, and walnut. The various colors may be called by those names only, a coined name, or a name that is generally accepted as a shade of one of the colors. The colors and shades are as follows:

Oak—light oak (yellowish); dark oak (brownish-yellow); golden oak (slightly reddish dark oak).

Maple—maple (brownish-yellow); honey (reddish-brown); Vermont (brownish-red).

Mahogany—mahogany (reddish-brown); dark mahogany (brownish-red).

Walnut—variation of brown to blackish-brown.

The colors on the charts may vary greatly from the color found in the can, so, when making a purchase, it is well to have the can opened and the color tested by placing a small quantity on a piece of paper, into which it is quickly absorbed and on which it soon dries, because the wet color varies from the dried. All stains should be mixed in the daylight.

Water Stain

Water stain is considered by most professional workers the best for all-purpose use. It is by far the most universally used stain for mass production in factories. For use in a home shop, it has both advantages and disadvantages.

The principal advantage in its use is that it may be readily mixed by dissolving aniline dye powders in hot water, producing a concentrated solution that may be stored in glass bottles indefinitely and diluted to tints as needed, resulting in low-cost dye. Also, with proper materials colors may be made and intermixed that harmonize with true wood colors of various shades and tones, that don't fade or bleed, and that may be applied to a prepared wood surface without a preliminary sealer coat.

The disadvantage in the use of this stain, for an amateur, is that for even application it is better applied with a spray gun than with a brush. Also, many workers do not care to take time or trouble to mix and store water stains when they are able to purchase the newly developed nonpigmented oil and other types of penetrating stains that are now

available in small containers, ready mixed for use and in colors to match various woods. Too, these stains do not raise the grain, while a water stain will. Another disadvantage in the use of water stains is that many paint stores do not carry the powders in stock.

The method of mixing and using water stain is as follows: Heat water to just below the boiling point in a vessel other than aluminum. Pour the aniline powder into the water slowly while stirring. Allow to cool, and store in a glass bottle. If the water is "hard" (containing lime) or not pure, use distilled water. The mixture should be in proportions of 4 ounces of powder to 1 gallon of water. Dilute this solution with pure water to the density of color or tint desired.

APPLYING WATER STAIN. To apply water stain, the procedure is as follows:

1. First moisten a surface. Then apply stain with a brush, using long, straight strokes. Free the brush from stain on the edge of the container or by shaking it, then go over the surface, picking up surplus stain. Continue doing so, using long strokes, until the surface is even in color. Remove all excess stain from cracks and crevices with a small scrub brush.

2. When brushing is completed, wipe the surface with a cloth, using light, full-length strokes, picking up stain remaining on the surface, making the surface uniform in color and without streaks.

3. The end surfaces should be thoroughly wetted before stain is applied to an adjacent surface. Don't let such end

surfaces become dry. Stain the end surfaces while wet and wipe off immediately, repeating if necessary. This method will keep the end surface from absorbing too much stain and becoming too dark.

When spots will not absorb the stain to match the surrounding area, rub them with 3/0 steel wool to open the pores while the surface is wet with stain.

NON-GRAIN-RAISING STAINS (NGR). Because water-soluble colors offer the best types of stain, except for their grain-raising qualities, finishing manufacturers have developed stains in which powders are dissolved in a solvent other than water. Stains of this kind are known by various descriptive trade terms such as *non-grain-raising, fast-to-light,* and *non-sand.* They are, of course, more expensive than water stains because of the solvent used, but they offer one of the best types of stain for new work. Their rapid drying makes brushing difficult, but smooth coats are easily applied by spraying. Strictly nonbleeding, they can be used under any type of finish coat. They dry for recoating in from 10 minutes to 3 hours, depending on the manufacturer's recommendation. Ready-mixed colors are numerous, but if you wish you may obtain concentrated primary colors and mix tints to suit your individual taste. It is possible to mix the stain powder and the solvent, but the cost is about the same as for the ready-mixed product.

NGR stains are best applied by spraying. Because of their quickdrying nature (some of them are ready for recoating in 10 minutes), brushing is difficult.

Also, because of the wetness of a brush coat, the stain tends to raise the grain of the wood, although it is strictly non-grain-raising when sprayed. These stains can be slowed down a bit with the addition of about 10 percent Carbitol or Cellosolve.

Use a large brush and apply the stain in a very wet coat. The cutting-in technique with a small brush is perfect for varnish top coats (see Chapter Six), but with NGR stain the edges will be dry before you get over the surface. Always break up the job into convenient areas; do the legs, rails, and top of a table in separate operations. If it is impossible to do a lap-free job, dilute the stain to half strength with an equal amount of solvent. Apply two coats of this weak stain. Another way is to wash the work quickly with the stain solvent and then apply full-strength stain immediately.

When you spray NGR stains, apply a moderate coat, not too wet. Shoot all inside edges first; do the top last. Use a small spray pattern but fan it out by holding the gun a fair distance from the work. Always have a good light on the work, so that the color density can be properly evaluated. By spraying heavier on light wood and less on dark wood, it is easy to obtain a uniform color on mixed or off-color wood.

Oil Stains

Oil stains are best for the beginner and amateur worker to use, whether such stains are purchased ready-mixed or are homemade. These stains not only are rich in tone and produce lasting colors, but are generally available, inexpensive, and easily applied and stored. They do not raise the grain, causing wood feathers, nor do they conceal the natural wood grain or wood patterns, and those of similar type may be mixed together for shades of color.

Oil stains are made of coloring matter with linseed oil as a vehicle, japan drier to hasten the drying of the oil, and turpentine used as a thinner, which carries the mixture into the pores of the wood and later evaporates. There are two distinct types of oil stains, as follows:

PIGMENT OIL STAINS. This type of stain is often referred to merely as an *oil stain* or a *wood-finishing stain,* without mention on the containers of the fact that it is a pigment type. The coloring matter is the same as that used in so-called colors in oil. The pigment settles to the bottom of the can and must be stirred before using.

Pigment oil stains are best on close-grained woods such as basswood, birch, cherry, gumwood, maple, pine, and poplar. If the stain is properly applied and wiped off, the small and closely spaced pores of these woods will not become clogged with the finely ground color pigment.

PENETRATING OIL STAINS. This type of stain is usually either referred to on the containers as a penetrating material or described by a coined word, indicating that it is of that kind. Since the coloring matter is in liquid form, these stains are transparent. They are best for use on coarse-grained woods such as ash, beech, chestnut, elm, hickory, mahogany, oak, rosewood, satinwood, sycamore, and walnut. Since these woods have large pores and coarse texture, they will often clog up too much with a pigment stain, which would be detrimental to the finished appearance.

Penetrating oil stains should be used by preference on woods that are not well seasoned or old enough to have had their natural oils dried out, and on surfaces that are quite smooth, as they will penetrate better than stains of the pigment type. Some workers prefer them to other types of stains and use them exclusively, when available.

The greatest drawback to this type of stain is that when it is used on an extremely porous surface it penetrates deeply and is very difficult to remove, should the occasion arise. If prior tests are made for color, tone, or shade, there should be no need for their later removal.

INTER-MIXING OIL STAIN COLORS. Practically all the variation of colors you may need for staining furniture woods may be made by inter-mixing stains of but three basic colors—maple (brownish-yellow), mahogany (reddish-brown), and walnut (true brown).

If the maple contains too much brown, it will be necessary to add light oak to the list, and should the walnut contain too much black, you'll need raw umber or burnt umber. To lighten the other colors, add gum turpentine to oil stains.

Those who doubt this can satisfy themselves as to its truth by buying all the colors available (including the oaks)

COLOR GUIDE FOR MIXING STAINS

To Stain Woods	Start with Base of	Add to Base
Brown (reddish)	Walnut stain	Reddish-brown mahogany stain
(yellowish)	Walnut stain	Brownish-yellow maple stain
Yellow (brownish)	Maple stain	Walnut stain

COLOR GUIDE FOR MIXING COLORS IN OIL
IF YOU MIX YOUR OWN

Color You Want	Use Base of	Add to Base Very Small Amount of
Cherry (light)	Burnt sienna	Raw sienna
(dark)	Burnt sienna	Burnt umber
Mahogany (reddish)	Burnt sienna	Burnt umber
(brownish)	Burnt umber	Burnt sienna
Maple (yellowish)	Raw sienna	Raw umber
(reddish)	Burnt sienna	Burnt umber
(blend)	Raw sienna	Burnt sienna + raw umber or burnt umber
Oak (light)	Raw sienna	Raw umber
Pine (warm brown)	Raw sienna	Ultramarine or deep Thalo green
(honey)	Yellow ocher	Raw sienna
Walnut (dark brown)	Burnt umber	Vandyke brown
(reddish-brown)	Burnt umber	Burnt sienna
(yellowish-brown)	Burnt umber	Raw umber

Mix together: 3 parts commercially boiled linseed oil
1 part gum turpentine
1/2 part japan drier

and applying them to a clean light-colored wood surface. Write on each the color used, allow to dry, and then brush over with a white shellac or clear varnish finish.

If this test is made, there will be no variation in color, or only one of the slightest degree, between the various oak stains and light maple. The mahogany and walnut, however, will show their own distinctive colors.

A small amount of oil stain goes a long way, especially when thinned with turpentine for lighter color tone. Buy only quality stains of the three colors and intermix for various shades of color. If necessary, you may add to these colors, as described earlier. To dull or gray color that is too bright, add a small amount of deep Thalo green (blue-green) color in oil to an oil stain. To mask refractory or other stains, add a small amount of blue-green color, as when you dull or gray color. *Caution:* Use a very little green to dull the red stain and to produce a reddish-brown wood tone. Don't stain the wood green!

Never buy cheap grades of stains. They are off-color, particularly the mahogany stain, which may be much too red. The walnut stain also may not be the true color of the wood it is to represent.

If you wish to mix your own oil stain colors using tubes of colors in oil, the basic colors are:

Red—burnt sienna

Yellows—raw sienna, yellow ocher

Browns—burnt umber, Vandyke brown, raw umber

Greens (to dull reds)—deep Thalo green, medium green chrome

Blacks—lampblack, ivory black

Combine the colors in oil according to the color guide below. Soften the pigments in turpentine and add slowly in small amounts to the mixture described below the chart, mixing thoroughly, until the desired color is attained.

APPLYING OIL STAINS. To apply oil stain, proceed as follows:

1. Test stain color on the underside of the piece to be sure it's appropriate.

2. Brush or wipe on an even and moderately thin coat of stain without overlaps, after having thoroughly stirred the stain, especially if it is the pigment type.

3. Allow to remain on wood long enough to penetrate and give the desired effect. Wipe off surplus with a lintless cloth before it sets. The stain should be allowed to dry 24 hours. Smooth lightly with 3/0 steel wool to remove roughness.

Spirit Stains

Stain powders soluble in alcohol make penetrating spirit stains, but they are also available in ready-mixed liquid form with various blended solvents. Spirit stains have the advantage of drying quickly. When you use them, a surface can be stained and filled or shellacked and varnished all on the same day. Because they dry rapidly, they are generally not suitable for brushing, but they can be sprayed. Spirit stains bleed and will strike through almost any type of finishing coat, including shellac. Bleeding causes a slight muddiness in the finish, but this is not a serious defect. Since spirit stains will penetrate an old varnish finish, they are often used for refinishing. Other uses include touch-up work and staining sap streaks. Spirit stains fade quickly when exposed to strong light unless well protected with finishing coats. They dry for recoating in 10 to 15 minutes.

Because the average stain of this type dries almost instantly, the best method of application is with a spray gun. If applied by brush, the work must be done rapidly and without backtracking. A small amount of shellac added to the stain will make it easier to brush evenly. Don't apply a coat of shellac over spirit stains, because shellac, which is also soluble in alcohol, will lift the stain and cause a muddy appearance.

Penetrating spirit stains always bleed, and will strike through any number of finishing coats. Wood finished with spirit stain shouldn't be exposed to strong sunlight until coated with varnish.

Pigmented Wiping Stains

Pigmented wiping stains, or stain sealers, are available in a wide range of color tones, which can be intermixed to offer an even wider variety. The pigments are in suspension in a penetrating-resin vehicle. This type of stain, which must be stirred constantly to assure even distribution of the pigments, is effective in uniforming the wood or in staining a piece of furniture made from different woods. Wood should generally be smoothly sanded to secure a uniform appearance. Soft, porous woods darken heavily, since they soak up more of the color, while harder woods absorb less stain. Pigmented wiping stains generally perform best on white pine and other softwoods. They also furnish a good method by which to create a "distressed" effect to a finish, since they help accentuate cracks, dents, and scratches.

Follow the manufacturer's label directions when applying pigmented wiping stains. Be sure to stir frequently and to give a uniform coverage to the entire area. If you are going to use more than one can of stain, mix the cans together in a large container to insure uniformity of color.

While all stains are wiped, wiping is the most important step in the application of this type of stain. After brushing the material on, allow it to penetrate. Then wait until it starts to dull over or has penetrated to the desired degree. Then wipe clean.

Should the color remain too dark after you have wiped all you can, dampen a cloth with paint thinner as per the manufacturer's directions, and carefully wipe again. You can also use this same technique to blend the wood grain more uniformly. That is, darken portions of the wood that are too light, like sapwood.

Although staining is usually employed to darken wood, pigmented wiping stains can be used to lighten it or create a "blond" effect. White wiping stain is brushed on, permitted to penetrate the wood surface, and then wiped off. This blond stain, like all pigmented wiping stains, works best on coarse-grained woods. Incidentally, all pigmented wiping stains in a penetrating resin help seal the wood to a degree.

Varnish Stains

These are not often used for fine wood finishes. However, there are occasional quick, cheap, temporary, or repair jobs where a varnish stain may be used to advantage. Varnish stains are simply varnish to which coloring matter has been added in sufficient quantity to produce a decided color, but not enough to completely obscure the surface. Transparent colors are used. These stains fill, color, and add a gloss to the surface, all in one coat. They do not penetrate the surface to any extent, they dry in from 3 to 12 hours, and they do not fade when exposed to strong light.

For really high-grade finishing, skilled craftsmen don't use this kind of stain. When a project is made from the cheaper grades of lumber, varnish stains may be used successfully because they give a uniform coloring to woods streaked with very soft and porous parts. This result is impossible with other stains unless you do a great deal of expensive preliminary work. If varnish stains are made too dark in color, they completely hide the wood grain and give the appearance of an enameled surface. They are applied in the same manner as varnish (see Chapter Six).

Other Stains

Other materials are often used by wood finishers as stains. Below are a few of the more popular ones:

Warm pine stain is recorded as having been made from plug chewing tobacco. The plug is broken up and allowed to stand in a half pint of household ammonia, then steeped for 15 minutes. Two coats should be applied to give varying degrees of light to dark tones, depending upon the strength of the material.

Brown stain is recorded as having been often and successfully made from tobacco soaked in water.

Nut-brown stain is often made by professional refinishers from potassium permanganate, which may be purchased in drugstores. It is violet in color but turns brown when applied to wood.

The so-called vegetable stains are extracted from roots, bark, and other vegetable matter. At one time they were used extensively, but have now been replaced by water-soluble aniline stains. Vegetable stains are mixed and applied in the same way as water stains, but have a tendency to fade when exposed to sunlight. The following are some of the vegetable stains: dragon's blood (red), alkanet (red), madder (red), logwood (black), indigo (blue), and fustic (yellow).

USING A SEALER COAT OVER STAIN

A sealer coat should be applied to a wood surface after a stain has been used, unless otherwise directed. It should also be applied before a wood filler (for an ultra-smooth, fine finish) and over the filler before the final coat, as related later in this chapter.

Wood finishers have never come to complete agreement as to the type of undercoat to be used beneath succeeding coats, but it is now generally conceded that the sealer material should be a thin coat of whatever is used for the final finish.

The purpose of the sealer coat is to keep the stain from bleeding into succeeding coats by sealing the pores, to ready the surface for a filler or smooth it for the final finish. The sealer prevents liquids from entering the wood fibers and reducing the stain materials, which often causes a gray cast or light-colored area surrounded by small rings.

Sealer coats should be so thin that they will leave no shine. Only one coat is applied (with a brush) and later smoothed, according to the final finish to be used, as follows:

For a *varnish finish* (or mixture containing varnish), reduce 1 part of varnish with 1 part of pure turpentine. A synthetic type of varnish should not be used, as it may not blend with turpentine. The 4-hour drying or spar varnish containers usually state thereon that they may be thinned with turpentine, while a synthetic varnish may mention no thinning material.

For a *shellac finish*, reduce 1 part of pure white shellac (4-pound cut) with 8 parts of denatured alcohol.

For most *lacquer finishes*, use two thin coats of pure white shellac, thinned one-half. Another popular sealer for lacquer and varnish is a special product known as sanding sealer. It is made of a lacquer-shellac base and it dries ready to recoat in about an hour. It brushes easily, has a good hard surface, and contains a sanding agent that permits clean, powdery sanding without gumming.

If a filler is to be used on a sealed stained surface, merely knock off any roughness by rubbing very lightly with 3/0 steel wool. If the final finish is to be applied over the sealer coat, the surface should be completely smoothed. Do this with worn 6/0 to 8/0 garnet paper or grade 3/0 steel wool. When using either type of material, great care must be exercised not to go too heavily on the edges or the corners, for fear of cutting through the stain. Should this be done, the spots will have to be restained, dried, and a new sealer coat applied.

Sealing Fir and Other Softwoods

Fir and some other softwoods need a good sealer because of the special character of the grain figure, which is made up of alternate hard summer growth and softer spring growth. If you do not use a sealer, the first coat of paint or finish penetrates unevenly and results in a wild, overconspicuous grain.

To tame or quiet this grain, several special types of resin sealers have been developed. They may be purchased from lumber, paint, or hardware dealers. If the resin sealer is used properly, it allows the stain to soften the darker markings and deepen the lighter surfaces. The finish will be soft and lustrous, and the wild grain figures pleasantly subdued. For application details, follow the manufacturer's directions.

FILLING THE WOOD SURFACE

Certain woods, such as oak, mahogany, walnut, and chestnut, have an open-grained structure with large, noticeable "pores," which make it difficult to achieve a smooth, even finish. With these woods, best results will be obtained if a paste wood filler is used. Filler is sometimes applied to bare wood, and sometimes over stain and washcoat sealers, depending on the effect desired. Fillers are available in colors to match different woods, or in natural (not colored) types. The natural can sometimes be tinted with oil colors to match the color of the wood (or the stain). It is best, however, to buy the shade you wish, to be sure your filler's color will be permanent. If unusual effects are desired, contrasting colors can also be used. Most fillers stain the flake of the wood as well as coloring the pores, so stains may not be necessary.

Fillers can be obtained in two forms —paste and liquid. Paste fillers, used on open-grained wood, are either semitransparent or opaque; liquid fillers, normally used on close-grained wood, are transparent. In general, fillers should be as transparent as possible so the natural color and beauty of the wood will not be hidden. However, opaque fillers have their place in wood finishing when special effects, such as a two-tone finish are desired.

Paste Fillers

Paste fillers are made with silex, a crushed and finely ground rock, crystalline in character and with no chemical action. It is transparent and similar to glass. When the paste is thinned, the application is a simple, fast operation

FILLER MIX REQUIRED FOR VARIOUS WOODS

No Filler Needed	Thin Filler	Medium Filler	Heavy Filler
Aspen	Alder	Avodire	Ash
Basswood	Beech	Butternut	Chestnut
Cedar	Birch	Kornia	Elm
Cypress	Cherry	Mahogany	Hickory
Ebony	Gum	Orientalwood	Locust
Fir	Maple	Primavera	Mahogany
Hemlock	Sycamore	Rosewood	(Philippine)
Pine		Tigerwood	Oak
Poplar		Walnut	Teakwood
Redwood		Zebrawood	
Spruce			

that greatly enhances the beauty of the wood grain, as it is seen through a smooth glasslike finish (except when enamel is used). Paste fillers can usually be bought at stores selling paints and painter's materials. They are made by many paint manufacturers and are often sold under the name *wood filler*.

Paste fillers are usually found only in neutral (grayish) color. However, sometimes they may be purchased in colors to approximate those of the wood surface to be filled, in which case they do not need to be colored.

Of course, you can easily make a paste filler. To do so, mix the following:

1 part pure boiled linseed oil

1/3 part "4-hour-drying" type of varnish

1/3 part pure japan drier

1/2 part pure turpentine

Mix with this enough powdered silex to form a heavy paste. When silex is not available, fine silica may be used, even though it is not transparent. The varnish used must be of the type that, as stated on the can, may be thinned with turpentine, for synthetic varnishes (made otherwise) won't mix.

THINNING PASTE FILLERS. Commercial paste fillers, as they come in the can, are a thick, heavy paste and must be thinned considerably for use, after which they should be colored to match the wood to which they are to be applied.

General directions for thinning and material used will be found on the containers, but they may be confusing, as they often seem to be directed to the professional shop. There they are measured, by the weight of the base stock, to the gallon of thinner. You will also find various thinning materials or combinations of them recommended by different firms.

Manufacturers of paste fillers and authorities recommend as a thinner pure turpentine, benzine, or naphtha. A good mixture is 1 part of turpentine and 1 to 2 parts of white gasoline (ethyl is poisonous). The purpose of thinning is for ease of application, and the medium used must evaporate. You may use any one mentioned above for good results.

A filler is used for the sole purpose of filling the grain of the wood surface to achieve a smooth finish. It is best that the filler be thinned to various consistencies of thickness, according to whether the wood is close-grained or coarse-grained.

There is but one rule to remember. It is difficult to handle and remove a filler that is too thick, and while, if it is too

PROPORTIONS FOR MIXING VARIOUS QUANTITIES OF FILLER
Heavy Mix (16-lb. Base)

Approx. Amt. Needed*	Paste	Thinner
2 gal.	16 lb.	1 gal.
5 pt.	5 lb.	2 1/2 pt.
2 qt.	1 qt.	1 qt.
2 pt.	1 pt.	1 pt.
1 pt.	1 lb.	1/2 pt.
1/2 pt.	1/2 lb.	4 oz.

Medium Mix (12-lb. Base)

Approx. Amt. Needed*	Paste	Thinner
1 gal. 3 qt.	12 lb.	1 gal.
3 qt.	5 lb.	3 pt. 5 oz.
2 qt. 10 oz.	1 qt.	2 pt. 10 oz.
1 qt. 5 oz.	1 pt.	1 pt. 5 oz.
1 pt. 20 oz.	1 lb.	10 1/2 oz.
9 oz.	1/2 lb.	5 1/4 oz.

Thin Mix (8-lb. Base)

Approx. Amt. Needed*	Paste	Thinner
1 1/2 gal.	8 lb.	1 gal.
1 gal.	5 lb.	5 pt.
3 qt.	1 qt.	2 qt.
3 pt.	1 pt.	2 pt.
1 1/2 pt.	1 lb.	1 pt.
12 oz.	1/2 lb.	1/2 pt.

*One pint of thinned filler covers approximately 36 square feet.

thin, a succeeding coat of the filler may be, applied should there be bare spots, too thin a coat may be injurious to a stain, if the stain is not properly sealed.

COLORING PASTE FILLERS. Paste fillers are used *over* stain, rather than depending upon the color of the filler for a stain. When a paste filler is used, it is best that it be approximately of the same color as the surface to which it is applied, except when the final finish is to be paint or enamel. Otherwise, if the filler is not correctly applied or properly wiped off, it might show through a transparent finish.

Neutral paste (usually a gray color) may be changed to match the wood, whether it be stained or natural color, by the use of colors in oil or colors in japan, which are available for this purpose.

Dry powder colors mixed in turpentine, and oil-soluble aniline colors thinned with turpentine, are sometimes used for colors in paste fillers, and a shade of color may often be had by using a pigment stain or a penetrating wood stain as it comes from the can.

STANDARD FILLER COLORS

Black—Add drop black (a tint of black) to natural filler. Suitable for blackwood or dark mahogany.

White—Color natural base with zinc oxide. Used for limed oak and similar effects on chestnut and ash.

Amber—Tint natural base with yellow or orange oil colors. Suitable for ambered walnut, harvest wheat mahogany, and other bleached finishes.

Light brown—Tint with Vandyke brown to the required shade. Can be used on any light brown-color wood.

Dark brown—Vandyke brown with a touch of drop black. For walnut, mahogany, etc. Suitable for any medium-to-dark color wood.

Walnut—Half and half Vandyke brown and burnt umber.

Light red—Use any red color (Indian red) in oil or japan, toning darker or lighter with drop black or zinc white.

Figure 5-8. Applying wood filler: (1) Before applying a filler to a surface, open the wood pores by rubbing water over the surface with a sponge. It's best to test the finish on a sample piece. (2) In place of wetting the wood, you can rub the surface down with a stiff wire brush. This can also be used in combination with wetting.

Dark red—Equal parts of burnt umber and rose pink. Add drop black for a darker shade. Used for Sheraton mahogany or any other red finish in which dark pores are desirable.

The mixing of colors to match a wood is not at all difficult, and may be quickly learned by a little experimenting. Thin the mixed color in turpentine and add to the thinned paste. Before applying this to furniture, it is best to make a test on scrap wood of like color to see if the color is satisfactory. Remember that a color in turpentine will lighten when it

dries. Actually, on most surfaces it is desirable to have the filler a trifle darker than the wood itself, to emphasize the grain pattern. Exceptions are the lime-oak filler, which is almost white, and the blue and green fillers used for special effects.

To summarize briefly, a thinned paste filler may be used without coloring if it is applied and wiped off in a manner that won't show the paste in the wood grain, but it is better to have the filler color approximate the color of the wood and best of all if it is the same shade of color.

Figure 5-8 *continued*. (3) If you don't want filler to darken the wood, apply a wash coat of shellac after opening the pores. Use half shellac and half alcohol. (4) Work the filler into the grain with a stiff brush, squeegee, or heavy cardboard. Wipe excess off across the grain. The filler here is plaster, varnish, and oil color. (5) When the filler has dried—about 24 hours—sand smooth in the direction of the grain. If the filler was not stained, stain it now. Finally, varnish or shellac.

USING PASTE FILLERS. There is a difference of opinion as to how the thinned paste fillers should be applied. If the following method and the correct timing for padding are used, the work should be a success, providing the filler is applied to a surface properly prepared for its acceptance. Have on hand a supply of clean burlap (15 to 18 inches square) and clean rags.

1. Clean dust from the surface with a stiff brush.

2. Apply the filler quickly and generously but to a limited area at a time, with an old, stiff, short-bristle brush, *with* the grain of the wood, rubbing it in a little. Then brush it smooth, with the grain. Stir the mixture thoroughly before each application.

3. Fold a piece of burlap several times to about the size of your hand. When the surface of the applied filler flattens and loses its shine appreciably (usually 5 to 10 minutes), rub the filler into the wood surface with the *cross-grain* and a circular motion and without changing to a new surface of the cloth. This operation pads the powdered silex particles into the wood pores and smooths the surface. The time when this work should start is most important, for, with conditions favorable, the filler sets up quickly.

4. Follow immediately by wiping off the surface, *across* the grain only, with clean pieces of burlap squares, followed by fresh rags, until all the surplus filler is removed and the surface is clean and free from smears. Finally, when you look at the surface against the light and it shines, you may stroke the surface with a clean cloth *with* the grain, to remove all traces of surplus filler and fingerprints. This must be done lightly, or the filler may be pulled from the surface.

5. Carvings, joints, moldings, etc., should be scrubbed with a small brush packed with the filler. When the surface "flattens," wipe with clean burlap, followed by cloths, etc. Hold a bit of cloth over the point of a wooden meat skewer or a small, sharpened dowel stick to clean out the depressions and corners.

6. A filled piece should dry at least 24 hours in a warm room, but 48 hours or even more would be better. Fillers that have colors added to them take longer to dry.

When the work is correctly accomplished by the above steps, the surface should be smooth and ready for a sealer coat. If the surface shows evidence of the filler, remove the filler and smooth with worn 6/0 to 8/0 abrasive paper dipped in white gasoline.

If the surface has blotches or smears not seen until the filler has dried, moisten with a cloth with the same thinner as used in the filler and wipe the spots carefully to avoid creating a light-covered area. If this will not remove the excess dried filler, the spots or area must be sanded lightly with a worn 6/0 to 8/0 abrasive paper dipped in white gasoline. If the area is then too light in color, dip a rag in the filler and work over that part of the surface until the color is blended. Then allow to dry and use the sealer coat on the entire surface.

If a filled and dried surface is found to lack a sufficient amount of filler, fill the entire surface again by starting at the beginning of the process.

Liquid Fillers

For close-grained woods like maple and birch, use liquid filler or paste filler thinned to a liquid consistency. Transparent liquid fillers are available in pint, quart, half-gallon, and gallon cans.

Commercial liquid fillers composed of glass oil, hard oil, or other cheap varnishes are not dependable. Some of the cheap fillers bleach out white in time and make a mottled, cloudy appearance under the varnish. Some are brittle and crack easily. However, when made of first-class varnish by a well-known manufacturer, they are excellent. The filler should be applied as directed by its maker.

Shellac makes a good liquid filler. White shellac is best for natural and light-colored finishes, and orange shellac is best for dark colors. For medium-dark finishes, mix white and orange shellac. For use as a filler, shellac should be a 2-pound cut (see page 160), thinned with shellac solvent or denatured alcohol. Apply one or two coats and allow each coat to set completely hard before applying the next coat. Be sure to sandpaper each coat when dry.

SEALING THE FILLER

Apply a sealer coat to a surface that has been treated with a paste filler. This should be a very thin coat of the same material used for clear final coats. Thin shellac with alcohol or varnish with turpentine as previously directed (see page 138). This coat will penetrate the filler and, being of the same material as the sealer coat applied prior to using the filler, it will leave the same adhesion and expanding factors, and assist in leveling the surface. Sand with 6/0 to 8/0 grade abrasive paper to prepare for succeeding final coats after the sealer coat has dried for 24 hours.

Use a varnish sealer coat over paste fillers on wood surfaces when the final coat is to be enamel as this product is also thinned with turpentine. When a shellac sealer coat is used, it fails to give proper adhesion between the enamel and the filler, allowing the enamel to chip more easily.

CHAPTER SIX

Applying the New Finish

You were previously advised to plan your work in advance, not only for the type of finish you decide to use, but for the type most suitable for the piece.

The finish best suited for a particular piece depends upon these factors:

1. The wood from which the piece is made—pine or mahogany, etc.

2. The utility of the piece, that is, for what used—chair, cabinet, table, etc.

3. The quality of the workmanship or fineness of the piece—a highboy as compared with a cobbler's bench.

4. The customary finish for the type or period of the piece, that is, the kind and smoothness of a finish that is or should be found on certain types of furniture—as, for example, a crude piece of pine furniture as compared to a mahogany dining room table, that has been smoothed with a paste filler.

It is just as bad to overfinish as to underfinish, depending upon the factors outlined above. There are, however, many cases that are not in the extreme; a worker should use good judgment.

You were also instructed to plan ahead any change of color or degree of smoothness desired, in order to decide on a stain to be used (for color), or whether to apply a paste filler (for smoothness). This work must be completed, and a sealer coat applied after each, before putting on a finish coat.

When all work of preparing for a new finish has been successfully completed, you are then ready to apply a previously chosen finish material, to be left in a:

High gloss finish, which is the natural gloss left after the application of several coats of finishing material. A finish seldom desired for indoor furniture.

Satin rubbed finish, a finish secured by smoothing a high gloss finish with abrasive papers of steel wool and then waxing. The most used and liked finish.

146

Polish rubbed finish, a finish requiring a paste filler before the final finish. A finish to be used on that type, period, or quality of furniture requiring it.

The most employed clear final finishes are varnish, shellac, oil, penetrating wood sealer, and lacquer finish. The first of the procedures that follow will give full and complete information and instruction for the application of a varnish finish. The balance of this chapter will give information, specific uses, and instructions for the other finishing material, leading up to or for a high gloss, satin rubbed, or polish rubbed finish.

VARNISH FINISH

The most satisfactory finish coat for the do-it-yourself operator to apply is varnish. Varnish is available in high gloss, medium gloss, satin finish, and completely flat. A good furniture varnish is resistant to water, alcohol, and other liquids, and should be relatively easy to apply. The number of coats determines the "depth" and smoothness of the finish.

A good finish requires at least two and preferably three or more coats with light sanding between each. Avoid working in dusty locations, and never apply varnish when the air is damp or cold. Where possible, lay pieces horizontal to simplify brushing.

Varnish is best applied with a good quality bristle brush, although a pad of lint-free cloth can also be used .

The Material

Most varnishes today are made of synthetic resins—alkyd, phenolic, vinyl, or urethane—that dry fairly rapidly to form a hard surface coating that is exceptionally resistant to rough wear. In the first edition of this book there were over six special mixtures of varnishes mentioned. Today, with the man-made resins, there are still three basic types—glossy, satin, and flat—but the mixtures depend on the synthetic used. It is almost impossible for the average home handyman to judge the quality of the varnish in advance of its use, for it is measured in whiteness, in resistance to yellowing, and thickness of film. Vinyls and urethanes are the clearest, and show very little color change. Some urethane and vinyl varnishes are even water-clear and often are sold as such. Phenolic varnishes are usually the most yellow, and tend to turn yellow more readily. Alkyds vary to an extent, and your best assurance of quality is a well-known manufacturer. This, of course, is true of any varnish you purchase. Don't buy a cheap varnish. A small quantity of varnish covers a large area and a cheap grade will never result in a good or lasting finish.

Brushing Varnish

Although brushing varnish is the most difficult of all ordinary brush work this should not discourage the beginner. Varnish should be "flowed" onto a surface with a brush, and with thin, even coats. The process is called "laying" it on and "tipping" it off. Most of your varnish work won't require exacting smoothness or freedom from foreign particles. It's

Figure 6-1. How to apply a varnish finish: (1) Sand the entire surface of the furniture. (2) Mix stains to obtain the right color, then test out on a scrap of wood before using it. (3) The stain may be applied by either a cloth or a brush. (4) Hold the brush at this angle for varnishing. (5) Sand lightly after each coat has set. (6) Complete the job with a protective coat of wax over the last coat of varnish.

important to have a good brush for varnishing. There are brushes especially made for use with varnish. (For general information regarding brushes and the type to buy, see pages 245–49).

If workers inexperienced in applying varnish will follow instructions carefully in their first few jobs, they will soon qualify for doing precision work. Instructions for brushing varnish (and similar materials) are as follows:

1. Never varnish in damp weather or on surfaces that are not thoroughly dry.

2. Both the room and the varnish should be 70 degrees F. or warmer. There are times (as in winter) when the work must be done in a colder room. In such cases, or if it is desired to use varnish warmer than the room temperature, place the unopened can in a pan of warm water for about an hour before using it.

3. Surfaces to be varnished should be free from dust. Wipe surfaces with a clean, lintless cloth (shaking often), then remove dust from cracks, deep pores, etc., with a clean, dry brush, and finally wipe again with the cloth. The surface is then ready for the first coat of varnish, if preparing for a high gloss finish or a satin rubbed finish.

4. Any dust or particles left on a surface will be picked up by a wet varnish brush and spread elsewhere on the surface, or go into the varnish container, contaminating the clean varnish therein. (A very limited amount of dust, etc., is not detrimental to a high gloss finish, as the procedure calls for smoothing. However, it is detrimental to a polish

rubbed finish.) In preparing for a polish rubbed finish, the surface should finally be wiped with a tack rag to remove every last particle of dust, lint, etc., before varnish is applied (see page 259).

5. Never shake or agitate varnish before removing the lid, since this will cause the formation of small bubbles that will be detrimental to smoothing out a coat. Hold the can in your hand and rotate it gently back and forth a few times to mix the varnish before removing the lid. When some of the varnish has been taken from the can, immediately place the lid (loosely) back on top so that the vehicle for thinning won't evaporate.

6. Varnish sets very rapidly. When varnish thickens to a point where it does not flow easily from the brush, it should be thinned as directed by the manufacturer on the label. A little thinner goes a long way, and it should be thoroughly mixed.

7. A brush is prepared for use before starting work by being dipped into the varnish and worked back and forth on clean paper to distribute the varnish evenly through the bristles. Too much varnish on a brush will cause it to drip or run onto the handle.

8. Never dip the brush into the varnish by more than one-third its length, and always flow on liberally with a minimum number of brush strokes. Do not remove excess varnish from the brush by dragging the bristles across the rim of the can. This causes tiny bubbles to form in the varnish and will make it almost impossible to achieve a smooth

finish. Instead, tap the bristle tips *lightly* against the inside of the container, above the surface of the liquid. Better still, use a "strike wire" for removing excess varnish from the brush before applying it to a surface (see page 260).

9. When brushing varnish, apply only a moderate amount of pressure on the handle. Do not bend the bristles. Flow on with parallel strokes, then cross-stroke immediately by brushing at right angles to the original direction. Finish off by stroking lightly with the bristle tips, using an almost dry brush and working parallel to the grain only. This eliminates brush strokes and will assure a coating of uniform appearance. Remember, that first coat of varnish should be "brushed" on very thin; later coats should be "flowed" on.

10. On horizontal surfaces, the varnish is laid on with very little brush work. Only lay an area about 6 to 8 inches at a time, working from the unfinished to the finished surface, and taking about two strokes. Then tip off the varnish, to smooth it and wipe out any bubbles, by holding the brush straight up and going lightly over the surface with the tip of the bristles. Inspect the surface against the light.

11. On vertical (standing) surfaces, the procedure is different, to prevent curtains (sags) on the finished work. Working an area of about 6 inches square, use short, quick strokes, back and forth across the surface by brushing down halfway and up halfway, so that the brush is lifted from the surface in the central portion.

12. Start strokes from a center toward an edge, rather than from an edge toward the center, to avoid wiping the varnish from the brush over the edge.

13. On turned parts, such as chair and table legs, brush around turnings but stroke lengthwise on the long, plain sections, tipping off halfway up and halfway down.

14. When varnishing small furniture (chairs, tables, etc.) that may be easily lifted, turn the article upside down, place on a workbench (boards on saw horses are good), complete all the understructure first, and then do the upper.

15. To wipe the varnish on with a cloth pad, dip the folded pad into the varnish, getting a generous quantity into the cloth. Spread the varnish on with long strokes applied parallel to the grain. Don't rub hard, and make no attempt to work the varnish into the surface. Wipe up runs or sags as soon as they are noticed, since varnish seldom levels out completely if allowed to set.

The common causes of varnish problems are as follows:

Pinholes often appear when a varnish has dried because the varnish was applied on a damp surface, a poor thinner was used, or the thinner was not thoroughly mixed with the varnish.

Crawling may be caused by coats being too thick, atmospheric changes, or the preceding coat not having dried.

Chipping or "crackling" may come from using a type of varnish that becomes brittle, or by placing one kind of varnish over another, the two having varying degrees of elasticity.

Sweating usually occurs when a varnish is rubbed before it is thoroughly dry.

Brush marks usually result from using too small a brush or brushing the varnish too long.

Drying a Varnished Surface

Under no circumstances should a varnished surface be rubbed with any type of abrasive (steel wool or an abrasive paper or cloth) until it is *completely* dry. If a surface is rubbed before it is thoroughly dried out, the result will be disastrous, in some cases requiring a complete removal of the finish and a new one to replace it. For good results, be guided by the general information given herein regarding the time for drying, tests for dryness, the removing of "fatty edges," "curtains," etc., as follows:

1. For high-quality work such as a polish rubbed finish, the first (thin) coat should be given a minimum drying time of 24 hours, 48 hours for the second, and 3 to 5 days for the third or final coat.

2. When insufficient time is allowed for drying, an abrasive rubbed on a surface will pick up any little particles of foreign matter (dust, etc.) imbedded in the finish and cause them to scratch or wear through the hardened face of the varnish. When this hardened face is damaged, the partially dried under material piles up on abrasive paper or is torn out by steel wool, leaving pinholes or spots on the surface.

3. Make a test with a thumbnail for hardness. If the surface seems hard, then make a test with the ball of the thumb for a print. Wipe the thumb clean and dry. Press it down hard on the surface, wipe the spot with a clean cloth, and examine for a print. If any is noticeable, set the piece aside for further hardening (a warm room is best).

4. It takes a long time for fatty edges, drips, sags, and curtains to become completely dry because of the thickness of the varnish in them. If an attempt is made to sand such a defect before it is hardened throughout, it will cut through to the bare surface, making it necessary that the work be done over, as no later coats would cover such a depression.

5. When such defects have completely dried, they may be sanded down with a fine grade of abrasive paper, well lubricated with a white soap, if great care is taken while doing this work. It is best to cut a thick defect (raised surface) down only part way. Then it should be washed and dried, and set aside to dry for some days. This extra precaution often avoids the necessity of removing the entire finish and starting over again.

Sanding Between Finish Coats

When more than one finish coat of varnish is being applied, each dried coat should be lightly sanded before the next one is applied. This sanding is done with a very fine grade of aluminum oxide paper, or with "super fine" (no. 400) waterproof sandpaper. Use the aluminum oxide paper after the first coat is dry, and the waterproof paper after the second coat is dry. With the latter, soapy water is often used as a lubricant. The use of very fine steel wool is also excellent between coats of varnish.

Remember always to sand the finish by working parallel with the grain and sand with *light* pressure only. Use enough pressure to dull the sheen and produce a uniform, satiny-smooth finish—but be careful to avoid cutting through the finish. The smoothness can best be determined by stroking lightly with the fingertips after wiping off the abrasive dust that has accumulated.

When sanding a large surface, such as a tabletop, rub with the grain of the wood toward the ends first and then near the sides, taking extreme care not to sand the finish from the edges or the corners. Then sand the center section with the grain, using long strokes, and an even pressure. Never sand cross-grain or in circles.

Avoid cross-grain sanding on furniture parts made of several pieces of wood with the grain running in different directions. For example, it is best to sand a paneled type door as follows:

1. First sand panel moldings, if any.
2. Then sand the panel, in straight lines, with the grain.
3. Then sand the top and bottom rails, protecting the side members of opposite grain from scratches by holding a piece of stiff paper at the joint.
4. Finally sand the side members, protecting the top and bottom rails.

When sanding is complete, dust thoroughly by wiping with a tack rag before applying the next coat of varnish.

High Gloss Finish

It is usually preferred that furniture for use in the house not be finished to a high gloss. There are, however, many articles, such as porch and patio furniture, on which you may wish to have a smooth and glossy finish.

Very often a two-coat job will suffice, but if a very smooth finish is desired, it may require three or more coats, and perhaps the surface should first be filled.

The final coat of any high gloss finish should be smoothed to knock off any raised particles that have settled on it while drying. On extremely smooth surfaces, this can be done best by a very light rubbing with 360-A or finer waterproof finishing paper, dipped into lukewarm soapy water. The less smooth surfaces may be rubbed lightly with 3/0 steel wool. Neither should be used until the finish coat has dried completely. If the work is done with a "light hand" and not too much rubbing, it should improve the high gloss, rather than dull it.

Satin Rubbed Finish

This finish is the most preferred and used of all the degrees for a final finish. It is a general purpose finish that is most satisfactory from the standpoint of wear and general appearance. It is adaptable to most types of wooden furniture and other wooden objects, and is recommended as a final finish for all antique furiture, except for period furniture and those pieces of fineness or quality of workmanship that have been smoothed with a paste filler and require a polish rubbed finish.

The soft, satiny sheen of this finish, which is gained by merely rubbing down a completely dried high gloss finish of sufficient coats and smoothness, may be had on all the finishing materials that are applied in coats, and that dry to a high gloss. These include varnish, shellac, varnish oil, penetrating wood sealers, blond, pickled, and lacquer finish.

Some workers leave the finish "as is," after it has been rubbed down to the satin sheen smoothness.

This finish is the easiest to accomplish, doesn't require a high degree of craftsmanship or too much exacting care in the application of the finishing material, looks and lasts well, and is suitable for virtually all woods. It should have *sufficient* coats of finishing material to bring the surface to a high gloss.

The final coat is smoothed as follows:

1. Sand the final coat very lightly with 8/0 to 10/0 wet or dry finishing paper—lubricated with water. This is to remove dust particles, etc., that can only be smoothed by sanding.

2. Rub the surface with 3/0 steel wool, with the grain, until the desired sheen has been obtained.

3. It is best and customary to wax this finish (two coats are best).

Polish Rubbed Finish

This is the pinnacle or acme of all final finishes, except perhaps the French finish, now seldom used. The most sought-for polish rubbed finish is a soft gloss with a high luster. The degree of smoothness of this finish is in direct proportion to the care taken in the application and smoothing of a paste filler and the sanding between coats of the finishing material.

The most practical material to use for this finish is a high-quality varnish. However, it may be accomplished with other finishing materials, including some penetrating sealers, lacquer, and shellac, if sufficient coats are applied (over a paste filler) to secure a hard and smooth high gloss.

A polish rubbed finish is seldom used on other than high-quality antique period furniture, or more recently made furniture of fine workmanship and design, made of choice hardwoods. It is customary that such furniture have this finish.

This finish is the most difficult to attain. It requires exacting work in rubbing with powdered abrasives, and the knowledge or judgment of just how this work should go for the desired degree of polish, which can only be obtained through strict obedience to directions and practice.

There are several things of importance done by professionals that should be followed to accomplish good work. They are as follows:

1. Pumice stone is used as the abrasive to rub a surface for a smooth and soft luster, after the final finish coat has been carefully sanded. The best grade for use

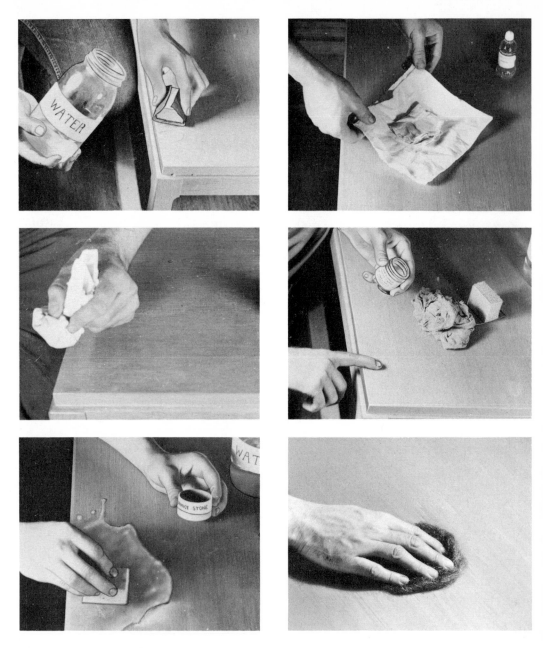

Figure 6-2. Finishing a final coat of varnish: (1) Sand the final coat lightly with 8/0 to 10/0 wet or dry finishing paper. (2) It is easy to make a rubbing pad. (3) How to hold a rubbing pad. (4) Applying rottenstone to a varnished surface. (5) Using pumice stone on a varnished surface. (6) Steel wool may also be used in final finishing.

is 3/F (triple-floated), which should be sifted through a fine cheesecloth into a clean container (a small pie pan is best), to remove lumps or foreign matter.

2. Paraffin oil (readily purchased) is recommended as the lubricant to use with pumice stone for an oil-rubbed finish. Sewing machine oil or a thin mineral oil may be used as a substitute. Many professionals prefer crude petroleum oil, but it is hard to remove.

3. Rottenstone (one grade only) is used for rubbing with water, for a high gloss finish, after a "pumice-oil" rub.

4. Rubbing pads should be carefully inspected before use for glazed spots, grit, bits of steel wool, etc., which might scratch a rubbed surface. They are used with the pumice-oil rub, the pumice-water rub, and the rottenstone rub. Rubbing pads used with oil may be scrubbed with a clean rubbing brush and white gasoline, while those used with water may be washed.

5. Dusting brushes used by professionals come in standard widths of 1/2 inch, and 1 inch, with the brush part about 6 inches long and a handle extending from one end. They are also used for dusting benches and the pieces being worked upon. A scrub brush with soft bristles used for the hands will suffice.

6. An old blanket or padding laid under the piece or parts being rubbed is a great help to avoid scratches. These should be covered with clean old newspapers to catch unavoidable splashes and drippings.

7. Three or more coats of finishing material (depending upon the kind used) are required for a quality finish. The final coat should have a *high gloss* and be very smooth.

FINAL COAT SANDING. Use the same method for sanding the final coat, as for a satin rubbed finish. You have already been given instructions for between-coat sanding.

RUBBING THE FINAL FINISH. A final polish may be obtained by rubbing the final sanded surface with either pumice stone and water or pumice stone and oil. Expert finishers often have a preference, but sometimes both are used for a desired effect. The highlights of their advantages or shortcomings are briefly as follows:

Water rubbing requires more skill, closer inspection, and better judgment. If any defect shows up, the surface can be easily cleaned, dried, and touched up or recoated. The work is faster and cleaner. It leaves a brighter gloss when oil-polished as a final operation.

Oil rubbing is best for use on a shellac finish (see page 163). The mixture of oil and pumice may be removed from a shellacked surface with soap and water, or gasoline, without injury to the finish. If all of it is not removed from a hard finish, like varnish, and it becomes necessary to touch up or apply a new coat, the material slows up in drying or doesn't dry at all. Oil rubbing is best for a soft, satin sheen.

Rottenstone is used for final rubbing to attain a highly polished finish. This operation is not necessary with a water-rubbed finish when full directions are followed.

EQUIPMENT FOR A RUBBED POLISH. The following items are used in accomplishing a rubbed polish:

pumice stone (3/F)

rottenstone (occasionally used)

rubbing pads (distinctive ones for water rubbing and oil rubbing)

2 flat containers, for abrasive powder and fluid (a small pie pan is good)

paraffin oil (or a substitute)

white gasoline

1″ wide rubbing brush

white cotton waste (better than rags for this purpose)

clean cloths

clean old newspapers

water

Water-pumice rubbing is accomplished as follows:

1. Place some sifted pumice stone in a clean, shallow container. Dip a rubbing pad in water, and then in the powder, or sprinkle the powder evenly over the surface to be rubbed and use a pad dipped in water only.

2. Rub the surface with the grain of the wood, using even pressure, taking fairly long strokes, and avoiding a twisting or circular motion.

3. Start on an end of a surface (at a side), next working an adjoining space until the entire surface is covered, trying not to overlap the rubbing. Then go over the entire surface again in the same manner, without the addition of more pumice stone.

4. Inspect the work by pulling the side of a thumb toward you at a spot, using a quick, snappy motion.

5. Continue the rubbing until the entire surface has an even sheen, without any highlights or without cutting through in any place. Add water to the rubbing pad, if necessary.

6. When you are satisfied that the surface has the degree of smoothness and sheen desired, wipe it off with damp cloths and polish with a dry one.

7. Then inspect the surface by looking at it against the light. Should there be any dull spots remaining, rub them with the rubbing block, *without* using any more pumice stone.

Pumice stone grinds finer and finer as it is rubbed. When a high gloss finish is desired, no more pumice should be added to the original amount put on a surface. The addition of pumice stone during the operation results in a much duller sheen.

A soft and satiny sheen may be had by leaving the water-rubbing sludge on a surface. Then dip a pad of white cotton waste in water, squeeze it out, and dip it in a rubbing oil. Use this instead of a rubbing pad for rubbing the sludge, working in lines with the grain and occasionally making thumb tests.

Oil-pumice rubbing is accomplished as follows:

1. Place a mixture of equal parts of paraffin oil and white gasoline in a clean shallow pan. Put some sifted pumice stone into another pan. Dip a rubbing pad first into the liquid and then into the pumice.

2. Rub the surface, adding more of the

liquid and pumice as necessary, following the same procedure as directed for water-pumice rubbing to produce a soft, satin sheen.

3. Wash the surface off with lukewarm, soapy water, or with white gasoline, if necessary. A final cleaning with a cloth slightly dampened with carbon tetrachloride (non-burning cleaning fluid), will remove the last traces of oil. Then give the surface a final polish with a soft cloth (chamois is better).

A better sheen may be had by leaving the oil-pumice sludge on the surface, rubbing it with cotton waste dipped in a *rubbing oil* (instead of water), squeezing it out, and otherwise following the same directions as given for the soft and satiny finish in the directions for water-pumice rubbing.

Plan to let the final finish season and harden before polishing with oil and pumice stone.

Rottenstone rubbing is a way of attaining a high polish after the completion of a water-pumice or oil-pumice rubbing. Dip a clean rubbing pad first into water and then into the rottenstone. Rub carefully in one direction, as already directed. A high gloss finish isn't usually desired.

Plan to leave a week after the completion of an oil-pumice rubbing before rubbing with rottenstone. The finish will soften slightly with the oil rub, and it needs time to harden well. The effect will be much better than if one followed after the other immediately.

RUBBING TURNINGS AND CARVINGS. It's advisable to delay the finish rubbing of turnings, carvings, beads, moldings, etc., to avoid marking the slightly softened flat surfaces, already finished.

1. The work should be done with the same mixture (water-pumice or oil-pumice) that was used on the flat surfaces.

2. Dip a rubbing brush into water (or oil) and shake out the fluid a little. Then dip it into sifted pumice stone and rub carefully, without much pressure, into detailed surfaces and on turnings.

3. Rub the surfaces with thin rubbing pads, moistened with the medium used. The high portions of carvings, etc., may be carefully rubbed in any direction, but turnings should be rubbed lengthwise.

4. Wash off, as previously directed (according to the mixture used), and inspect for highlights. Rub these with the pumice already on the pad.

"PICKING" VARNISH FOR A POLISH RUBBED FINISH. A varnished surface should be "picked" free from dust and other foreign particles as soon as possible after the varnish is applied. No matter how much care has been taken to free the room in which varnishing is done from dust, and even though all the necessary precautions are strictly adhered to, it is impossible to avoid foreign particles on a newly varnished surface.

Picking is best done with a "pick stick" (see page 259), which consists of a very thin wooden rod with a pear-shaped ball of "burned" varnish on one end. As a substitute, a small artist's sable brush (no. 3 or 5 is good) may be used for picking lint or dust.

A pick stick is used by touching a freshly varnished surface with the ball of burned varnish and lifting the speck of dust, lint, etc., *upward* with the stick. Before using, tap the ball against your hand and the burned varnish will become sticky.

An artist's brush is used by inserting the tip between the lips and withdrawing it to draw the bristles into a fine point. This point is used by *slipping* it under a particle and lifting the particle out.

If this work is done when the varnish is fresh and before it has a chance to set, the varnish will immediately flow over the spot from which a particle was removed. When varnish has set, it is too late to remove specks. Then allow the varnish to harden a bit and test the raised spot for hardness with the surface of a fingernail, as it might be an air bubble. All spots that have no give will have to be sanded or rubbed out when the varnish is thoroughly hard.

Foreign particles cause fresh varnish to pile up around them in a small mound by capillary attraction. The type of foreign matter can be recognized as follows:

1. *Dirt* will show as a dark speck.
2. *Bubbles* show a light-colored top.
3. *Varnish specks* are soft and transparent granules. They may be removed by the rubbing operation.
4. *Lint* will show a crooked line. It may be removed or rubbed out later, if not too large.

POLYURETHANE FINISHES

In addition to the conventional furniture varnishes, there are several other synthetic clear coatings that make excellent finishes for furniture. Of these finishes, the clear, oil-modified urethanes, such as the polyurethane finishes, are the most popular because they:

1. Are highly resistant to abrasion, scratching, water, chemicals, grease, solvents, food stains, alcohol, and oils.
2. Do not penetrate (they form a coating on the surface).

Polyurethane finishes may be applied to bare wood (new or wood with its old finish removed) that is smooth and free of dust and grease, or over a sealer or varnish finish that has been cleaned and deglossed. Do *not* apply a polyurethane finish over a shellac or lacquer finish or a paste wood or liquid filler unless especially formulated for polyurethane finishes. They are available in gloss and satin types. The gloss type is, of course, very shiny, while the satin type produces a sheen if wiped on, in, and off.

To apply polyurethane finish to bare wood, this procedure should be followed:

1. Thin the first coat of the polyurethane finish with mineral spirits according to the manufacturer's recommendations. Apply a smooth, even coat over the surface of the bare wood with a lintless cloth. First, apply crosswise to the grain. Then apply lengthwise to the grain. Rub on, in, and off.
2. Allow to dry 24 hours with ample air circulation. Then, rub gently with 3/0 steel wool. Remove all filings with a vacuum or cloth and tack cloth.
3. Within 48 hours the second coat (unthinned) *must* be applied over the

entire surface. Dry 24 hours with good circulation. If additional coats are desired, remember that successive coats of polyurethanes must be applied within a 48-hour period.

To apply polyurethane finish over a sealer or varnish, prepare the surface by applying a cleaning fluid solvent to remove grease (see pages 107–8) and gloss. Use 3/0 steel wool to remove any remaining gloss. Remove the filings and sanding with a vacuum cleaner or brush and cloth, and lastly, wipe gently with a tack cloth.

If areas are damaged, apply the polyurethane finish to those areas—"feather out" the edges. Dry 24 hours with ample air circulation. Steel-wool gently, then remove filings. Apply the polyurethane finish within 48 hours over the entire surface if you had to touch up the damaged areas first.

SHELLAC FINISH

For years, shellac was a favored finish of home handymen because it was quick-drying and quite easy to apply. In recent times, the so-called modern finishes—the synthetic varnishes and penetrating wood sealers—have replaced it to a degree. But for many purposes shellac still is a superior finish. For instance, it is perfect for chairs, settees, benches, desks, display racks, picture and mirror frames, clocks, etc. It is better not to use it on such items as tables, stands, chests, cabinets, bureaus, etc., on which may be placed articles that are hot or contain water or alcoholic beverages, since shellac stains easily and white rings develop when wet glasses, vases, etc., are placed on it.

Almost any kind of wood may be finished with shellac, but it is more complimentary to pine and the lighter-colored woods, particularly when white and orange shellacs are mixed to just the right shade to do justice to the wood involved, in which case it intensifies the wood colors.

The main reason why a shellac finish is so easy to apply is that in a correct mixture it is greatly thinned with alcohol. Many amateurs (and some professionals) attempt to hasten the work by applying shellac that is too thick. The result is a "botched" job, unsightly in appearance. Also, many people apply a succeeding coat before the previous one has dried thoroughly, fail to rub surfaces between coats, and often leave the last coat glossy, instead of removing the shine and applying wax.

The Material

Shellac is made from the secretion of the lac insect. Proper thinning of the shellac purchased in commercial mixtures is a vital part of its correct application.

The concentration of shellac in alcohol is known as its cut. Most shellac on the market is 4-, 4 1/2-, or 5-pound cut; that is, 4, 4 1/2, or 5 pounds of granular shellac are dissolved in 1 gallon of alcohol. The cut is indicated on the label. For almost all purposes, commercial shellac will require thinning with alcohol. Here is a table showing how to convert one cut to another.

DILUTION TABLE FOR
REDUCING SHELLAC TO DESIRED CUT

Original Cut	Desired Cut	Mixing Ratio Parts* Alcohol	Parts* Shellac
5 lb.	3 lb.	1	2
5 lb.	2 lb.	1	1
5 lb.	1 lb.	2	1
4 lb.	3 lb.	2	1
4 lb.	2 lb.	3	4
4 lb.	1 lb.	2	1
3 lb.	2 lb.	2	5
3 lb.	1 lb.	4	3

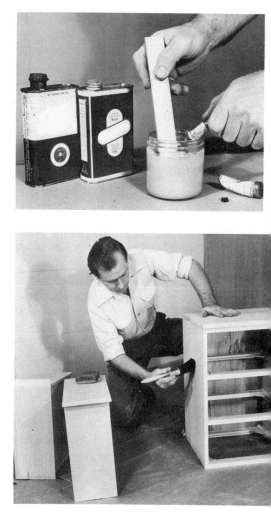

Using this table, you will be able to convert any quantity. That is, the proportions are the same even if you are thinning only a pint of shellac. For example, if you wished to thin a pint of 4-pound cut (the best cut for general use) to a 2-pound cut, you would use 3/4 pint of alcohol to 1 pint of shellac. When thinning the cut, use only pure denatured ethyl or grain alcohol. Never use acetone, gasoline, benzol, or the antifreeze grade of alcohol.

Before you use shellac, shake or stir it thoroughly. The first two coats should be thinned to 2-pound-cut consistency, while a 3- or 4-pound cut is best for final cut.

* "Parts" refers to liquid volume. Any convenient unit, such as pints or cupfuls, can be used. Proportions given are not precise, since minor variations in the resulting cut will have little or no effect on the final results.

Figure 6-3. Applying a shellac finish: (1) Prepare your own stains with equal parts turpentine and linseed oil, plus ground-in-oil pigment. (2) Apply the prepared stain heavily but evenly along the grain to hide defects such as board joints.

Figure 6-3 *continued*. (3) Apply three coats of shellac after the stain has dried, thinning shellac 50 percent for each application. (4) Next, prepare a paste of powdered pumice and blooming oil, a special acid-free variety of finish oil. (5) Saturate a wad of steel wool in the paste and work over the surface with a light touch to glaze. (6) After removing oil residue, apply a coat of clear paste wax, rubbing briskly with a wad of clean cloth.

Shellac is available in three types: orange, bleached (or white), and de- waxed. Orange shellac has a pronounced reddish-brown color and is cloudy in appearance. White or bleached shellac is a similar solution, but it is made from bleached resin. Dewaxed shellac is usually light in color, but unlike the other two it is wax-free and thus perfectly clear.

The three forms are very much alike. However, white shellac is best for most work and is essential for blond finishes. Orange shellac is used for dark wood or over darkly stained woods. Intermixing white and orange shellac to obtain color effects isn't advisable. Should deeper colors be desired to tone a finish where the stain doesn't seem exactly right, a transparent toner, which can be made by mixing alcohol-soluble powder stain with alcohol and adding it to the shellac as required, may be used. The same method can be used to darken lacquer and varnish finishes, using lacquer- and varnish-soluble powder respectively.

One fault of shellac is that in time it goes stale. About a year after it has been made, a chemical change causes the shellac to become so gummy that it will not dry. For this reason, shellac should be purchased in small amounts as needed, from a store where there is a good turnover.

Satin Rubbed Finish

This finish is ideal for most furniture or other wood articles. It is perfect for the cruder type of furniture and pieces made of pine and other light-colored woods on which it is advisable to use a little orange shellac in the mixture for added color. Here are some points to remember about applying shellac to obtain a satin rubbed finish:

1. Apply enough coats (usually four or more) of the shellac mixture so that the last one shines. Allow time for each coat to dry thoroughly (the first will dry much faster than the later ones). Test for dryness by trying to make a thumbprint.

2. Whenever roughness is felt with the fingertips, rub the surface (with the grain) between coats, using an 8/0 abrasive paper. Dust with a brush and wipe the surface with a cloth after each coat.

3. Allow several hours for the last coat to dry completely (overnight is preferred) and then rub it with 3/0 steel wool until there is absolutely *no* shine remaining. It is important to shake the shellac dust from the pads of steel wool and refold them, as steel wool becomes dull with use. Too much rubbing in one spot causes heat from friction, softens the finish, and tends to roll it up. Use great care at corners and edges to avoid cutting through the finish. When many minute bright spots still remain on a surface after the gloss has been removed by rubbing it with steel wool, sprinkle the surface with dry 3/F (triple-floated) pumice stone and brush it lightly. Use a small hand scrub brush with soft bristles on flat surfaces, and an old shaving brush (held by the bristles) on carvings, angles, etc. When the spots have disappeared, give the entire surface another light rubbing with steel wool.

4. Dust and wipe off the surface.

Then apply at least two coats of wax. (See *Wax Finish,* page 174, and *Waxing and Polishing,* page 236.)

Polish Rubbed Finish

This finish is for high-grade furniture and that type which calls for extreme smoothness and high polish. Surfaces should be completely smoothed with a paste filler before this finish is applied. Here is how to accomplish a polish rubbed finish with shellac:

1. Apply enough coats of the shellac mixture (usually six or more) until the last coat shines. Allow each coat to dry thoroughly. Test for dryness by trying to make a thumbprint.

2. Rub the surface (with the grain) between coats, using a 10/0 abrasive paper dipped in a linseed oil mixture (half raw linseed oil and half pure turpentine) whenever the slightest roughness is felt with the fingertips after the first few coats. When you can notice the finish beginning to build up toward the final coat (or to shine), rub the surface between each coat. Rub carvings and moldings lightly with a small hand scrub brush with soft bristles, dipped first in the oil and then in the pumice. Turnings may first be rubbed with the steel wool dipped in the oil mixture and then a 3/F pumice.

3. After each rubbing with the linseed oil mixture, wipe the surface clean with rags and allow a few hours for it to dry completely.

4. When the last coat shines, first rub the surface (with the grain) with 3/0 steel wool dipped in the linseed oil mixture, taking only a few strokes and gradually working across the area, until you believe the entire surface is completely dulled. Then sprinkle the surface with dry pumice stone, dip the rubbing pad in the oil mixture, and rub the surface lengthwise (with the grain), taking long, even strokes, until the entire surface is polished. Wipe off and examine for shiny spots. These should be rubbed without addition of more pumice. When the entire surface has been completed, wipe it off with soft rags and allow to dry completely. When a highly polished finish is desired, it may be obtained by a final rubbing with rottenstone and the oil mixture after the surface has been completely cleaned, following the use of the pumice.

5. Apply at least two coats of wax.

French Finish

The French finish dates back at least three centuries, and is the finest finish known and probably the most beautiful of all. This finish is acquired with shellac and raw linseed oil, building up coat after coat. The work is painstaking and tedious. It requires time, patience, and skill. You are given but a brief outline of how the work is done, from the standpoint of knowledge rather than for practical use, as most refinishers hold this finish in high regard. It is sometimes called the "lost art" of finishes.

The finish must be applied to woods that are extremely smooth, whether or not they are filled, and over a water stain.

Thin shellac with alcohol to the consistency of water and apply with an old silk stocking made into a ball, squeezing out a little of the material at a time.

Dip the pad in the shellac solution and apply with straight strokes. As soon as dry, continue to apply more coats until a sheen or gloss is acquired. If cracks appear on the surface, sprinkle on a little pumice stone and rub. Then apply more coats of the shellac until the cracks are filled.

Allow time for the surface to dry completely. Then put only a few drops of raw linseed oil on the pad, and rub with a circular motion over the entire area, adding a few more drops of the oil as needed. When a high polish is seen, add no more oil, but continue rubbing until the surface is thoroughly dry. Allow to stand overnight, and repeat the rubbing with the oil.

This hard and rugged process will give a high polish. It can't be had by rubbing a surface with so-called French polish.

OIL FINISH

An oil finish is one of the oldest and most satisfactory of all finishes on hard or close-grained woods, if you have the time, patience, and willingness to do an endless amount of rubbing. It produces a rich color that is considered by many to be the most beautiful of all finishes. It is particularly good for tables and furniture that may be easily spotted or scratched. When this finish is properly applied, the wood is impervious to water, heat, scratches, and most stains. The furniture may be used during the process of finish, which may take up to a year to complete. The finish requires no waxing when sufficiently oiled and rubbed. The oil finish doesn't look well on cherry, and it should not be used on walnut, since it will turn the wood black.

Applying Oil Finish

The oil finish is accomplished by using a mixture of two-thirds (commercially) boiled linseed oil and one-third pure turpentine. When applying this mixture, do so as follows:

1. The wood must be free from any old finish, repaired, sanded, wiped with a dry cloth, and then tack-ragged.

2. Apply the mixture (hot or cold) generously with a rag and rub into a limited surface for 10 to 20 minutes. A hot mixture penetrates more quickly but produces a darker color. It should never be applied hot to carvings or grooved parts as it sets too quickly. When applied hot, the mixture should be heated in a double boiler to prevent danger of ignition.

3. Wipe off all excess oil with soft, lintless cloths, taking care to get it out of all crevices or carvings, as excess oil becomes sticky or hardens quickly. It must then be removed with alcohol or a commercial paint and varnish remover.

4. Rub each surface vigorously (one area at a time) with a hard polishing cloth for 10 to 20 minutes. This rubbing with a hard cloth develops heat by fric-

tion and is essential in bringing out a luster.

5. From five to about twenty coats of the oil mixture should be applied as directed above. The process is repeated until no dull spots remain. It should also be repeated once or twice a year to keep the furniture in good shape. Allow at least two days between the first two coats (in warm weather), and from a week to a month between later coats. Each coat must be dried before another is applied. If it isn't, the following coat will become sticky. Test a surface by holding a hand on it for several minutes. If the surface is oily, it is not dry enough for the next coat. Repeat oiling once or twice a year to keep the furniture in good condition. Oil table leaves *on the underside* as often as the top to prevent warping.

If the grain of the wood is raised with oiling, rub the wood until smooth with 3/0 steel wool. If the oil hardens in the crevices, remove it with a paint remover.

It must always be remembered that oiled rags are easily combustible. To prevent fire, they should be burned or washed soon after being used. Should there be any delay, spread them out flat or hang them on a line. If left too long they will harden. Store the rag that was used for applying the mixture in the container with any unused portion of the mixture.

Quick-Method Oil Finish

Here's a quick, four-coat oil finish that may be employed for those who don't wish the long procedure for the regular oil finish:

First coat: Apply one-third *raw* linseed oil and two-thirds turpentine. Allow 24 hours to dry.

Second coat: Apply pure *boiled* linseed oil (purchase commercially boiled linseed oil). Dry 24 hours.

Third coat: Apply *boiled* linseed oil, and dry 24 hours.

Fourth coat: Mix and apply half *boiled* linseed oil and half japan drier.

While applying, watch closely for any tackiness and rub off with burlap. Complete the finish by rubbing with pumice and oil, then with 3/0 steel wool in the manner described on pages 153–55.

Modern Oil Finishes

There are several so-called modern oil finishes available at paint stores that are easy to apply and offer the following advantages:

1. They resemble the mellow satin luster of old oil-type finishes that required hours of hand rubbing.

2. They accent the beauty of natural grain patterns; finish and appearance improve with age and use.

3. They saturate the wood and fill and seal pores; therefore, water spots, stains, and even minor burns may be steel-wooled away and the spot retouched with the oil finish.

4. They dry and solidify to provide a permanent finish needing only occasional reapplication.

5. They do not gum up in warm temperatures or feel greasy.

To apply these natural wood oil finishes (for wood with beauty in grain and color):

1. Pour the oil as it comes from the can on the surface and spread uniformly with a lintless cloth or roller; or dampen a lintless cloth with oil and apply to the surface.

2. Allow the oil to penetrate the surface for a few minutes.

3. Wipe the excess off, leaving the surface dry (to prevent dust particles adhering).

4. Allow 6 hours or more between coats. Three coats may be sufficient for most surfaces except dining tabletops and chair arms.

5. Allow the final coat to dry 24 hours before using.

PENETRATING WOOD-SEALER FINISHES

Penetrating oil finishes, like linseed oil, have long been used to beautify and preserve gun stocks and other fine woods. Penetrating *resin*-oil finishes are a second generation in this family of finishes and preservers. They actually improve the wood permanently without hours of hand rubbing; a simple application imparts to the surface a lustrous hand-rubbed look that is long lasting, seldom needs replenishing, and never needs resanding.

The exciting thing about this finish is that anyone can do it. It doesn't run, no tell-tale application marks are left behind, and no dirt or bugs can stick and stay in the finish. You get this beautifully rich wood finish by simply wetting the wood, waiting until penetration stops, and drying the surface. Resin-oil finishes withstand stains, watermarks, minor burns, and scratches. Should damage occur, it doesn't necessarily mean ruin, since the finish may be steel-wooled, replenished with more penetrating resin-oil, and become good as new. Old-style surface finishes cannot be repaired so easily. The use of penetrating resin-oil finishes is surprising to anyone familiar with lacquer and varnish. It is quite an experience.

Besides beauty, the resin-oil finish has other important qualities. Once application has been completed, the wood is ready for immediate use. There is no sticky surface to dry. After about a month, the resin-oil will have turned to a tough but flexible solid mass inside the wood that effectively preserves it. The wood will have become harder and will have remarkable dimensional stability. There is less shrinkage or expansion in extremely hot and cold weather and little or no warping, even in unusually wet climates. Wood-boring insects cannot enter, and decay and fungus are kept out.

Choose the sealer to suit your purpose, one resistant to heat and cold for dining tabletops, for instance. Read the labels carefully, and follow the manufacturer's directions. The available literature on these products generally states that they are made from a base of synthetic resin or tung oil (obtained from tung trees, mainly found in China but grown in some southern states, and valuable for

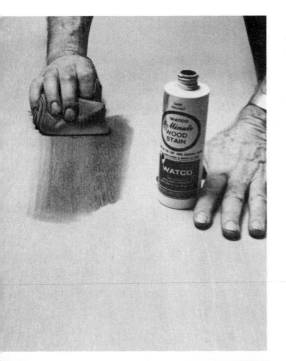

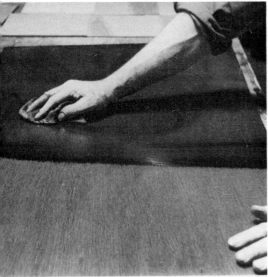

Figure 6-4. Applying a penetrating wood-sealer finish: (1) After sanding, apply a quick-dry nonsealing alcohol or water-base stain with a clean cloth or brush. (2) Let the stain dry for about 45 minutes, then pour on liberal amounts of the penetrating oil-resin finish. (3) Allow to soak for about 30 minutes, or until penetration stops, keeping the surface uniformly wet.

Figure 6-4 *continued.* (4) This is the most important of all. Wipe the surface completely dry, using a soft, absorbent cloth. (5) For more luster, let dry 4 hours, then wet-sand lightly with small amount of resin-oil finish. (6) After wet-sanding, dry wood thoroughly with a clean cloth, then polish briskly with another cloth.

quick drying, penetration, and hardness). Some of the mixtures contain varnish, others plastics. Read the label and literature and ask the sales person for the best type for your use. Buy a heavy type for open-pored wood.

Sealer finishes are of two general types: those that contain wax and those that do not. For furniture, it is preferable to use those which are *free* from wax and contain *varnish*, in order to bring the surface to a high gloss. This gloss is then rubbed down for a satin rubbed or a polish rubbed finish. In addition, thin, medium, and heavy consistencies are available. The thin-type sealer is recommended for furniture woods.

The mixtures containing wax harden to a soft luster and, if enough coats are applied properly (by smoothing between them), they are ideal and give a lastingly satisfactory finish on most furniture. They may be applied with a rag and completed with little effort. It is recommended that a hard waterproof wax be applied over most of the penetrating wood-sealer types of finish.

The penetrating sealers that contain wax result in a soft sheen that is pleasing on simple early American pieces requiring a rich mellowness rather than a high gloss. The sealers that dry to a high gloss are especially fine for a finish with a high degree of luster on, for example, mahogany Empire pieces and most modern pieces.

Applying a Sealer Finish

Apply the penetrating sealer within 12 hours after smoothing the wood, or 24 hours after applying stain. Before applying the finish, wipe the surface with a dry cloth, then a tack rag.

Strain the sealer each time it is used by stretching a piece of nylon hose over the top of the open can. Dip a clean, lintless cloth (rayon or nylon fabric) into the sealer that wells up through the nylon hose. Apply the sealer to the wood with a cloth.

The procedure for the *first coat* is as follows:

1. Apply the sealer with a cloth to one section at a time. Use a circular motion, working across the wood grain. Immediately remove all surplus sealer, wiping with the grain, before applying sealer on the next section.

2. Rub the sealer in and off with your hands. The warmth of your hands helps the sealer to penetrate into the wood. Rubbing removes the air bubbles and ensures even lapping of the finish.

3. Apply the sealer one at a time to any rungs on the piece, using another piece of nylon hose or fabric. Wipe the surplus away immediately with your hands. Remove the surplus sealer from the edges and carvings with your fingers.

4. Don't let a heavy, glasslike coating of sealer build up on the surface. Wipe off any excess that is not absorbed. Allow the sealer to dry 24 hours.

5. Before applying the next coat, and before every succeeding coat, smooth the surface gently with 3/0 steel wool. This removes the bubbles and makes a "tooth" for the next coat. Wipe the surface with a dry cloth and then with a tack rag.

For the *second coat*, apply the sealer as for the first coat. Rub the sealer on, in, and off. When smoothing and for extreme smoothness on dark woods, use crocus cloth. (Crocus cloth is coated with jeweler's rouge—iron oxide—which tints light woods a reddish color that cannot be removed.) Wrap the crocus cloth around a smoothing block for wide surfaces. Crocus cloth may be obtained from hardware stores.

For *succeeding coats,* apply the sealer as for previous coats. Apply several coats to the undersides of table leaves and the insides of drawers. Allow each coat to dry 24 hours in good drying weather—36 hours or more if humidity is high. Then rub the surface lightly with 3/0 steel wool. Wipe with a dry cloth, then a tack rag.

Continue to apply finish coats until no dull spots appear. For an even, satinlike smoothness and a hard finish, apply three to five coats on chairs or legs of a piece. Apply nine to twenty-one coats of finish on dining and coffee tabletops, depending on the degree of smoothness you desire and the intended use. Let the final coat dry 1 week. For extreme smoothness on dining tabletops and similar surfaces, rub the surface when thoroughly dry with 500A silicon carbide abrasive paper and a mild soap (not detergent) solution. Dip the 500A silicon carbide abrasive paper in the warm soap solution and wrap around a smoothing block. Smooth gently with the grain, but not on the edges. When the abrasive begins to drag, dip in the soapy water again, then proceed with the rubbing as described.

For a handsome satin finish, you can eliminate the rubbing. Simply wait about 4 hours—preferably overnight—after drying the surface of excess resin-oil, then, using a small amount of resin-oil finish or carnauba (palm oil) stain wax

as a lubricant, wet-sand lightly with superfine paper, wait about 10 minutes, and wipe clean and dry. Polish with a soft cloth.

LACQUER FINISH

Lacquer has generally replaced varnish and shellac as finishes in the furniture-making field as well as in custom finishing. But for the home handyman the lacquer system of finishing isn't widely used because spray equipment is necessary. In recent years, several so-called brushing lacquers have appeared on the market.

Lacquer offers a hard, durable, waterproof surface that is able to withstand high heat without becoming sticky. A lacquered surface is mirror-smooth and transparent, enhances the colors over which it is laid, and brings out the beauty of the wood grain when a natural finish is desired. Some varieties of lacquer are resistant to acids and alcohol—ideal for bars and tabletops.

Lacquer is the fastest drying finish ever developed. The drying time is 1 1/2 to 2 hours, as compared with the quick-dry paints, varnishes, and enamels, which require at least 4 hours. But due to its speed in drying, the best way to apply lacquer is by spraying. This produces an even coat unmarred by brush-marks. When applied with a brush, the lacquer must be "slowed up" to prevent marking and sagging.

Before applying lacquer, the wood surface must be perfectly smooth and ready for the final finish. But before discussing application of lacquer, two words of warning:

1. Lacquer is extremely flammable and all precautions should be taken to prevent fire and explosion. Make sure there are no lighted cigarettes, pilot lights, etc., in the room.

2. Dust in the air from sanding, floating lint, etc., will ruin your work. Clean up well before you begin to apply lacquer.

Spraying Technique

The best spraying method requires a pressure of 30 to 40 pounds. As a rule, with a spray gun of this pressure a single coat will suffice. When the air pressure is lower, the lacquer must be thinned to a point where two or more coats will be necessary.

Before beginning the spraying job, be sure the equipment is clean, and make sure it works properly by trying a test pattern on waste material. A heavy-centered pattern indicates too much liquid weight, which is corrected by thinning or increasing the air pressure. A "peanut"-shaped pattern results from clogging of the gun. Rotate the tip of the gun, and if the pattern rotates, clean the air cap. If the pattern remains the same, clean the fluid line. Too much air pressure sometimes results in a split pattern.

Handling a paint sprayer is an art that comes quickly with practice. Apply the spray in even lines across the surface, moving the sprayer parallel with the work rather than turning the spray head from side to side in an arc, which will produce an unsatisfactory wavy surface. Some common errors in spraying with lacquer are (1) dry spots from holding the gun too far from the work; (2) sags from too heavy fluid mixture in the gun, or from lack of speed in applying, or from holding the gun too long in one place; (3) pinholes produced by holding the gun too close to the work or by using too much pressure, which blasts the area already covered. More on spray-gun techniques can be found in Chapter Ten.

Furniture finishing lacquer is now available in aerosol pressure cans. For full details on operating these cans, see page 254–58.

Brushing Technique

As stated earlier, there are a number of slower-drying lacquers prepared especially for application by brushing. However, with a bit of skill, and by cutting down on the quantity of thinner, almost any lacquer can be brushed on. Just remember that you are using the fastest-drying finish available. The more thinner used, the quicker the drying process becomes. Speed in application is essential, and mistakes are hard to correct.

With that thought in mind, first look to your brush. A cheap one won't do. If bristles drop out, they are hard to retrieve from a lacquer surface without marring the work. Nylon bristles can sometimes be dissolved in lacquer thinners, so avoid them. A good brush is a must.

When you buy lacquer, buy twice as much thinner. Some will go to thin the

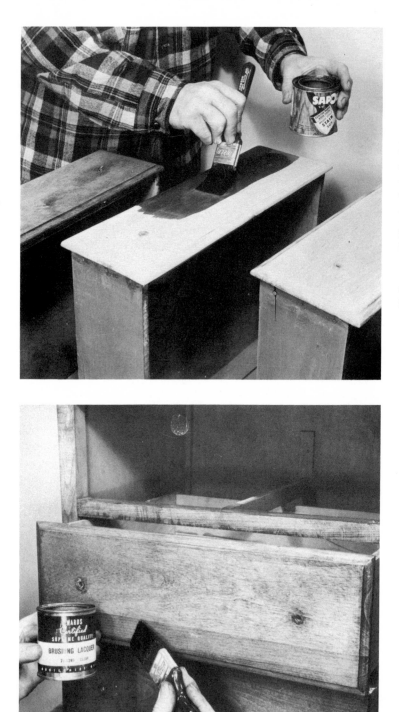

Figure 6-5. Applying a brushing lacquer: (1) The first step after preparing the surface is application of the desired color stain. Apply along the grain and wipe off excess with a cloth. (2) After the stain has dried, apply the first coat of lacquer. A large brush is best, as lacquer dries rapidly. Apply along the grain. (3) Rub each lacquer coat lightly with fine steel wool wadded into a ball and frequently turned inside out. Use even pressure. (4) Rub the final coat of lacquer (and there may be from 3 to 5 coats) with blooming oil and fine-grit waterproof sandpaper.

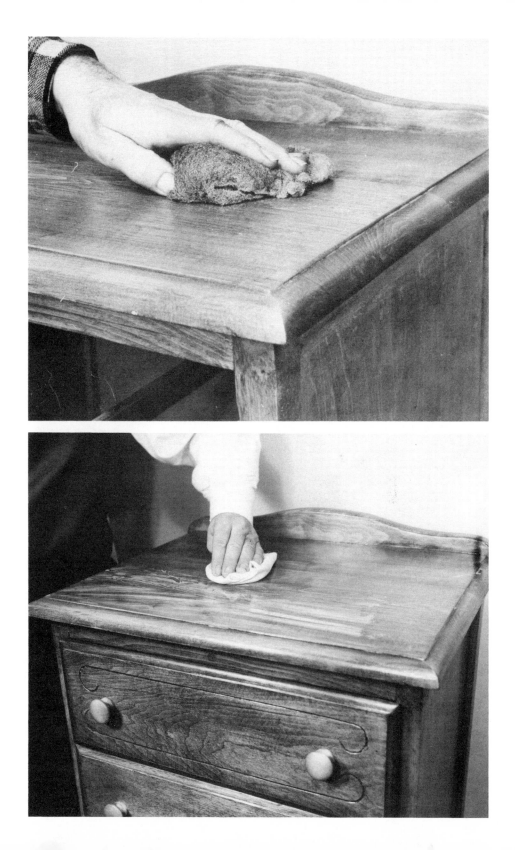

lacquer for application. More will be needed to keep the brush in shape, and still more for "mopping up" spots and sticky fingers.

To apply, fill a container half full of the lacquer. Add your thinner. Then soak the ends of the brush thoroughly in the mixture, but do not rub off excess on the rim of the container as you do with paint or the quick-drying lacquer will become sticky and foul the brush on successive trips to the container. Instead, squeeze off any excess against the inner side of the container.

Make your brush strokes bold and rapid. Carry each stroke as far as you can go without running out the lacquer into thin, separate lines. Overlap prior strokes slightly. If the surface is large, work from opposite ends, blending the strokes in the center.

When putting lacquer on uneven surfaces, such as beading and carving, take care not to allow the lacquer to accumulate in the hollows. Pick up the excess with the tip of the brush.

Once you've finished the lacquer application, let the work stand for 24 to 48 hours. Then for the final process—rubbing.

The lacquered surface upon drying is hard, brilliantly glossy. Most people prefer it reduced to a satinlike quality by rubbing. This is done as described on page 152–53.

WAX FINISH

One of the most ancient, simple, and effective ways of finishing wood is with wax. It provides a soft, velvet, mellow, luster that is easy to apply. Actually, a thin film of polished wax over all final finishes (except polish rubbed varnish) is applied by most finishers, and desired in most homes, yet there are some who never use it or desire it. Many such people depend upon furniture polish, which may be a detriment to a finish. Waxing gives a soft, pleasing luster, and, if it is renewed before the underlying coat is harmed, will enable the finish to last indefinitely.

As we just stated, waxing is neither difficult nor involved. However, if it is not properly done, especially on a surface that is not completely smooth, or over dark woods, light yellow waxes may sometimes show white in cracks and pores. In such cases, it is best to use a brown wax.

Never use anything but a *paste* wax on furniture or other wood articles. Those commonly available in grocery stores are satisfactory, but there are carnauba-type waxes obtainable. These can usually be bought in furniture, hardware, or paint stores. Some waxes come in yellow only, while others are colored brown, reddish-brown, and red, to blend with different woods.

Generally, the wax is applied over a dried and sanded *sealer* coat of shellac or varnish. *Under no circumstances* should any type of wax be applied to bare wood. Wax should always be applied over some kind of finishing material. Most professional shops will not accept a piece of refinishing if wax has been applied to bare wood. Grime works into it, making it almost impossible to remove the wax if you wish to refinish the piece.

For good results, apply the wax as follows:

1. Remove dust deposited from the air and that left after smoothing the piece with an abrasive. Use a dusting brush and then a dusting cloth.

2. Lay a 10-inch-square heavy linen or closely woven cloth flat and place in its center about two heaping tablespoons of paste wax. Fold the cloth over the wax into a pad. Using a circular motion, rub the entire surface of the piece with the pad, thus leaving thereon a thin coat of wax.

3. Allow time for the wax to dry, as per the directions on the container.

4. When dry, brush all surfaces briskly with a soft bristle brush; then rub thoroughly with a soft cloth (cotton flannel is good) and finally with a very tightly woven or hard cloth. The brushing aids in removing any surplus wax from the pores and grooves in a surface. A thorough rubbing with the soft cloth removes surplus wax and smooths it out, while a brisk rubbing under pressure with the hard cloth polishes the wax. Remember, don't "pile up" the wax by applying too much, for then it is next to impossible to brush or rub it out to a smooth, satin finish. The application through the close-grained cloth prevents lumps of wax from being applied.

5. Follow the same directions and apply at least two coats. Three coats are often required for best results.

6. For a final test, attempt to make a thumbprint. If it can be seen, the surface should be rubbed again briskly with the hard cloth until no thumbprint is visible. This rubbing creates friction and tends to heat the wax, causing the polish desired. Each surface should have an equal luster with no dull spots. A surface thus finished may be brightened from time to time by rubbing with a soft cloth and then a hard one, without the addition of new wax.

ANTIQUE-LIKE FINISH

The finish often preferred on antique pieces is softly dull and brought up slightly with surface wax. A piece of rubbing felt charged with a paste of 3/F powdered pumice will provide proper cutting on your final surface of shellac, lacquer, or varnish. Sometimes the final surface wax can be ordinary shoe polish. For instance, to enrich old red mahogany, a soft hand rub with red mahogany shoe polish will add a deep red tinge.

There are all kinds of so-called antiquing. Another antiquing procedure is to remove all badly scuffed finish, fill all blemishes, then brush on a glaze of 3 parts of turpentine and 1 part of varnish mixed with burnt-umber oil coloring. Wipe off the glaze as soon as it is brushed on, working from the center to the edges. Antiquing systems using paint are discussed in full in Chapter Seven.

UNIQUE MODERN FINISHES

As previously stated, light-colored stains used on bleached woods, then finished off with lacquer, shellac, or varnish as previously described, will provide a clear blond finish. What many people think of as blond, however, is actually a "pickled" finish. This is achieved with a stain or tinted filler that is applied with a brush, then wiped off so that it remains only in the pores and grain indentations of the wood. The tinted filler is then sealed, and the work is then completed with clear finish.

Limed Oak

Cover the bleached wood with a wash coat of water-clear lacquer. Apply flat white paint or white filler (made by adding zinc-white oil pigment to natural filler) to the surface, then wipe. Finish the surface in water-clear lacquer.

Amber Walnut

After bleaching, tone the wood with a light application of amber stain, thinned until the stain is slightly darker than the bleached wood. Wipe while wet and seal with a wash coat of shellac. Cover the surface with a natural filler and, when dry, proceed with your clear finish.

Blond Mahoganies

Bleached mahoganies are finished in many tones. Filling and wiping with white filler produces *heather* mahogany, red filler (red oil pigment added to natural filler) produces *tweed* mahogany, and natural filler produces *bronze* mahogany.

CHAPTER SEVEN

Painted Finishes for Furniture

During the past three centuries many styles or pieces of furniture were painted rather than finished with oil, shellac, lacquer, varnish, or wax. In some instances, however, lacquer and varnish may have been colored to give a painted appearance. Painted finishes made it possible to obtain a uniform appearance from woods of different color, grain, or unequal quality used in one piece; they also helped to preserve the wood, and they provided a background for such ornamentation as freehand painting, stenciling, or gilding.

Painted furniture in America was influenced by English cabinetmakers and architects, French monarchs, designs from ancient Greece and Rome, lacquerwork from the Orient, and the creative ability of early American cabinetmakers and individuals. Today it's not necessary to be a professional or experienced person to paint furniture. But the furniture should be worth the energy, patience, and time spent in applying the painted finish.

In general, there are three reasons for painting furniture:

1. Some furniture styles were painted originally, and may need repainting. Such styles include variations of the following: Louis XV and XVI furniture; Italian seventeenth- and eighteenth-century furniture; Sheraton fancy chairs; Windsor and Hitchcock chairs and rockers; and Pennsylvania German.

2. Many new unfinished pieces of furniture are available, but may lack beauty of color and grain. Such pieces are made of pine, poplar, or beech, and come knocked-down or assembled.

3. The appearance of some furniture may be improved by painting. Such furniture may include Mission style and late Victorian pieces, and furniture that has been damaged by stain or wear.

PAINT SELECTION

Alkyd resin-base enamel is the most satisfactory paint for wood furniture. It provides a hard, durable finish that is resistant to wear, water, marring, and chipping. Do *not* use latex-base paint and polyvinyl acetate-base paint on wood furniture. Water in these paints raises the grain of the wood, and they are also difficult to remove.

There are two basic types of paints used in furniture work:

Undercoat, which may be labeled undercoat, flat, or primer, depending on the brand. It should have no gloss, and is used as the undercoat for the final finish. An undercoat used alone won't give serviceable wearing qualities.

Finish coat, which may be a high gloss, semigloss, or satin enamel. High gloss enamel has a high luster, and gives the hardest and most durable finish. Check the brand label for specific wearing qualities. Semigloss or satin enamel gives a low luster finish, usually less durable than a high gloss.

A beautiful enameled finish may be obtained by rubbing down the last coat to a fine and soft polish with pumice or rottenstone and water. This is accomplished by the same method as used for varnish. (See *Polish Rubbed Finish,* page 153.) This finish may be obtained only after several thin coats of enamel have been applied and sanded lightly after each coat, except the last, with a 6/0 or 8/0 abrasive paper, and the use of a paste filler before the undercoat.

When selecting paints for small children's furniture, make sure that it contains no ingredients that would be harmful if chewed or swallowed by them. If a paint contains even small amounts of lead, antimony, arsenic, cadmium, mercury, selenium or soluble barium, it is not advisable to use it on children's furniture. Have your paint dealer check the label of the paint you are purchasing to assure its suitability for such use.

Color Selection

When selecting paint color for a piece of furniture, look for one that will harmonize with other furnishings in the room and with the room interior. The color may be chosen from a picture, the draperies, rug, wallpaper, or other accessory. But, when selecting color from paint chips, remember that most colors are lovely in small areas. Applied to large areas, these same colors may be too intense, dull, dark, or light. Also, paint colors change in intensity or value when they dry. Flat paints dry lighter than they were when wet, and enamels dry darker.

Also consider the size of the furniture, its location, and background provided by the wall. Furniture painted the same color as the wall will seem a part of the background; if painted a contrasting color, it will stand out and attract attention.

Select the paint of a reliable manufacturer and buy from a reputable dealer. Colors are available as follows:

1. *Ready-mixed paints* can be purchased in a variety of colors to harmo-

nize with interiors. If these are unsatisfactory, many dealers will mix paints from formulas supplied by paint companies.

2. *Formula-mixed paints* can be purchased in large paint stores. The formulas are prepared by manufacturers on paint chips. After the customer selects the desired color from the paint chips, the dealer mixes it at the store on a special machine.

3. *Mix-your-own paints*. Start with a base coat of white or a color. To obtain the desired tint or shade, use colors in oil; these may be purchased at paint or art stores. Keep a record of the amount of each color used for each sample chip. Look at each paint sample where it will be used—both by sunlight and incandescent or fluorescent light.

Be sure to purchase enough paint for at least two coats of undercoat and finish—especially if the color is mixed at the store. Four coats may not be necessary for every piece of furniture, but sometimes it is difficult to match paints if they are specially mixed. Be sure to remember that, if mixing paint colors, use one brand, one kind, and one type. Each manufacturer has his own formula. Never mix different brands or kinds of paints.

SURFACE PREPARATION

The surface of furniture (or other articles) to be enameled is one of three classes, namely:

1. Bare wood that has never been painted.

2. An old finish in good condition.

3. An old finish that is cracked or damaged.

Hardware should be removed, if possible, before applying the remover or paint. Its removal will prevent possible damage to the hardware and alleviate tedious work during the paint removal, smoothing, and painting processes.

Old finish, if cracked, chipped, sticky, rough, or too thick, should be removed with paint and varnish remover. Small chipped areas can be smoothed with abrasive paper and/or carefully touched up with undercoat several times. If the old finish is in good condition but very soiled, wash the surface with detergent and water. Use mineral spirits or gum turpentine on a cloth to remove grease and old wax. Allow the piece to dry 24 hours before applying new paint.

New wood should have the hair grain removed or controlled to obtain a smooth surface for painting. Wipe the entire surface with a cloth dampened in clear water. This will raise the hair grain. Dry for 24 hours, then smooth with very fine and extrafine grit abrasive papers folded over a padded smoothing block.

New unfinished furniture, especially pine, needs sealing to prevent knots and sappy spots from bleeding through painted finishes. Follow the directions below for sealing. If these methods do not stop the sap, the wood is improperly cured and therefore will continue to bleed until it dries out over a period of months.

Knots, sappy spots, mahogany-stained

varnish, and other stains often bleed through painted surfaces, if not sealed. They can be sealed or removed with one of the following methods:

Sealer Method

Apply two coats of clear modified or white-pigmented shellac-base sealer with a brush to resinous or stained areas. Follow the directions on the can for drying time between coats. Smooth lightly between each coat. White-pigmented shellac sealer also serves to prime and mask the wood. Clean the brush with alcohol solvent.

Bleach Method For Stains Only

Prepare a solution by placing 2 ounces of oxalic acid and 2 ounces of tartaric acid in a 1-quart glass jar. Fill the jar with hot water and stir until dissolved. Label *Poison*. Never keep this solution in a metal container, and don't breathe the fumes. Apply the hot solution to stained areas with a cloth, protecting the hands with rubber gloves. Do not apply the solution for longer than 20 minutes at a time, as it may split the wood. Neutralize the bleached area with an ammonia solution, prepared by adding 1 tablespoon of regular household ammonia to a quart jar of water. Apply this solution with a clean cloth. Finally, wash the surface with clear water. Dry for 24 hours. Smooth the surface with a medium-grit abrasive paper. Avoid breathing the sanding dust. Do *not* use this method on veneer.

Holes and cracks should be filled with an oil-base filling compound such as wood dough, plastic forming wood, surfacing putty, or spackling compound. Do not use water-base fillers in large holes and gouges. The water in the filler may cause the wood around the filler to swell and expand, and when the wood dries it will shrink and pull away from the filler. Apply the filler with a spatula or putty knife. When dry, smooth level with fine-grit abrasive paper.

Coarse- or open-grained woods—such as oak, chestnut, and ash—need filling before paint is applied. Mix a small amount of paste wood filler with gum turpentine to thin, if necessary. Apply across the grain with a stubby brush. As the filler starts to dry, giving a dull, flat appearance, rub off the excess filler with a piece of burlap, going across the grain. Don't rub the grain because this will pull the filler out of the open pores. Dry for 24 hours. It may be necessary to repeat this process two or three times to completely fill the open grain to a level surface.

Dents and bruises can be removed from bare wood by laying several layers of damp woolen cloth over the surface and pressing with a hot iron. Moisture causes the wood to swell and raise to normal height. It may be necessary to repeat this process. Do not use this method on veneer.

If no surface repairs are necessary before applying the first coat of paint, smooth bare wood or previously painted surfaces with very fine-grit abrasive paper and a sanding block. Always smooth in one direction. Follow with extrafine-grit abrasive paper, using steel wool on curved surfaces. Remove sanding dust with a tack rag.

STEPS IN ENAMELING

An enamel is actually a pigmented varnish, so its application procedures and brushing techniques are basically the same as described in Chapter Six on varnishing.

As with all finishes, plan the order of painting so that the piece may be picked up and turned without marring the fresh enamel. That is, when painting furniture always do the hard-to-reach parts first: legs, cross spindles, and back of chair—then proceed to accessible parts.

To finish a chair, proceed as follows:

1. Begin by turning the chair upside down and placing the seat of the chair on a table or box. Paint all bottom surfaces of the seat, legs, and back.

2. Then stand the chair upright on its legs and do all the top surfaces, finishing with the seat.

To finish a table, proceed as follows:

1. Begin by turning the table upside down and painting the bottom and its edges.

2. Then paint the legs, doing the inner sides first.

3. Finish the legs with smooth strokes lengthwise.

4. When enameling turned or round legs or braces, brush around them; do *not* attempt to finish with smooth strokes lengthwise.

5. Now turn the table right side up and do all the top edges.

6. Finish the tabletop last, applying

Figure 7-1. Steps in enameling furniture: (1) All finishing work starts with sanding, either by hand or power. (2) Apply both undercoat and the enamel from the inside out, starting with hard-to-reach points, then the sides, then the top, edges last.

Figure 7-1 *continued*. (3) The wide brush is held at an angle, enamel being flowed on with even strokes. Always follow along the grain lines of the wood. (4) Most important—the stroke should continue out past the end of the surface. Hold the brush at a near-right angle, and move in steady strokes. (5) Excess enamel should be picked up by the brush to keep it from filling grooves or other recesses in the piece being finished. (6) Removable trim: knobs and hardware are removed and enameled separately. Provide a place such as this for these to dry alone.

the enamel across the table width, and then smooth the entire surface with light brushing along the table length, using only the tip of the brush to achieve an even finish.

To finish a cabinet or a chest, proceed as follows:

1. For dressers, buffets, and cabinets that have drawers, remove the drawers. Take off handles and knobs. You will do the drawers separately.

2. Paint the molding (if any) surrounding the panels, and then paint the panels, picking up any runs or sags at the corners.

3. Paint the frame and top. Finish the top and panel surfaces with cross brushing.

4. Begin the drawers by enameling the side about 6 inches back. Do all the edges. Then finish the front panel (do the interior of the drawer firsrt, if desired). Stack until dry.

First Coat: Undercoat

Thoroughly mix the undercoat. To keep the paint as free as possible of dirt and dust, pour a small amount into a container for immediate use.

Dip the brush in the paint to about one-third of its bristle length. Work the paint through the bristles by brushing back and forth on clean paper. Dip the brush in the paint again and wipe off the excess. Apply the paint to surface brushing in all directions. Then "tip off" by removing excess paint from the brush. Hold the brush at a right angle to the surface. Brush in one direction only, gently skimming the freshly painted surface to remove any excess paint and to level the painted surface. Do not paint too large an area at one time. Dry 24 hours or more.

Between First and Second Coat

Smooth lightly with extrafine-grit abrasive paper and a smoothing block. Waterproof abrasive paper and water may be used on painted surfaces for more rapid smoothing. Dry.

Second Coat: Undercoat, Semigloss, or Gloss

Sometimes it is necessary to apply a second undercoat to dark surfaces. But if this is not necessary, the surface is now ready for the first coat of satin, semigloss, or high gloss enamel.

Semigloss and high gloss enamels should not be stirred rapidly because bubbles form and are difficult to remove from the painted surface. Stir the paint slowly but thoroughly. Apply the paint in the same manner as for the undercoat. Do not overbrush. While wet, enamel will "level" itself. Do a small section at a time and work rapidly.

Between Second and Final Coats

Let the surface dry, then smooth. The gloss must be cut to make a "tooth" for the next coat of paint. Use the same smoothing method as before.

Final Coat

Follow the directions as for the preceding coats. Drying and thorough curing may take several days to two weeks, depending upon the weather and the paint used.

Final Rub

If a satin of low luster finish is desired rather than a high gloss, the painted surfaces, as previously mentioned, may be rubbed with pumice powder and oil after the surface has thoroughly dried and cured. Use 3/F or 4/F pumice powder and lightweight oil.

For curved surfaces, make a paste of pumice powder and apply with the hands to remove the gloss.

For flat surfaces, sprinkle pumice on the surface. Dribble oil on top of it. Then, with a new blackboard eraser or other clean felt padding, rub in one direction until a satin finish is obtained. A satin or low gloss finish gives a more finished look. Several rubbings may be needed to obtain the type of finish desired.

Wipe the surface with a clean, dry cloth to remove the excess pumice and oil.

ANTIQUED FINISH

Antiquing over enamel is a glaze or toner coat that is used to obtain a mellow or soft appearance rather than a finish that will simulate great age. The finish is achieved by a glaze coat colored with oil colors applied over a base-coat enamel in a lighter value. When the glaze coat is sparingly and carefully applied, the result should give a pleasing effect.

A glazed finish is more effective when applied to furniture with carved surfaces, moldings, and turnings rather than to a piece that is entirely flat in design.

A new, unfinished piece of furniture or a piece that has all the old finish removed will require the following applications for a glazed finish: An undercoat or primer, two coats of enamel, a glazing liquid and a protective coat. Some pieces, with the old finish in good condition, will not require the undercoater and perhaps only one coat of enamel. Some commercial glazes do not require a protective coat over the glaze coat.

Glazing kits may be purchased complete with all of the necessary products and supplies for refinishing an article. The supplier may also have each of the products and needed supplies for sale separately. Will the quantity of the paint products be adequate or too much in excess of the size of the article being painted? Compare the convenience, quality, desired colors available, and the cost of the kit with separate unit purchasing. Some kits may contain items you have already on hand.

The furniture piece to be painted is prepared in the same manner as a piece that will not have a glazed finish, with the *exception* of the final rub of pumice and oil. Make a "tooth" for the glazing liquid on the final coat of enamel by lightly rubbing with 3/0 steel wool or a fine-grit abrasive paper. Wipe the sandings from the piece with a clean cloth or tack rag. The piece is now ready for the glaze application.

Glazing Liquids

You may prepare your own glazing liquid or purchase one that is ready mixed. Prepare a glazing liquid by mixing 3 tablespoons gum turpentine, 1 tablespoon varnish or boiled linseed oil (varnish preferred), and 1 teaspoon of the desired oil color(s). Stir well until uniformly mixed.

Examples of glaze oil colors to use over ivory or off-white base enamels to achieve a mellow look are:

Raw umber (grayish tone)
Raw sienna (reddish tone)
Burnt umber (brownish tone)
Burnt sienna (reddish-brown tone)

Other hues are equally effective, depending upon the enamel color and the color scheme of the room in which the finished piece will be used.

As previously stated, ready-mixed glazing liquid can be purchased from a paint or art store in a variety of colors. Follow application directions.

Applying the Glaze

Wipe the enameled undercoat surface with a tack rag to remove all traces of dust and dirt. Then mix the glazing liquid and oil colors thoroughly. If using a commercial glazing liquid, stir it thoroughly with a wooden paddle and read the label instructions carefully.

Apply a thin coat of the glazing liquid with an oil paint brush, painting one side of the piece of furniture at a time. Long, even strokes with the grain of the wood will produce the best results. If the piece has prominent legs, turn it upside down and paint the legs first, then the top, working downward. Pay special attention to carved trim and crevices, painting them first to allow more absorption of the glaze.

Let the color glaze set for 10 to 30 minutes before beginning to rub or wipe.

Wiping the Glaze

Once the glaze has set enough to be slightly "tacky," use cheesecloth to wipe lightly at first and then more heavily in those places where you want more highlights—usually the high points of carving and the center of panels. Wipe in long, straight lines in the direction of the grain (usually the long way to your piece).

Blend further by patting the surface with clean cheesecloth and finish blending with a dry paint brush. Work the brush from the center toward the edges. Wipe the brush off on a cloth to remove excess glaze. Wiping off and blending is not at all difficult when only a small amount of glaze material remains on the surface. It gives a slightly noticeable but most effective appearance.

Rub large, flat areas in long, even strokes, beginning with a light touch and applying more pressure as you get along. If you find that you have allowed the glaze to set too long, simply dampen your rubbing cloth with mineral spirits. If wiping shows that you haven't allowed the glaze to set long enough, simply apply another coat and wait again.

For carved surfaces, moldings, and turnings, proceed as for flat surfaces. Remove excess glaze material from depressions with a dry paint brush. Wipe the brush off on a cloth. Highlight by wiping the glaze off the raised areas with a clean cloth, leaving the glaze in the depressions for contrast. Difficulty in rubbing intricate carved trim can be overcome by using a cotton tip in those hard-to-reach areas.

Other materials may be used for wiping to get still different results. Try the texture of Turkish towels or paper towels, for instance. For extra-fine grain, try wiping with fine 3/0 steel wool. Experiment—just apply a layer of imagination.

For example, dry brush is the one most often used by professionals for furniture antiquing. It gives a more "grainy" texture than wiping. If your piece seems to lack interest after wiping, apply the dry brush technique right over it. First, wipe your brush dry and spread the bristles by pinching so that they will deposit the color in irregular separate lines. (Here is where a cheap brush works better than a good one.) Instead of dipping your brush in the paint can, spread some glaze on a saucer or sheet of aluminum foil. Pick up the glaze with the tip of your brush. Apply the glaze in long straight but irregular lines with this almost dry brush. Work in the direction of the grain. For beginners it may be easier to get the "dry brush" effect by wiping with coarse material of some kind—a Turkish towel, paper towels, even a square of carpeting.

If you use the steel-wool method to achieve a wood-graining effect, don't try to copy the wood grain. If you follow the simple straight-line wiping directions outlined below, you will be surprised at the amazing ease with which a close-grained, fine hardwood effect reveals itself without any special effort to imitate or copy the grain of the wood. Remember that grain usually runs the length of the piece or part. So, wipe the long way of each section in long, straight lines—remembering that wood grain lines are straight, but not mathematically straight.

With your 3/0 steel wool, wipe lightly with a long, sweeping motion. Don't start your wiping motion from a still position—rather, have your hand in motion before the steel wool touches the surface. Pick up lightly on the finish of each stroke with a follow-through of motion. This gives a light, brushing attack to the job that lets you blend one stroke into another without depositing smears of glaze at the beginning or finish of each stroke. To touch up rough or unsatisfactory areas, use a light whisking motion.

To avoid "directionalism" in wiping and to get the natural random look of wood grain, *walk around* your piece as you wipe. Attack it from both front and rear. If you stand in the same place throughout the wiping, you will get an unnatural *slanting* appearance. Working from both front and back cancels out the slant and results in a blend that is more natural looking.

Inside corners are difficult to get at with steel wool. It's generally best to start the wipe from the corner with a dry brush, continuing with steel wool.

On tabletops, dresser tops, etc., finish wiping with an outward sweeping motion that continues out into the air at the end of the piece. In this way you can maintain the illusion of continuing grain.

Your steel wool will fill up with glaze quite quickly. When glaze begins to "ball up" on the surface of the wood, remove excess glaze by pressing the steel wool against cheesecloth or paper towel—or change the steel wool to another position. You may need to do this every two or three strokes if you are working on a large surface. It's a good practice to unroll your steel wool and cut it with scissors into short pieces—about six inches long. This gives you a number of good handfuls, each of which can be turned several times as it fills up. After cutting, shake each piece several times to free it of loose particles.

Glaze and wipe one area at a time. This method allows you to work in an unhurried manner. If interrupted, you have only to finish wiping the glazed area and then resume work at your leisure. Also, stop to judge the effect frequently while wiping; maybe you're finished and don't know it. Don't overwork your piece, but try to get a fresh, free feeling. While you are busy working, you are "too close to the woods to see the trees" and thus a poor judge of the effects you're getting. You may be underrating them . . . getting too "fussy." It is advisable to work quickly (but not hurriedly), without going back over your work too much. Relax! Tell yourself, "If I don't like this I can wipe it off and start over." Now go away and leave it for a while. When you come back, your transformed piece will surprise you. You may decide that this is exactly the effect you want.

When you've finished wiping, allow enough time for the paint to dry thoroughly, usually 24 hours. In some commercial antiquing systems a second coat of glaze is required. This second coat is applied in the same manner as the first.

A glazing liquid you have prepared yourself should have a protective coat for greater wear and durability. When the glaze is completely dry, apply a coat of *water-clear* varnish. (Do not use regular varnish as it has a yellowish color.) Allow one week for the varnish to dry. If the surface is too shiny, rub carefully with 4/F or 3/F pumice powder and mineral oil. Make a paste of the powder and mineral oil and apply with your hands. Rub the surface until a satin finish is obtained. Wipe the surface with a clean, dry cloth to remove the pumice and oil.

A commercial glazing liquid may also require a protective coat. The label will state if a protective coat is needed. If it is, then purchase the protective coat in the same brand as the glazing liquid.

With either commercial or homemade glazing liquid, if you wish to wax the surface, it is best to allow the paint to dry for at least a week before applying.

Special Effects

After applying the coat or toner or glaze there are a few tricks that can be used to achieve interesting special effects:

SHADING. To get a shaded effect, glaze more thinly in the center of large areas such as door panels, dresser and table-tops, end panels, etc. The lightest area of your shading should be roughly oval in shape. Shaded areas will curve softly around the oval, dissolving into deepest shadows at the corners. For shading, use slightly more glaze to start. Then, with cheesecloth, wipe out some glaze from the center oval area. Before wiping with steel wool, "feather" the hard edges of the wiped-out oval by brushing back into it with an almost dry brush.

FROSTING. If the work is delicately done, beautiful effects may be secured by using white to glaze over furniture enameled light opaque colors, resulting in a "frosted" effect. White primer material or enamel is used in the glaze mixture in place of the oil color. This is applied, wiped off, and finished in the same manner as for antiquing.

SPATTER. (*A Speckled Texture*). The spatter technique requires a stiff brush. Try an old toothbrush for small areas or a small whisk broom for larger surfaces —or any other stiff household brush. Flip the glaze off the bristles in a coarse spray. Bend the bristles with your fingers or a stick to get a spring action that will throw the spray. To avoid blobs, don't overload your brush. After reloading your brush each time, try out your spatter on a newspaper to get rid of blobs and to judge your "aim."

Spatter makes good imitation worm holes on antique furniture. It is a good finish procedure because it will blend patterns together. Because spatter is a "chancy" method, apply it over work that has dried overnight. Then you can wipe off and try again.

SPATTERN. (*Splatter with a Pattern*). While the glaze is still wet, spray mineral spirits, using the spatter technique above. The mineral spirits will cause the glaze to "crawl," pushing it back into little circles or "star" patterns, revealing the undercoat.

Spray once, then watch! The clear droplets will "flower" slowly on the surface. This should take several seconds to a minute. Wait for the full development of the "flowers" before applying the "spattern."

Spattern should be applied only to a flat horizontal surface. If applied vertically or on a slanting or rounded surface, the mineral spirits may run and streak your work. Remember that the addition of mineral spirits may slow the drying time.

WATER-STAINED WOOD. This traditional and interesting look can be achieved by first rubbing the toned surface, and then splattering it with mineral spirits. The toner will spread out in the spots where the liquid has fallen, creating an authentic water-stained look.

STIPPLING. (*Fine Texture*). One of the best stipple patterns is made with a piece of carpet cut to fit your hand. (The "twist" type carpet is fine.) Apply glaze with a brush and then, holding the carpet in a flat position, pounce lightly over the surface. (To pounce:

pound with a bounce.) This makes an even-textured pattern, not unlike a leather finish.

The more usual method of stippling is done with a brush. Using the tip end of a dry brush, pick up paint from a shallow surface. (Use a paint-can cover, a saucer, or a sheet of aluminum foil.) Apply stipple with a pouncing motion, holding the brush at right angles to the surface you are painting. For a uniform pattern, turn your brush this way and that with each pounce.

For a mottled effect, pounce more in some spots, less in others. For shaded effects, start at the darkest point with a freshly loaded brush and work out toward lighter areas as the glaze in the bristles is used up.

CRUMPLE. (*Coarse Texture*). This is a method of applying coarse texture with a pad of crumpled material. You can use almost anything that will crumple—paper, cheesecloth, burlap, to name a few.

Plastic is best of all because it is non-absorbent. It will not get soggy and change shape. (Cut up a plastic bag or use sheet plastic.) Crumple your plastic to fit the hand and press it lightly onto a previously glazed surface. If your surface is thinly glazed or wiped, add more glaze with your crumpled plastic, picking it up from aluminum foil or some other shallow surface. Pounce, turning your hand with each motion to assure a random pattern. If your first try doesn't please you, redistribute the glaze by brushing it in one direction. Start over. For a different effect, give your plastic

wad a slight roll or twist each time you touch the surface.

MARBLE-LIKE TEXTURE. For a marble-like texture, crumple a sheet of plastic and shake it out. Spread it out over a freshly glazed surface. There should be some air bubbles under it. If not, give it a twist and turn or push it together in some places. Pat with your cheesecloth to get good tight adhesion in several spots. Now, pick it up quickly but carefully (without dragging it across the surface). The resulting texture is very much like marble veining, or travertine marble. Spray "spattern" over this texture for a good-looking marbleized surface.

A similar marble effect can be achieved by using a sponge, burlap, a feather, or a combination of these.

VEINING. The classic tool for marble veining is a turkey feather. Drag it across the glaze to make a straight, thin line; twist and turn the feather a little to vary the width of the line. Occasionally change direction—but at an angle, not with a curve—keep veining lines straight. A string, saturated with glaze and dragged across the surface several times at different angles, makes a fair imitation of veining.

Beginners, note: Let your piece dry overnight before attempting veining. This allows you to wipe it off and try again. Also, with a dried surface, it is possible to obscure your veining line if it becomes too dark. Pick up excess glaze by laying a paper lightly over the surface and lifting it gently.

THE RANDOM EFFECT. The random or

chance effect is most important to successful marbleizing. Planned irregularity is more difficult than an ordered arrangement because almost from birth we have been trained to arrange things in an orderly manner. To "think random," reverse this training— check the following points:

Avoid: Lines or configuratons that start from a corner or from the center of any side.

Avoid: Concentration of interest in the exact center.

Avoid: Lines parallel to each other or to the outer edges of your piece.

Avoid: "Directionalism"—that is, a slanting effect, like handwriting. This comes from working always from the same position. Offset this by walking around your piece. Work on it from different angles.

TORTOISE SHELL. This effect is best created by working on one small area at a time. Apply a heavier than usual amount of toner glaze, then tap the surface lightly with your fingertips, changing the angle of your hand each time. For a random effect, walk around your piece—let each tap be from a different angle. For bigger shells, use heavy rubber gloves. For a less-distinct shell pattern, put your hands inside a plastic bag.

A similar appearance is achieved by tapping the surface with a short bristle brush, beginning in the center of the area and working toward the edges.

HIGHLIGHTING. After the glaze coat has dried thoroughly (overnight) you can increase and heighten the light-and-dark effect by highlighting. The object of highlighting is to emphasize the shading you achieved in the wiping step. With highlighting you reveal the full gamut of color from the clear, unglazed paint to the depths of the glazed shadows. These touches are still different from those achieved by wiping—and should be explored. Try them in an inconspicuous place. The highlight step also makes it possible to correct some deficiencies of wiping.

With finest sandpaper or steel wool, rub lightly all over to flatten any nibs, dust particles, etc. Rub in the direction of the grain. Avoid corners and edges because paint will wear away very quickly at these points. For spindles and other rounded or curved surfaces, use steel wool.

With medium sandpaper, sand more vigorously in the center of panels and large areas—bear down just enough to remove some of the glaze. Always sand with the grain, and leave a heavier coat of glaze around the edges. Gently "feather" edges of highlight so as not to leave an abrupt and obvious line between highlight and shading.

As you sand, the glaze will disappear first from atop the ridges formed by the brush strokes of the undercoat paint. These brush-stroke lines will lend additional interest to the texturing. Add highlights gradually. Stand back and judge the effect from time to time.

Work on the following areas:

1. Highlight the centers of panels and of all areas large enough to reach with the sandpaper.

2. Highlight high points of carvings

and spindles. (Use finest sandpaper or steel wool here, proceeding carefully. Paint wears off quickly.)

3. Highlight normal wear spots on chairs—that is, arms, front of seats, center of back, etc.

Don't worry about "chalking" or the light powdery look that first results from the sanding step. It will disappear in the finishing process. If you find that too much glaze has been removed, simply dry-brush on more fresh glaze, wipe, and let dry overnight.

STRIPING. For really professional striping, get a long-bristled, sign-painters stripping brush, available at any paint or art store. Before striping, let your piece dry overnight. This will allow you to rest your hand on the piece to guide your brush and also to repair your stripes by wiping the edges, or to wipe them off and try again.

To stripe, dip your brush deep into the glaze, coating the full length of the bristles. Remove excess by drawing each side of the brush against the edge of can. Your brush should be loaded but not dripping. To stripe effectively, use the brush wth a careful slow dragging motion.

For a wide stripe or border, lay the brush flat along the stripe line with the full length of the bristles in contact with the surface. Drag the brush in the direction of the stripe. When you run out of glaze, reload and resume your line, overlapping a little.

For a narrow stripe, turn your brush to the side of the narrow edge and proceed as for a broad stripe. The width of

line is a little harder to control in this position.

The easiest kind of striping is where you have a beveled edge or the concave indentation of a molding to act as a guide for your brush.

Where there is no such guide, more skill and practice is needed. On a table-top or border where you want a line to represent a panel on a door or drawer, draw one light guide line with a pencil. Keep your brush to the right of the line (if you are right-handed). Keeping your eye on the line, draw your brush along it with a motion swift enough to keep the line from wavering. Do not go back over it. The grain of the line will give it a finished look.

GOLD EFFECTS. Some pieces look better with the addition of gold, others don't. If you're not sure, try adding gold touches to a small area or one corner and then think about it awhile. In general, gold will be applied to formal period furniture such as English and French eighteenth-century. Gold is used less often on French Provincial designs, and very little gold appears on early American and Victorian.

Use gold powder and bronzing liquid (buy them at any art supply department or paint store). Mix the powder with the liquid only as you need it. When you become much more expert, try gold leaf for striping and larger gold areas.

Gold striping: See directions for striping.

Gold highlighting: With a dry brush (see page 186), touch high spots lightly. If too much gold is deposited, wipe lightly before the gold sets.

Gold wipe: Apply gold lightly with a dry brush (see page 186). Wipe thoroughly and quickly before the gold sets. This distributes the gold in small amounts over the entire area, to create gold *glints* rather than gold spots.

Gold spatter: See *Spatter*. This is still another way to achieve gold glints.

Gold in wax: Now on the market is gold in wax. Quite widely distributed, this paste form of gold may be rubbed on with the finger or a cloth, dried, then buffed to a fine sheen that resembles gold leaf. Use very small amounts—a little goes a long way. It is excellent for striping a concave molding line that may be traced with the finger. For flat or textured surfaces, thin with turpentine and apply gold, using dry-brush technique. Thin with turpentine to spatter or for use with a striping brush. To repair or remove gold in wax, use turpentine.

DISTRESSED. Distressed wood is one of the most popular antiquing effects, and if your piece of furniture isn't naturally worn, the effect can be simulated. Make your own scratches and mars by beating the surface with a heavy tool or a burlap bag filled with chains. Sand the scratches and apply artist's oil paint, using the color raw umber, straight from the tube. Rub off excess oil paint vigorously.

DISTRESSED PAINT. This effect is achieved by applying two layers of contrasting colors to your furniture, allowing each to dry thoroughly. Then take a coarse sandpaper and lightly sand the surface, until the initial color is in evidence. Do this only in the spots where normal wear would occur.

THE UNFINISHED LOOK. The white "unfinished" look seen in some ultramodern settings is not as simple as it seems. Only the extra-white woods like birch, ash, and cottonwood can get by with just a water-white varnish. More ordinary cabinet woods—pine, for instance—will require a white stain to equalize strong grain patterns and to delay the tendency of all woods to yellow with age.

EXTRA-DEEP WOOD COLOR. A deep black/brown color will give wood a Spanish, Mexican or Mediterranean look and will also conceal unmatched wood colors and undesirable grains. This effect is fine for many of the applied designs today that are rough-hewn and rustic looking, and also for rough-finished lumber that is cross-sawn and weathered looking.

On some of the rustic furniture handcrafted in the village industries of Mexico, this black/brown color is obtained from materials most unorthodox by any modern paint standards—would you believe tar and gasoline?

But more dependable are the pigmented stains or penetrating oil stains (see Chapter Six). A satisfactory deep color may require several coats of stain.

PAINTED-ON WOOD FINISHES. More often than you know, those furniture finishes that look the most mellow and shaded are completely painted on. They are the ones that seem most to glow with "the patina of age." The new painted-on wood finishes show only a subtle indication of grain.

Three separate color coats (one opaque, two transparent) assure color variation and a remarkable illusion of "depth" of wood grain. The first coat is paint, coats 2 and 3 are two different glaze colors.

Painted-on wood finishes are particularly effective on traditional cabinets and doors with decorative detail. Panels, carving, and molding trim can be shaded and distressed with spatter to give a mellow "old" appearance.

Painted-on wood finishes are useful for "matching" radiator covers, baseboards, or other metallic or nonwood surfaces to surrounding wood color to maintain a continuous wood effect, as in a paneled room.

EBONY FINISH. Any close-grained wood may be given a good imitation ebony finish with a black stain made by pouring 2 quarts of boiling hot water over 1 ounce of powdered logwood extract. After the extract has been dissolved, add to it a solution made by dissolving 1 dram of powdered potassium chromate in a few drops of hot water. Combine these two solutions and allow to cool before using. If the first coat does not produce a sufficiently deep black, apply a second and a third coat. The water stain has a tendency to raise the grain of the wood. It is a good idea, therefore, to sand the surface after each coat has dried. The last coat will usually not cause any noticeable raising of the grain. Protect the ebonized finish by ap-

plying a thin coating of shellac after the stain has dried. Rub lightly with extra-fine sandpaper to remove the gloss of the shellac.

FROSTIQUE. This is a new textured look in a light, bright key. It is paint plus glaze, but not traditional antiquing. Six sharp modern pastel colors are each modified with a white glaze to make a series of soft flowery tints. They are excellent for dressing rooms, baths, kitchen, feminine-looking bedrooms, and girls' rooms. They can be wiped in the traditional antique method or textured for a modern look.

MODERN PAINT TREATMENTS. The "wet look," strong, bright colors with a high gloss finish are in great demand now for ultramodern treatments of cabinets, bookshelves, and built-ins. But there are not a lot of high gloss colors to choose from—only a few ready-mixed enamel colors.

For a "wet look" custom color, first paint the color coat, using a flat-finish high color. Give it the "wet look" with a high gloss water-clear varnish. This makes a color that is ever so much brighter and stronger than a semigloss of the same color.

DECOUPAGE

You've admired those museumlike pieces in antique stores and expensive gift shops—those small furniture items and plaques decorated with art prints preserved in clear lacquer or varnish finishes. An artist created them with decoupage—an art that dates back to the seventeenth century—and now you can practice the same art of decoupage easily and economically.

Actually, decoupage means to decorate surfaces with cutouts of favorite art prints, unusual designs, photographs, old maps, documents, wedding and birth announcements—any collection of designs, stamps, or cherished printed mementos you want to preserve and display.

The steps in decoupage are as follows:

1. The surface of the object to be decoupaged must be completely clean and smooth. Sand carefully, fill cracks and holes with wood plastic or filler, and sand smooth. If the furniture piece or object was previously painted and can't be sanded smooth, remove the paint with paint remover and then sand smooth. Wipe clean with a soft cloth. Apply an undercoat or wood stain basecoat in the desired color (which should complement your selected print). Allow to dry thoroughly.

2. Choose a cutout (print) of suitable size to cover the object or to be centered attractively as desired. Cut out the print by feeding the paper into the scissors, rather than cutting along the edges as you would normally do. Some artisans prefer to tear around the print following the shape of the picture, creating a ragged edge. If you tear the print, sand lightly on the reverse side to smooth out the torn edges. *Note:* If the print or picture has printing on the back, you must seal it by coating the back with white glue slightly diluted with water; allow to dry thoroughly. This prevents the printing from showing through on the surface of the print.

3. You are now ready to glue the print to the object. Apply some slightly diluted white glue to the surface on which the print is to be placed and also to the back of the print. Place the print on the object and press out all air bubbles with your fingers, or with a roller. Place waxed paper over the print and, using the roller, press out all excess glue and wipe clean with a damp cloth. Now, brush the print with the diluted white glue to seal the surface of the print. Allow to dry thoroughly.

4. Brush on the first coat of lacquer, varnish, or decoupage coating. Allow to dry. If you desire an antique effect, apply antique glaze, wipe lightly with a soft cloth for graining effects, and allow to dry. Continue to apply coats of lacquer, varnish, or decoupage finish, sanding lightly and wiping with a soft cloth between coats—until the print is completely submerged in the clear lacquer, varnish, or decoupage finish.

5. The final step achieves a deep, rich finish. Using very fine steel wool or fine sandpaper wet with water, rub the object until the finish is uniformly dull. Apply one or two coats of a good-grade paste wax, polishing vigorously with a clean, soft cloth. Your masterpiece is now completed.

FABRIC OR WALLPAPER FINISHES

Fabric or wallpaper is sometimes used to cover furniture, the inside of drawers, and other surfaces. The fabric or paper should be carefully cut to size with a razor blade, wallpaper knife, or similar cutting device. Then apply wallpaper paste to both the area to be covered as well as to the paper or fabric.

The paste should be mixed and applied according to the directions on the package. Always smooth the paste out well, covering all areas so there will be no loose sections. Smooth the paper firmly in place, working the strip down gradually so no air bubbles are left under the surface. Wipe smooth with a clean dry cloth, but use a damp cloth to remove any paste that has smeared over the edges. Remove these spots before they have a chance to dry. After the paper or fabric has dried, it may be treated to a surface coating of special wallpaper wax (wallpaper wax *only*) or it may be painted or sprayed with a thin coat of clear shellac, lacquer, or varnish.

FIR PLYWOOD FINISHES

One of the most popular and most economical types of plywood is made of fir. As previously stated in Chapter Five, fir plywood needs a good sealer, because of the special character of the grain figure, which is made up of alternate hard summer growth and softer spring growth. Without the use of a sealer, the first coat of paint or stain penetrates unevenly, resulting usually in a "wild," overconspicuous grain.

To tame or quiet this grain, several special types of sealers which may be purchased from your neighborhood lumber, paint, or hardware dealer, have been developed. If the sealer is used properly, it allows the stain to soften the darker markings and deepen the lighter surfaces of the fir wood. The effect will be soft and lustrous, with the wild grain figures pleasantly subdued.

To obtain a light natural finish, first sandpaper the wood smooth with fine sandpaper, and then apply an even coat of resin sealer. Lightly sand when dry and follow with a thin coat of pure white shellac. It is suggested that the shellac be reduced to 2-pound cut. Sandpaper again when dry and apply either a satin-finish lacquer or a gloss varnish. If a flat finish is desired, a flat or dull varnish may be substituted. After drying thoroughly, steel-wool and complete with white wax.

The blond or pickled effect may be had for fir plywood panels by using a white plywood sealer or interior white undercoater, thinned as follows: 6 pounds of flat undercoat, 3 1/2 quarts of pure turpentine, and 1 pint of linseed oil. If the white sealer is used, it may be thinned 10 to 15 percent with mineral spirits or turpentine. Paint the sealer on and allow it to set for 3 or 4 minutes. Then rub into the pores and wipe clean, taking care not to leave a painted effect. Let dry overnight, and next day lightly sand with fine sandpaper. Apply a thin coat of pure white shellac and sand when dry. Follow with a coat of lacquer or varnish. Steel-wool when dry, and wax.

An inexpensive but attractive finish may be had with a single coat of white sealer or interior white undercoater, pigmented to the desired tint and thinned sufficiently so that the grain of the wood will show through. A second coat of clear shellac or varnish will add to the durability of this finish and give it a deep luster.

For a painted surface on fir plywood, the sealer will provide a smooth, even base that will enable the paint to take evenly. The paint may be applied directly over the sealer, but, for the best results, the surface should first be made smooth with sandpaper.

HARDBOARD FINISHES

Hardwood plywood may be finished as described in Chapter Six.

Hardboard is reconstituted natural wood and is fabricated by reducing natural wood to fibers and then pressing the fibers together into panels of various thickness and surface dimensions. It is often used as a tabletop surface, in drawers and other furniture parts.

When painting hardboard, both surface preparation and the application of a good primer-sealer are essential for a smooth, uniform finish. The hardboard should be clean and dry. All grease and dirt should be removed with a suitable cleaner, and nail heads should be countersunk and puttied.

Good sealing by the primer is required to prevent absorption of the top coat. Good water-thinned and solvent-thinned primer-sealers are available for this purpose. Factory-primed hardboard is ready for painting unless the primer has been damaged. Damaged areas should be spot-primed or given another coat of primer-sealer to insure proper sealing.

After the hardboard has been properly sealed, the top coat can be applied. A smoother- and better-appearing finish will be obtained if the sealer is lightly sanded to remove irregularities before the top coat is applied. This is especially true if a gloss enamel is used as the final coat. Usually, two coats of paint—semigloss or gloss enamels—is a good idea, with a light sanding between coats.

PARTICLEBOARD FINISHES

Particleboard is the newest member of the family of man-made wood panel products used in furniture and cabinetry. Because it is competitively priced and offers certain woodworking and performance advantages, particleboard is one of the fastest-growing segments of the wood products industry.

In general, all particleboard surfaces within habitable spaces that are not covered with finished adhesive-bonded laminates should be painted. Unpainted, exposed particleboard is easily soiled, difficult to clean, and may sometimes develop an odor when used extensively within confined spaces.

When painting or otherwise finishing particleboard, it is well to know in advance the distinctive characteristics of the material. The basic particleboard surface is somewhat more porous than most finished lumber. Surface characteristics vary from one board to another, some boards providing a surface that can be painted without using a filler and others requiring a filler to reduce the porosity of the surface. It is a good idea to test scraps to determine the best method for obtaining the desired surface finish.

If a very smooth finish is desired, the particleboard surface should be filled with a paste wood filler or a sanding sealer prior to applying the finish. If the surface is unusually porous, both a filler and sanding sealer should be used. Factory-filled boards, with surfaces ready for painting, are available. Some manufacturers apply a resin-impregnated fibrous sheet to the faces of their particleboards to provide an excellent base for painting.

Particleboard usually contains a small amount of paraffin wax, which is added during manufacturing to retard the rate of water absorption. If the paint or finish contains materials that are good solvents for wax, some of the wax will be absorbed in the wet paint film and cause areas whose drying rate is slower. The wax can be effectively isolated from painted finishes by applying a thin barrier coat such as shellac, which isn't a solvent for wax.

Because of the shapes and color contrasts of the wood particles, interesting decorative effects may be obtained by staining particleboard. A variety of clear finishes and stains can be used to highlight the different colors and shapes of the wood particles. To create these finishes, apply one coat of stain, allow it to set for a few minutes, then rub and wipe off the excess. The desired color penetration may be determined on some sample material or scraps.

When painting doors or other free-moving units, it is especially important to finish both sides of the door with an equal number of coats. As with other wood products, particleboard will gain or lose moisture with changes in the atmospheric conditions, so, unless both sides are finished equally, the less-finished side will gain or lose moisture faster than the other side and the panel will warp. Tops and bottoms of doors should be well sealed with paint to reduce moisture intake.

The edges of particleboard have the same tendency to absorb paint as the surface, usually, in fact, to a greater extent. When edges are to be exposed to view, they should be filled with paste wood filler or other special filler formulated for the job before painting. Best results on edges are obtained by applying the filler with a putty knife or a coarse cloth applicator. Brush or spray application of filler may be satisfactory on certain boards, such as those having a density above 45 or 50 pounds per cubic foot.

Counter and Tabletop Finishes

Among the newest counter- and tabletop finishes—especially for fir plywood, hardboard, and particleboard—are the so-called seamless flooring systems, which were introduced a few years ago as an unique concept in commercial and residential flooring. They are colorful, decorative, extremely durable, and, as the name implies, "seamless." Most seamless systems consist of liquid base coats, colored chips or other decorative materials, and liquid sealer or wear coats. All coats are applied in a continuous flow, without seams—leaving a sanitary, smooth, and easy-to-maintain finished surface, which is ideal for counter- and tabletops as well as floors.

The type of seamless system used will determine the exact application techniques required. However, the usual steps are:

1. Fill the seams and cracks with wood plastic and sand level. Apply a seal or prime coat, if recommended.

2. Apply base coat and chips or other decorative materials. The latter add the color, excitement, and texture that makes seamless floor coverings *individually* yours. Don't skimp when you create your own "color" pattern. Be certain you have enough decorative materials or chips to create the pattern desired before you begin. Excess decorative materials and chips can be easily removed after the base coat has dried with a clean broom or vacuum. Sand high areas where the chips have overlapped and are not firmly bonded. Vacuum thoroughly. *Allow the base or chip-receiving coat to dry thoroughly before applying the glaze coat.* Some dry in 4 to 6 hours—others are recommended for drying overnight. (*Note:* If the base coat is *not* the chip-receiving coat, apply and let dry thoroughly. Then apply the manufacturer's recommended chip-receiving coat and apply decorative materials as above.)

3. Apply glaze, seal, or wear coat. If urethane or solvent-thinned wear or glaze coat is used, adhere to all safety precautions. Some final coats can be applied as soon as the chip-receiving coat is hard enough to use, while others require that the chip-receiving coat dry longer, more thoroughly. If only one coat is recommended, apply generously. Where more than one coat is recommended, apply a glaze or wear coat and allow to dry according to the manufacturer's directions; sand if recommended, and apply a second coat. Often extra coats are recommended if less texture is desired or to create a high-build, tougher surface.

Clean the tools immediately after application is complete. The manufacturers of most glaze coats recommend use of a thinner or special solution for cleaning tools.

Seamless floor coverings require little maintenance to retain their beauty and sparkle, being tougher and more durable than most counter- and tabletop materials. Clean with a damp cloth when dirty.

PAINTING LAWN FURNITURE

A lawn chair or table's life is a rugged one—exposed to rain, sunshine, moonshine, and even passing birds! You can't halt the weather, but you can make a protective shield for your furniture with paint. You will want a durable finish, one that will laugh at the weather and that will take to soap and water clean-ups with a smile.

Is your lawn furniture metal? Keep a sharp eye open for cracks in the old finish where moisture is apt to sneak in and promote rust and corrosion. Remove cracked paint with a wire brush, and sand away all traces of rust or corrosion with steel wool. After spot coating these problem areas with a protective anticorrosive primer (such as zinc chromate), the entire surface can be painted with colorful exterior enamel. Unpainted iron or steel furniture *must* be painted for protection. Galvanized steel will give its best performance when a primer such as a zinc dust–zinc oxide type is used. Other special primers specifically developed for coating galvanized steel will also give satisfactory protection. Apply the primer, dry overnight, and then apply one or two coats of a good exterior metal enamel for best results.

Aluminum furniture, shiny-bright when new, may develop unsightly pitting when left outdoors or in a corrosive environment. To restore a dazzling appearance, and to assure adhesion of the new coating, use a phosphoric acid cleaner or sand the surface to remove all dull film. Wipe clean with turpentine to remove dirt and grease, and then apply a clear, nonyellowing exterior acrylic or butyrate lacquer. Incidentally, if this lacquer is applied to new aluminum furniture (which you have wiped with solvent), you'll be rewarded by a shinier, longer-lasting finish.

Wood furniture is vulnerable to moisture attack from above and below. Moisture from the damp ground can ruin the legs and undersides of furniture. To avoid this problem be sure to protect the entire piece of furniture with a good-quality exterior enamel. First remove all loose paint by sanding or by using a chemical paint remover, and apply a good exterior enamel undercoat before applying the enamel.

Metal fittings on wood furniture need special attention. They should be protected from rust and corrosion by the same methods used for metal furniture. If the wood has been finished to accent the natural beauty of the wood grain, you'll want to use a spar varnish, a rough-and-ready urethane varnish, or a clear exterior lacquer to keep the furniture beautiful.

Exterior enamels come in exciting decorating shades. Why not turn your attention to exterior decorating and color—coordinate your lawn furniture with your patio or the outside of your home!

CHAPTER EIGHT

Applying New Seating Materials

One of the major repair jobs that must be done on many antique chairs is to replace the seating. This seating may be cane, rush, splint, or webbing. Let's see how to go about replacing these materials.

CANE SEATS

Cane for chair seating is made from a palm called *rattan*. The plants come from the Indian archipelago, China, India, Ceylon, and the Malay peninsula. They grow in dense forests and frequently reach tree height; then they fall over and form a matted undergrowth. The stem, which is covered with beautiful foliage, grows in length from 100 to 300 feet and is seldom more than 1 inch in diameter. For export, these stems are cut in 10- to 20-foot lengths. The outer bark is stripped in widths varying from 1/16 to 3/16 of an inch and is cut in strips. Then it is tied in hanks of 1,000 feet and is ready for the weaver. One such hank is enough for four chairs with medium-sized seats.

Seating cane differs from domestic sugar cane and from the cane known as *bamboo*, which grows in the southern states. Bamboo, which is shorter, straighter, and thicker, is used for furniture, walking sticks, poles, and the like. Neither bamboo nor sugar cane is suitable for chair seating.

You can buy cane at chair-seating and craftsman's supply houses, and at certain mail-order houses and department stores. Buy long, select cane (from 15- to 18-foot lengths) for medium or large chair seats. You can use shorter lengths but they have to be tied more often. Good cane is smooth, glossy on the right side, tough, and pliable. The "eye," or lump where the stem of the leaf grew out, should be smooth and un-

200

broken. Poor cane has rough and imperfect spots, does not weave easily, and is likely to split.

Plastic cane is also available. It weaves easily, does not require soaking, is strong, and costs slightly less than other cane because little is wasted. Its smooth shiny texture is suitable for painted chairs; real cane is preferable for fine old furniture.

Binder, to finish the edge of the seat, is cane one width wider than that used for weaving, and is included with the weaving cane.

The widths of cane to use depends on the size of the holes in the chair seat and the distance between them. The table below is a guide to the size of cane to buy.

SIZE OF CANE TO USE

Cane Size	Size of Hole in Seat (Inches)	Distance Between Holes in Seat (Inches)
Carriage (narrowest)	1/8	3/8
Superfine	1/8	3/8
Fine fine	3/16	1/2
Fine	3/16	5/8
Medium	1/4	3/4
Common (widest)	5/16	7/8

Getting Ready to Weave

Cut away the old seat, using a keyhole saw. Clean any pieces of broken cane or dirt from the holes and the seat rails. Pull out old nails and tacks. Be sure you can get cane through all the holes. If any are filled, bore a hole through them. Use a file to round the inside of the frame so no sharp edges will cut the cane. If you need to refinish the wood, do this before the seat is caned.

To prepare the cane, pull one of the strands of cane from the looped end of the hank, near where it is tied. As you pull, shake the hank so that the cane won't tangle or tear. Roll the strand, right side out, to fit in a 5- to 6-inch bowl. Fasten the ends with a clamp clothespin.

Fill the bowl with a 10 percent solution of glycerine, about 1 1/2 tablespoons of glycerine to 1 cup of water (warm water hastens the process). Soak the roll of cane in the solution. Or use a solution of urea crystals, available at drugstores in 1-pound jars, 1 tablespoon to 1 quart of water. Either solution helps to prevent the cane from drying out, but glycerine is preferable. Let the cane soak for about 20 minutes, or until it is soft and pliable.

Plastic cane, enough for one chair, is sold in a bunch with strands cut 6 to 7 yards long; if you buy it in quantity on a spool, cut it in strands of similar length. Do not soak it.

How to Weave Square or Oblong Seats

The usual form of weaving is called *seven-step weaving:* Weave from the upper side of the seat; first, from back to front, then from side to side, again from back to front, and from side to side, and then on the two diagonals. If you begin in the center of the back, you will find it easy to make sure the rows of cane are straight. Add the binder last.

STEP 1. Count the holes in the back rail. If there are an odd number of holes, put a peg in the center hole. If there are an even number of holes, put the peg in one of the holes nearest the center. Do the same on the front rail, pegging the same side of the center as at the back.

Take the roll of cane from the bowl and wipe off excess water with your fingers or a cloth. Put another strand in to soak while you work.

Weave the eye whenever you can to keep from roughening or breaking the strand. Pull out the peg from the back rail. Push about 4 inches of an end of cane down through this hole and fasten it with a peg. Bring the cane to the front rail, right side (smooth side) up; take out the peg there and push the cane through. Leave the cane slack, because the mesh tightens as weaving continues. Then replace the peg. Push the cane up through the nearest hole on one side of the center. Pull it across the chair and down through the opposite hole at the back.

As you weave, hold the cane so that it sags a little below the level of the wood seat frame. Weave large seats and plastic cane tighter. If the chair has a scoop seat, press the cane down as far as the bottom of the wood frame. Continue weaving toward the side as long as you can weave in opposite holes. Don't use

corner holes unless you are sure there will be room for the diagonal and binder canes that must also go through these holes. Leave the rest of the strand to use later. Fasten it with a clamp clothespin to keep it out of your way.

For seats wider at the front than at the back, weave separate pieces of cane, as shown here. Canes must not be carried across on the underside of the frame to block holes that must be used later. As you continue weaving you can keep the cane in position without using pegs, except to fasten the ends.

Weave the other half of the seat.

STEP 2. Start at the back on the right side rail as you face the chair, in a hole next to the corner. Pull the cane up through the hole and across the seat over the weaving you have already done. Continue weaving back and forth. If the front rail is curved, weave with separate pieces of cane.

STEP 3. Weave as in step 1. Keep the strands slack as in steps 1 and 2. Weave in line with, and on top of, the first and second weaving and to the right of the cane you wove in the first step.

Fasten the ends of cane on the underside of the frame by tying them to or twisting them around the cane crossing from the next hole. Trim the end wherever you can before starting step 4 and then tie as you go along, so the pegs won't be in your way. Moisten the ends of cane if necessary so they can be tied without breaking.

STEP 4. Real weaving begins, here, as you weave from side to side. Start at the back on the right as you face the chair

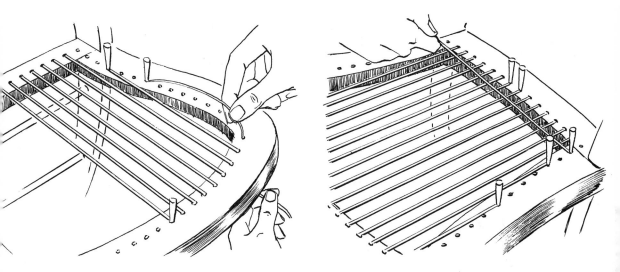

Figure 8-1. For seats wider at the front than at the back, weave the pieces of can as shown at the left. Pull the cane up through the hole and across the seat over the weaving you have, as shown at the right.

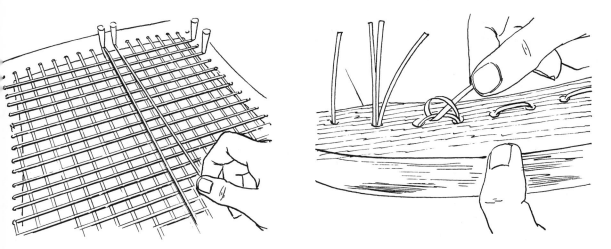

Figure 8-2. Continue weaving back and forth, as shown at the left. Fasten the ends of the cane as shown at the right.

and in a hole next to a corner. Weave over the canes on top and under the canes underneath. As you work, straighten the canes you wove in step 2 to help keep step 4 canes in place. When you are a third or halfway across, pull the length through that far, being careful that it does not twist or break. As you pull, keep your hand level with the chair rail. If you lift up, the weaving cane may cut canes already woven, especially if the cane is plastic. Continue weaving across the row. This draws together, in pairs, the canes from front to back and from side to side. When you reach the opposite side, put the end of cane down through the hole and peg it until you weave the next row. Pull the cane up through the nearest hole and weave back across the seat, so the cane passes over the same canes and under the same canes as it did the first time across. If you find it easier, weave with the end of cane.

Repeat for the other rows. At the sides, be sure the canes in step 3 are on top and at the right of the canes in step 1. Soak the woven cane with a wet sponge or cloth. Using two pegs, straighten the rows and force them close together in pairs with hollow squares between.

STEP 5. Diagonal weaving begins in this step. Start at the back corner hole on the right side as you face the chair, and weave the first row toward the left front corner. You will weave the cane diagonally *over* the pairs from front to back and *under* those from side to side, keeping the cane straight from the corner holes. First lay it in position to decide how to start. Weave with one hand on top of the seat and the other underneath. Pull the cane through when you are a third or halfway across. Be careful not to lift it and cut the strands already woven. The cane must lie flat and be so woven that the edges do not bind. The cane should pull through easily; it helps to moisten it with a damp cloth.

Weave the *back section* of the seat first, using holes on the left and back rails. For the second row, weave from front to back, going over and under the same rows you did before.

Weave two canes in each corner hole, making a "fish-head" or a "V." You may complete the fish-head on the back corner or finish it when weaving the front corner. Sometimes canes can be kept straight only by weaving a single cane in part of the corner holes. Keep the canes right side up. Don't skip holes on the underside of the seat.

Weave back and forth until you have reached a place near the center of the left side. If the seat is round or definitely curved, weave only a few diagonals and then begin to skip holes or double in holes. Keep the rows straight. If there are more holes on the sides than on the back, skip holes, usually not more than three on the side. If the seat is round, you may double in holes across the back as well as skip holes on the side. Make the canes lie straight across the back corner. Check to see that you have skipped enough holes so that the same number are left on the back as on the

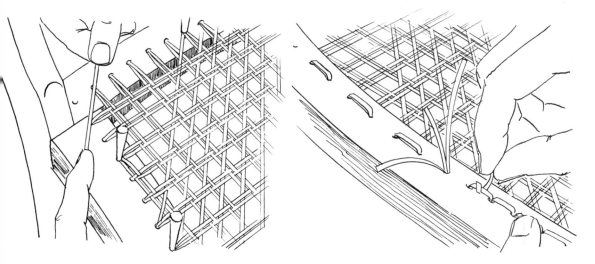

Figure 8-3. The canes should lie straight across the back corner, as shown at the right. At the right, one end is tied and the other cane out of the same hole can be tied to the same strap. Those from the other hole can't be tied until more straps are formed.

side. Use a new piece of cane when you need to, or use an end left from previous weaving if you can do so without crossing holes on the lower side of the seat. Experienced weavers use all ends of cane so that there will be fewer knots to tie.

The rest of the seat must be woven according to the pattern started on this section.

Since the first diagonal was woven from back to front, weave the first row on the *front section* from front to back, using holes on the front and right rails. Use a new piece of cane.

Check to keep the rows straight. Canes may curve slightly near the rail. Put them in the holes where they will curve the least. To make the pattern

alike on the two sides, weave twice (fish-head) in the hole or holes corresponding to those skipped on the left side of the chair. To prevent cutting the cane, you may fish-head in the hole above or below that directly opposite.

On the front rail, double in holes on the left and skip holes on the right. Note the four pegs. Tie ends as you go along, wherever there is a nearby strap to which to tie.

STEP 6. This is the second diagonal, woven in the opposite direction. Start at the back corner hole on the left side as you face the chair and weave toward the front right corner. Weave diagonally *under* the pairs from front to back and *over* those from side to side.

Weave the *front section* of the seat

first. Complete the pattern started in the first diagonal, so the corners and the two sides correspond. Each half of the front and back rails must also correspond. On the left side rail, weave twice in holes skipped by the first diagonal. Do the same on the front rail, right side. On the left side, skip those holes used twice before. Don't carry cane across holes on the underside of the seat. Instead, cut the cane if necessary.

For the *back section,* continue the weaving, using a new cane to weave from front to back; double in the back corner hole to match the opposite corner. Weave to the front and double in that corner hole. On the side rail, skip holes woven in twice by the first diagonal. On the back rail, skip any holes already used twice.

STEP 7. The binder cane is the next size wider than that used for weaving. It is used to cover the holes and to finish the edge of the weaving. If the seat is curved, use one strip long enough to go around. If corners are square or turns are sharp, cut separate lengths, each from 6 to 8 inches longer than the side of the seat where it will be used. Keep both binder and weaving cane wet and pliable. Lay one of the pieces of binder flat over the holes on one side of the seat, with the center of the piece at about the center hole. Push one end through the corner hole and hold it there with a peg.

Use as long a piece of weaving cane as you can handle easily. Or use a piece left from previous weaving, crossing the corner underneath if you wish. Fasten the binder at each hole or, if the holes are close together, at every other hole. Begin at the end where the binder is pegged. Pull the weaving cane up through the next hole, pass it over the top of the binder, and down through the same hole. Bring it up through the next hole on either side of the binder and repeat. Keep both canes right side up, flat and tight. Use an awl or a bone knitting needle if you need to force an opening for the cane.

If a continuous piece does not lie flat around the corner, start the second side by taking out the peg and pushing the end of the binder through the corner hole. Replace the peg, hammer it tightly, and file the top level with the chair frame. Repeat around the chair. When the cane is dry, it should be tight enough to ring when you snap it sharply with your fingers. The mesh should be level with the seat frame.

How to Finish the Seat

Tie and cut off any loose ends on the underside of the seat. Trim off rough places or hairs with a razor blade.

Cane has a hard, glossy surface that does not need a finish. If you want, however, you may apply a thin type of penetrating wood sealer to both sides to prevent drying and cracking. To blend the color of a new cane seat with the finish on the chair, apply a chair seat stain, available where you buy the cane. Rub the stain on the underside first, with a soft cloth or brush. Wipe off the surplus, and repeat on the upper side. When the

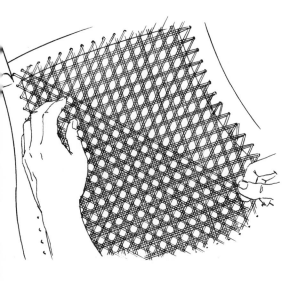

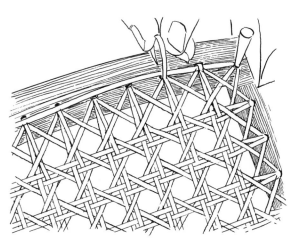

Figure 8-4. Finish the caning operation.

stain is dry, apply a second coat if you want a darker color.

CLEANING. Cane seats can be cleaned with a cloth wrung from a solution made as follows: Place 1 quart of boiling water in the top of a double boiler (or two old basins). Add 3 tablespoons of (commercially) boiled linseed oil and 1 tablespoon of turpentine. Put boiling water in the bottom of the boiler to help keep the solution hot. Do not place the mixture directly over a flame. Clean both sides of the seat.

RUSH SEATS

Chairs with round rails can have seats woven either of rush or of splint; the original seat usually shows which to use. Rush can be employed for chairs of simple design, such as the very early American ladder-back type. It always should be chosen for more elaborate chairs, such as the later Hitchcock type and the Sheraton. Rush can be used if seat rails are of the same height, or if side rails are slightly higher than those at the front and back.

Real rush or cattail is better than imitation fiber for chairs of good design, although more skill is required to weave it.

The kind of rush used for chair seating is known as *cattail*. Cattails grow in shallow fresh water, wet swampy places, along the banks of streams, and in lowlands and marshes. They are found commonly in most parts of the northern states. They can be gathered easily and with little or no expense, and, if properly chosen and prepared, are easy to use. Rush also may be bought. Stock ordered from a reliable dealer usually is well cured.

How to Collect and Dry Rush

You can tell cattails from other plants by their round spikes of flowers—the "bobs" or "cattails." The leaves are in two rows, with their flat sides back to back. There are two kinds: the broad-leafed (about 1 inch wide) and the narrow-leafed. The broad-leafed is more common; the narrow-leafed grows in lowlands and has much longer leaves. Choose the narrow, long leaves (about 7 feet) for chair seating.

Gather the rush when the leaves are full grown, when the stalks are still green, and the tips are beginning to turn brown. Late July, August, or early September is the usual time. Select perfect leaves and those from the stalks that do not have "bobs." Cut the stalks just above the surface of the water or ground. Gather an ample supply. Leaves shrink at least one-third of their weight as they cure; there is waste in weaving as well.

Pull the leaves from the stalks. Sort the leaves, placing together those of about the same width and length, and tie them in loose, flat bundles. Be careful not to bend or break the leaves. Dry them thoroughly for at least two or three weeks in a dark, airy room. An attic or storeroom floor is a good place for drying. Do not put the leaves in a damp room, such as a cellar, where mildew might form on the leaves, or in a hot sunny room where leaves might become brittle.

Rush carefully dried and stored should be usable for a year or more.

Getting Ready to Weave

Take out the old seat and remove all old tacks or nails from the rails. Smooth any uneven places in the wood and round the edges if they are sharp and likely to break the rush.

DAMPEN THE RUSH. Dampen the rush until it is workable enough to twist and weave without cracking or breaking. This may take 1 hour in warm water in a trough, or 8 to 12 hours if spread on the floor and sprinkled.

Fill the trough about three-quarters full of warm water. Add glycerine until the water feels soft, about 1 cup; or use a solution of urea crystals available at drugstores in 1-pound jars, about 1/4 cup to 1 gallon of water. Either solution helps to prevent the rush from drying out. Glycerine is preferable but costs more. Soak the rush, about a handful at a time, in the solution. You may have to change the solution once before you finish weaving a seat.

You would probably use only water if you dampened the rush on the floor.

CHOOSE AND PREPARE THE LEAVES. Choose long, unbroken leaves of about the same length, width, and thickness. The number of leaves to use in each strand depends not only on the leaves but on the size of strand you want. Usually, two leaves are twisted together; sometimes, if they are narrow or thin, three may be used. A thin strand is best for a graceful, delicate chair, but many strands are needed to fill the seat. Thick strands, although fewer would be needed, are too coarse for such a chair.

It is important to decide what size strands will look best on your chair.

Select and prepare the leaves and make them into strands as you work. Run the leaves through a wringer to take out air from the cells and to make the leaves workable. Set the rollers tight so that the leaves make a sharp crackling noise as they are run through. Good rush, well prepared, seldom stains the rollers. Draw each leaf quickly over the edge of a metal surface, to take out any air left in the cells.

PRACTICE MAKING TWISTS. Cut off about 1 yard of cord, and loop it around the back rail of the seat. Tie the ends of cord in a square knot; keep the loop about 5 inches long. Arrange two leaves with a butt end and a tip end together and the flat side of one next to the rounded side of the other, like stacked spoons. Put one end of the pair through the loop of cord for about 3 inches. Fold it toward the front rail and use the ends of string to tie around the bunch, making a square knot near the fold of rush. Tie the string temporarily around the side rail. Twist the leaves together, away from you and in such a way that the strand is smooth, even, tight, and of good color. Usually the thumb and first two fingers of one hand are used to make the twist, and the thumb and fingers of the other hand hold it. Keep the separate leaves straight and smooth as when making a braid; make long but firm twists, with the thumbs about 2 inches apart. Practice until you can make a smooth, even strand that is of a good size for your chair. Then untie the string around the side rail and take out this practice strand before starting to weave.

How To Weave

The weaving of a firm, smooth seat takes much skill and practice. How you do it depends on the way you like to do it and how you want it to look. One satisfactory method is described in the following paragraphs.

SEATS WITHOUT CORNER BLOCKS. With a carpenter's square as a guide,

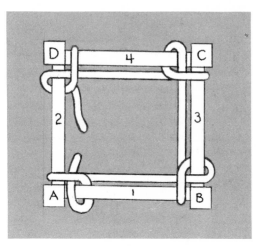

Figure 8-6. By numbering rails with pencil (at center), you can follow the steps without error. A short loop makes the fiber easier to handle in this work.

Figure 8-5. How to make the twists

make a square of stiff cardboard, with the long side about 15 inches. Use this to mark off a square center opening. Place the short side of the cardboard square parallel to either the front or the back rail and the long side against the inner edge of the corner of the back rail. Using a pencil, mark the edge of the square on the front rail. Do the same on the other side of the seat. The two corner measurements may not be the same, but the distance between pencil lines on the front rail must be the same as between posts on the back rail.

Weave the corners first until you reach the marks on the front rail and then weave as for a square seat. To do this, face the front of the chair and push the loop of string that was used for the practice twist close to the back post on the left side of the seat.

Begin with 4 leaves, each long enough to reach around three sides of the seat. Make 2 pairs, each with a butt and tip end together and the flat side of one leaf next to the round side of the other, as indicated on page 209. Place one end of the pair through the loop of cord for about 3 inches. Fold it toward the front rail and use the ends of string to tie around the bunch, making a square knot near the fold of rush.

Choose one pair of leaves, bring them almost to the front rail, and then twist them into a strand. Turn this twist away from the post; keep all other twists in the same direction like a rope. Draw the strand over rail 1, close to post A, up through the opening of the chair, over the side rail 2, again close to the corner

post A, and up through the opening again, thus holding the beginning of the twist. Lift up the strand from the underside of the seat to shorten its length and thus help to make the seat firm. Lay the strands in position to make a square crossing and a seam straight from the corner of the seat.

Pull the strand, without twisting the leaves, across the front of the seat. At post B, twist the leaves, bring the strand over side rail 3, close to post B, up through the opening of the seat, over front rail 1, again close to post B. Arrange the strands as at post A.

Pull the strand, without twisting, to the back and fasten it firmly by winding the ends around the back rail and tying them together, or by holding them with a clamp clothespin.

The strands should be twisted only over the rails where they will show, not on the underside of the seat.

Weave the second pair in the same way. Loop the ends tightly around the back rail and fasten them with a clothespin to the first strand. Tie more leaves, one pair at a time, in the same loop of string. About 5 twists fill 1 inch. Use a piece of rush or the cardboard square every 2 or 3 rows to make sure that the corners are square and the rows straight. Use the hammer and block of wood to force the strands in place. Keep the seam straight from the corner toward the center of the seat. Make a square crossing; add from 4 to 6 inches of another leaf, if needed, to fill the space.

After the corners are woven as far as the marks on the front rail, fasten the

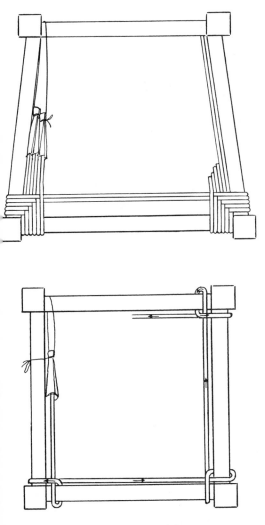

Figure 8-7. Weaving seats without a corner block is shown above, while square seat weaving can be seen below.

ends on the right-hand side: tie with a square knot a piece of string about 18 inches long around all the ends of rush. Loop the ends around the back rail and

tie another knot. Pull the strands taut and keep the rows straight and close together. Remove the clothespin and cut away the rush over the rail.

If the rush breaks, replace it with another piece.

PAD THE SEAT. After the front corners are filled in, pad them. The padding is put in the pockets on the underside of the seat at each side of the corner seams. Butt ends and short lengths of rush are folded the length of the opening and forced in flat bunches from the center toward the corner posts. To do this, turn the chair over. Use a wooden stuffer and poke a bunch of rush into the pocket on the underside of the seat, from the center to the seam. The finished seat should be hard and flat, or slightly rounded, but not overstuffed. Rush shrinks as it dries, so put in enough padding to make the seat firm but not "fat." Both front corners should be of the same thickness.

As you continue to weave around all four corners, add padding about every 3 inches. Back corners take less padding than do front corners. When you have finished the weaving, add the last padding by poking in bunches parallel to the last strands.

Square Seats

Seat frames may be square or have corner blocks that make the opening square. Weave these seats and seats that are wider at the front, after you have have filled the corners, as follows:

Weave the first strand, corner A. Use the same loop that you had for seats wider at the front, or make a similar loop if you are just starting to weave a square seat. Tie in the butt ends of two leaves, one of which is long, and the other short. Twist and weave around post A. Loops of string never have to be cut; weaving covers them.

JOIN THE RUSH. As you leave corner A, add a new leaf. Place between the weaving and the strand, with the butt end hanging down below the underside of the seat for about 6 inches, or the amount of the stiff end of the leaf, and with the curved side toward you. Twist this new leaf (about twice) with the other two, to hold them together. The butt ends make a seam on the underside of the seat and should hang down rather than be caught in the weaving. That is, always add a new piece of rush after you finish each corner so that when you are ready to weave the next corner the rush will be securely fastened and you will have enough to go around that corner.

ADDING RUSH. Occasionally you may need to use a third piece of rush to fill out the strand, as when crossing twists at the seam. Weave the first strand to corner B. If the strand is too "fat," drop the end of the shortest leaf. This can be cut off or folded in for padding. Twist and weave around corner B. As you leave this corner, again add a new leaf. Then continue to corner C and weave, as shown in the illustration here. Add a new piece of rush, and proceed to and weave around corner D, again adding a piece of rush.

SPLICING. If the rush breaks or you

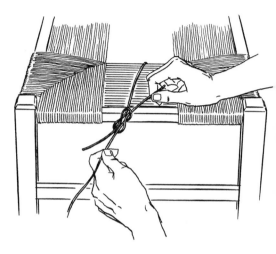

Figure 8-8. As successive rounds are placed, a pocket is formed between the top and bottom layers. Pack the pocket with wadded brown paper to form a bulge. Tie on new lengths of fiber with a square knot.

don't have enough to finish weaving the corner, another piece may be spliced in. After you weave the first half of the corner, add a new leaf at the seam with the butt end extending about 6 inches below the seat. Twist the old leaves once around the new to lock it. Then arrange the leaves parallel and twist all three together. If the strand is too thick, pull out the shortest leaf. Continue weaving the second half of the corner. On the underside of the chair these butt ends will stick down, but at an opposite angle from those used for joining, and will be cut off later.

WEAVE THE REST OF THE SEAT. Go on weaving, as for the first strand around

Figure 8-9. Use a small block of wood or metal to force the strands tightly against previously laid strands. This prevents a loose weave. Draw the free end tight after the new strand is tapped into place.

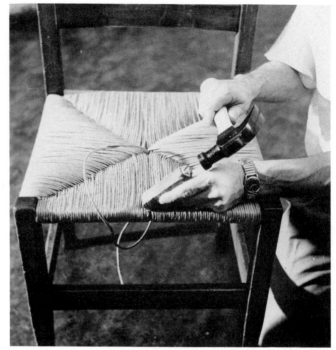

post A to posts B, C, and D, until there is only space for two more rows on the side rails. Continue to make the rush workable by running it through the wringer and zipping it with a metal tool. Smooth the twists. Join a new piece of rush after each corner. Pad the seat as you weave. Keep the strands taut, and rows straight, by pounding them with the block of wood, seams straight and the opposite sides of the chair alike. Check as you go along to see that the opposite openings measure the same and that you have the same number of twists over each rail. Occasionally force the metal tool quickly between the rows to straighten them and to smooth the strands. Also occasionally, and before

the rush dries out, roll and polish the strands with the round end of the stuffer until the seat is smooth.

If the sides are shorter than the back, fill the sides and then weave from back to front in a figure eight: To help prevent holes near the center, weave around the right side rail twice for the last two strands, then proceed to the left rail and weave around it twice. Then weave in a figure eight over the back and front rails until those rails are filled in. Sometimes this process is reversed. Join the rush at the center after weaving the front rail, or after weaving around both rails.

Pull the last few strands through the small opening with a hook made of wire.

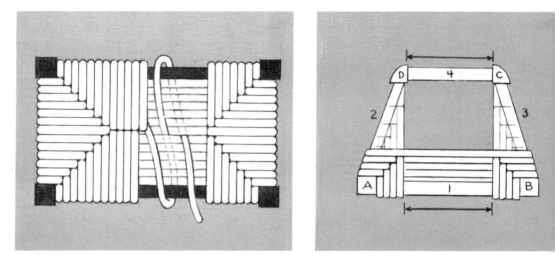

Figure 8-10. *Left:* For rectangular seats, make both ends as you did the square seat, then fill in the center with the back-and-forth weaving technique. *Right:* For irregular-shaped seats, fill in the front corners, then continue on the corner-to-corner technique as in steps 3 and 4 on page 210.

Weave in as many rows as possible; when you think the seat is filled, add one more strand. Fasten the last strand on the underside of the chair by separating the ends, winding each one around a nearby strand, and tying them firmly with a square knot.

If the unfinished seat is left overnight, fasten the last twist to the seat with a clamp clothespin. Cover the seat with wet cheesecloth, to keep the rush from drying out.

Seats Wider Than Deep

Weave until the sides are filled as directed for a square seat. See that the opening measures the same on one side as the other, and the front the same as the back. Complete the filling of the back and front rails by weaving the twists in a figure eight, going over and under the front rail, up through the opening, over and under the back rail, and again up through the opening. Don't cross the rush, that is, if you finish weaving the corners on the left-hand side of the seat, weave from there in a figure eight until the opening is completely filled. You may finish weaving the sides in such a way that you would reverse this, weaving from the right side or the back rail first.

Just before making the figure eight, you may weave twice around the side rail as directed above, instead of singly as shown here.

How To Finish the Seat

After you have completed the weaving and padding, trim the butt ends on the lower side of the seat to about 1 inch, so that they do not show as you face the chair. Trim any loose ends with a razor blade or shears. Use the rounded end of the stuffer to pound and even the seat. On the upper side, trim the loose ends, straighten the rows, and pound with the stuffer to mold and polish the twists. You may also use a piece of leather for polishing.

Immediately after you finish weaving, apply a protective coating both to the top and to the lower side of the seat. One treatment is as follows: Apply a mixture of half turpentine and half raw linseed oil (4 tablespoonfuls each) to both sides of the seat. The next day, when this is dry, apply a second coat (about 3 tablespoonfuls of each), and when this is thoroughly dry, apply a coat of dull varnish. Add coats of varnish until there are no dull spots on the rush.

When first and second coats are still "tacky," smooth and even the strands so that when the varnish sets they will be held in place. Shellac may be used instead of the above mixture.

Be sure no one sits in the chair until the finish has dried thoroughly, at least two weeks after the weaving is completed.

FIBER RUSH SEATS FOR CHAIRS

Fiber rush is made from a very tough grade of paper twisted into a strand to resemble rush. It may be purchased, in dark brown, in widths of 3/32 inch, 4/32 inch, 5/32 inch, and 6/32 inch to resemble antique rush seats, and, in multicolored strands, in a width of 6/32 inch to resemble new seats.

Getting Ready to Weave

Prepare the chair, as before (see page 208). Buy the fiber in pound or two-pound lots or in quantity on a large reel. That in pound lots costs a few cents more; that in reels takes time and patience to unroll and rewind. Handle that on a reel as you would wire; that is, roll and unroll it rather than pull it. Take off about 25 yards to work with at one time. Tie the end to a nearby strand, and wind it in a roll about 6 inches across. Twenty-five yards of 5/32-inch-width fiber weighs about one-half pound. Tie string in a slip knot around the roll so that it won't unwind or untwist.

How to Weave

Use one strand and weave as you do real rush, except that the fiber is already twisted. You may dampen the fiber by dipping the roll in and out of warm water; if wet, the paper softens and cannot be used. Fasten and join the fiber, and pad the seats as directed below. Cut separate lengths for each time that you weave around the two front corners.

To begin weaving, fasten the ends of the fiber as for real rush, except alternately hooking and tying ends to a nearby strand to make them less bulky. Each time you weave the corners, tighten the preceding strand.

Join the fiber by one of three methods: (1) Fold back the ends of fiber and wire them together; or (2) overlap the ends for about 3 inches and tie them together with very fine wire, fish line, or heavy thread; or (3) tie the end with a square knot on the underside of the seat.

PADDING. Heavy corrugated cardboard is desirable for padding. Other cardboard or heavy paper can be used but may rattle as the chair is sat in. Begin padding after 4 or 5 inches are woven on the front rail. If the rails are of even height, cut 4 pieces of cardboard, one to fit exactly each section of the seat. It may help to number them. Force them under the weaving from the upper side of the seat. If the rails are of uneven height, two pieces of cardboard may be used in each section. More padding may be added underneath and between. A hole about 2 inches square must be left in the cardboards at the center of the seat to get the fiber through. If brown paper is used, cut it in squares and fold it in triangles.

To fasten fiber ends after weaving is completed, pull each one to the underside of the seat, untwist the paper, cut it in half, wind it around a nearby strand, and tie. Unfasten joinings that are conspicuous, overlap the ends, and glue or wire them together.

Seats are finished with the oil and turpentine mixture used for real rush and then with a sealer or shellac.

SPLINT SEATS

Splint chair seats are made of wood that has been cut in long thin strips and interwoven in various patterns. The chair on which splint can be used must have seat rails so the splint can be wound around them. Such chairs may also have seats of splint-type materials (reed or wide binding cane) or of rush; the original seat usually indicates which to use.

Splint is suitable for chairs simple in design, with few turnings, such as early American ladder-back chairs. Often it is used when side rails are higher than front and back rails. If side rails slant so the front of the seat is more than 3 inches wider than the back, choose rush or a material no wider than 3/8 inch so the strands will stay in place easily. Splint and flat reed are used for indoor furniture, while flat oval reed and wide binding cane are used for outdoor furniture.

Splint is obtained from native ash and hickory and from tropical palm trees. The native splint is cut from selected second-growth timber with straight grain. Ash splints, machine-cut to a uniform width, wear well. Hickory splints often vary slightly in width, giving a pleasing effect.

The tropical palm tree from which materials like splints are made grows in the Indian archipelago, China, India, Ceylon, and the Malay peninsula. Without its leaves it is known commercially as *rattan*. The outer bark, stripped in different widths, is sold as cane; the core, split into round and flat strips of different thicknesses and widths, is called *reed*. These materials are available from dealers of seat-weaving supplies, mail-order houses, and local stores.

They are all sold either in bunches containing enough for one chair or in quantity lots. Costs per seat are about the same. Real splint makes a better-looking seat than does flat reed, but reed may be easier for beginners to weave.

Widths of splint vary:

Splint	1/2-inch, 5/8-inch, and 3/4-inch
	Buy 1 pound of 5/8-inch width for seat of average size (16 inches across front)
Flat reed	1/4-inch, 3/8-inch, and 1/2-inch
	Buy 1 pound of 3/8-inch width for 16-inch seat
Flat oval reed	3/16-inch and 3/8-inch
	Buy 1 pound for 16-inch seat; 1 1/2 pound for 18-inch or larger seat
Wide binding cane	About 3/16-inch
	Buy 1 bunch of 500 feet for 18-inch seat

The width you need depends on the style and size of chair and on the place the chair is to be used. Narrower widths take longer to weave than wider ones, but wider ones may look heavy or bulky.

Fiber (paper) splint is less durable than other kinds of splint, and isn't recommended.

Prepare to Weave

Cut the old splint away from the seat. You may find padding between the layers, but it can be omitted; shaped seats without stuffing are usually more comfortable than padded ones. Pull out all nails and tacks, and clean any dust from the seat rails. If you need to paint or refinish the wood, be sure the wood is dry before you begin weaving.

THE SPLINT. Pull one of the strands of splint from the looped end of the hank, near where it is tied. As you pull, shake the hank so the splint will not tangle or roughen. Bend the piece between your fingers. The right side is smooth; the wrong side splinters. With the smooth or beveled side out, roll the strand to fit the pan or bowl in which it is to soak. Fasten the ends with a clamp clothespin. Prepare 3 or 4 strands in the same way.

Soak the splint in a solution of glycerine, or of urea crystals. Either helps to shape the splint. The crystals increase its strength, but glycerine is preferred because it helps to retain moisture and keep the splint from drying out and cracking. To hasten the soaking process, use warm water in the solution. Lay the roll in the appropriate container and let it soak until it is soft and pliable—about 30 minutes for splint and about 20 minutes for flat reed, flat oval reed, and binding cane. Each time you remove a roll from the pan, put another one in to soak while you work.

How to Weave

Weaving is done in two directions: the first, called *warping,* is the wrapping of the splint around the seat rails. Usually this is done from the back to the front of the chair, or the long way of the opening, so that the second step, called *weaving,* can be done across the open rails, from side to side or the short way of the opening. Both sides of the seat are woven so that they look alike when finished.

All splints woven one way on the top of the seat are at right angles to those woven the other way. If the front of the seat is wider than the back, weave the center first and fill in the corners later with short lengths.

WARPING. Mark a center rectangle or square the following way: Using a carpenter's square, cut a cardboard pattern of a size that will fit within the chair rails. Fit this close against one back post, parallel with the back rail. Mark the front corner of the square on the front rail. Repeat on the other side of the seat. Check to see that you have enough space for the width of the splint. If the two sides vary, adjust by marking a slightly greater allowance on the shorter side and less on the long side. On the front rail, mark the center between these two marks. Mark the center on the back rail.

Take the roll of splint from the bowl in which it is soaking and remove the excess water with your fingers, sponge, or cloth. Put another strand in to soak while you work.

Work with the full length of the strand. Tie one end to the left side rail with string, with the right side of the splint next to the wood, so that you are working with the grain. Pull the strand under, and then up and over the back rail, close to the post, in the exact position and shape you want it to dry. Pull the strand to the front rail, with the outside edge exactly at the pencil mark. Pull the strand over and under the rail and then return it to the back rail.

Continue until you have used all the strand. Force the wet warpers close together so they will not slip on the rail—splints are apt to shrink more in width than in length—and keep them equally taut. Hold the end temporarily with a clamp clothespin.

To join strands on the underside, place a new piece under the old, with the right side down. Lay a stick of soft wood across the rails, under the strands, and staple the strands together in three places, 1 to 2 inches apart, so that at least one of them can be covered when you weave the other way. Pull the strand away from the stick and use pliers to flatten the sharp ends of the staples. Leave enough of the old strand to support the new, but cut off any that would make a double thickness around the rail. Pull the new strand under and around the rail.

Continue wrapping strands. When you reach the center mark, count the warpers to make sure you will have the same number on each half of the seat. When you reach the pencil mark on the right side of the chair, use a clamp clothespin to hold the warper. If the work is interrupted, sprinkle the seat and dampen the end to keep the splints pliable.

You may want to use the old seat as a guide in deciding the pattern of the weave. Or, you can use scraps and ends of splints to try out different designs, or, work out designs on squared paper, using one square for each warper.

Count the number of warpers on the back rail. This number may be evenly divisible by the number in the design you want to use: for example, 20 strands and a mesh of 2 over and 2 under, or 21 strands with a mesh of 3 over and 3 under. If the number is not evenly divisible, you may use the same design if you:

1. Plan from near the center of the opening and begin weaving accordingly. *Example:* If there are 23 strands and a mesh of 3 over and 3 under, weave over 1 to start the row, continue across until you have used 21 strands, and then weave the single strand as on the first side.

2. Plan to use a diagonal design. Emphasis then will be away from the side rails, where the design may or may not be completed. A diagonal design also is desirable if the side rails are uneven.

The second row determines how you use the design. You can move one or more strands to the left for a diagonal design from the right back to the left

front of the seat, or you may reverse the direction. For a geometric design, weave alternate rows alike.

Weaving that makes the design, frequently is:

> over 2 and under 2

With finer mesh, strands are difficult to push together closely.

Other designs are:

> over 2 and under 3
> over 3 and under 3

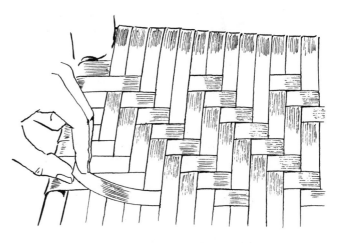

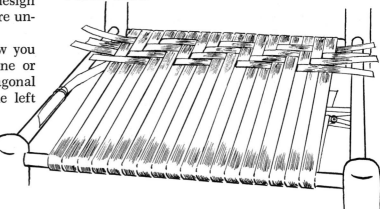

Figure 8-11. *Above:* Simple 2-over. *Below:* 3-under weave.

Large seats or seats using narrow strands, 3/8 inch or less, may be woven:

> over 4 and under 4
> over 4 and under 2
> over 5 and under 3

The above combinations may be reversed, such as over 2 and under 4. Coarser mesh may be used occasionally if long strands will stay in place and wear satisfactorily. See page 221 for other weaving designs and the method of planning elaborate designs on squared paper. The design you choose depends on the size and shape of the seat opening, the width of splint you are using, the number of warper strands and whether the number is even or uneven.

WEAVING. Be sure the strand of splint is long enough to weave across the top of the seat and to join on the underside. Loosen the last warper over the back rail, remove the clothespin, and bring the warper from the front under and over the back rail and under the preceding warper. Then bring the strand diagonally in front of the back post, under the side rail and turned so the right side is down. Pull all strands tight and then weave across, right to left.

Pull the weaver over the side rail and weave the underside like the top, going over and under the same warpers.

When you join strands, staple from either side, if you know the staples will be hidden under warpers. Or you can cover staples with short lengths of splint tucked under nearby strands. Flatten

the sharp ends of staples with pliers, as before. Continue weaving, cutting the old strand inside the rail, even if you waste some of it, and forcing the joining in position. You can't use the wrapper strand you tucked under until you get nearer the front.

The second row is over 2 and under 3, but one warper to the left of the first row. Or weave to the right if you want the diagonal in the same direction as on the top of the seat. Use a stick or a screwdriver to force the strands together. At the same time pull the strand across the rails so the seat will be firm.

On the underside, plan from near the center of the opening, where the design is established, how to begin the row and so continue the design used on the top. In this way you will weave over and under the same strands as you did on top.

When you have woven far enough to see the design, and have space, cut off a length of splint for a warper in the corner of the seat. Hook about 3 inches over the weaver that will continue the design, near the back of the seat, or just push the strand in rather than hook it over a weaver, if it fits snugly. Bring this warper to the underside of the seat and hook it over a weaver there also. The strands may be joined on top of the seat, under the warpers, to save splint.

If the joining is secure, cut off the old strand so two thicknesses do not show. Also cut the string holding the first strand. The weaving will hold this end in place.

Add other short lengths in the corners

of the seat, as you have room for them. Warpers should also be cut so the ends can be concealed under weavers. One or two staples and the weaving will hold the joining. Use a screwdriver or similar blunt tool to help with the weaving as you get near the front of the seat.

Continue weaving to the front rail. Finish the underside by weaving as far across as you can and tucking the end under a warper. If the back of the chair is to be woven, wrap strands the long way (up and down). Weave across from the bottom up so that you can push the strands in place easily.

OTHER WEAVING DESIGNS. Elaborate designs should first be planned on squared paper. Count the number of warper strands over the back rail. Estimate the number of rows from front to back by measuring with a piece of splint on one of the side rails. Allow one square on the paper for each strand across the back, and for each strand from back to front.

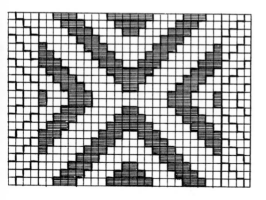

Figure 8-12. More elaborate weave pattern

For a geometric design, choose as square an opening as possible or a design that can be adapted to a wider front rail. Begin in the center and work toward the sides and ends. The side sections indicate that the design can be continued if there is space for added rows.

Weaving With Other Materials

Flat reed is thinner and more pliable than splint and consequently is easier for beginners to use. It is not as smooth, as sturdy, or as fine a quality as splint. The right side of reed is smoother than the wrong side. Follow the directions for weaving splint seats.

Flat oval reed is used mostly for porch furniture. The right side is beveled and the other is flat. Strands can be rolled smaller than splint, to fit in a bowl about 11 inches in diameter for soaking,

How To Finish the Seat

Trim off hairs or rough places with a razor blade or sharp knife. Splint that has a hard, glossy surface can be left without a finish. Or you may apply 2 or 3 coats of a thin type of penetrating wood sealer to both sides of the seat. Apply the first coat as soon as you finish weaving. Let each coat dry thoroughly before applying the next. If you want the seat darkened to blend with the color of the chair finish, apply one or more coats of seat stain, which you can obtain from the dealer from whom you buy other seating supplies. A sealer can then be used over the stain. Wax can also be used, but it may stain clothing and collect dust.

WEBBING SEATS

Webbing seats can be used to modernize old chairs, benches, and stools. Webbing also looks well on contemporary indoor and outdoor furniture.

The chair on which you plan to use webbing should be sturdy, and simple in line and design. Chair seat frames should be straight, rather than noticeably curved. The front of the frame should be no more than 3 inches wider than the back so the webbing will stay in place without slipping on the side rails. The wood of the frame should be 2 to 3 inches deep to support the webbing underneath. There must be enough space between the seat and back to bring the webbing through the opening.

Webbing can be used on round seat rails as well as on flat ones. For large openings, the frame must be sturdy and the wood able to hold tacks well so the webbing can support the necessary weight. Usually, wooden chairs with small seat openings are neither comfortable nor attractive with webbing. If webbing is to be used on the back of the chair, the wood in the cross pieces should be thick enough to take tacks without splitting.

Select the Webbing

Webbing is available in both plastic and cotton, 2 inches wide, in a variety of colors. It can be tacked or stapled to wood.

Plastic webbing can be cleaned easily with a damp cloth and used both on indoor and outdoor furniture. Cotton webbing stays in place better than plastic webbing but is not as easy to clean, nor as satisfactory on outdoor furniture. You can buy webbing at chair-seating and craftsman's supply houses, and at certain mail-order houses and department stores.

How To Weave

Before beginning the weaving process, the old seat should be removed and the chair refinished or painted. Then the new webbing can be applied.

SEATS WITH FLAT RAILS. Measure with a stiff ruler and mark the center of the front rail. Do the same on the other three rails. Place short strips of webbing loosely on the chair, to plan the number of strips you will need to use each way, or fold a long length and estimate the number of strips. As you plan, avoid the legs and the lower part of the back posts. Use tacks and clothespins to hold the webbing temporarily in place. Arrange crosspieces to see how the mesh will look. Allow space between strips so the seat will not look solid or bulky.

The right side is usually on the outside of the roll, is smoother, and has more sheen than the wrong side. Cut the number of strips you'll need back to front. Allow enough webbing for each strip to extend across the top of the seat, down the rails to the underside, or to the inside if there is room to hammer the tacks, and to turn under 1/2 inch.

Tip the chair so you can tack easily. The place you begin tacking is determined by the shape and construction of the chair. Tack only temporarily until you are sure the strips are where you want them.

Fasten strips first on the straighter of the two rails or on the one with a crosspiece, where you have less room to hammer. Then you can stretch the webbing and tack it on the more open rail. Since the back of this chair is curved, fasten the strips first on the front rail so they can be stretched taut from the straight edge. Fasten the webbing on the inside of the frame so that the lower edge of the front rail will look smooth rather than bumpy. Fasten the outside strips first, with the webbing close to the chair leg. Or you may find it easier to start in the center.

Put the tape over the end of the strip to prevent raveling. Turn the end under about 1/2 inch and fasten with 5 tacks, staggered to help keep the wood from splitting. Tack the center strip next, or those on each side of the center if you have an even number, and then the strips between. When you are sure the strips are evenly spaced and properly placed, pound the tacks all the way in. On the curving rail at the back, tack the center strip first so you can be sure it is straight. Tape the end.

Cut cardboard strips, one for each webbing strip, about 1/4 inch narrower than the webbing and the wood. Turn

under the taped end and insert the cardboard to help make the edge smooth. Pull the strip taut and tack it on the bottom of the seat rail, since this edge shows least. Or, if the wood splits easily, tack it on the inside of the frame.

When pulled tight across the top, the outside strips will be on a slant underneath the rail. Cut the end parallel with the rail. Tape the end, and tack the strip temporarily in place. Do the same on the other side, then fasten the strips between in the same way. The strips will be closer together on the back rail because it is shorter than the front rail. When you are sure the strips are placed correctly, tack them permanently.

Measure and cut all the side strips at once. (If you want to save webbing, you may find it more economical to cut each one as you work.) Fasten them together with a clamp clothespin, in the order in which you will use them from front to back.

Weave the front strip over and under to determine how you want the design and how the mesh will best be held in place. Weave the next strip under and over, and alternate the rest.

Fasten the strips on alternate sides. Since the side rails slant, the ends of the webbing will slant. Tape one end of each strand and tack the front strip, bringing the edge close to the front legs. Tack on the inside, if you have space, because the wood splits less, or tack on the bottom edge. Tack the back strip close to the back leg, then the center strip and those between. Pull the strips taut and

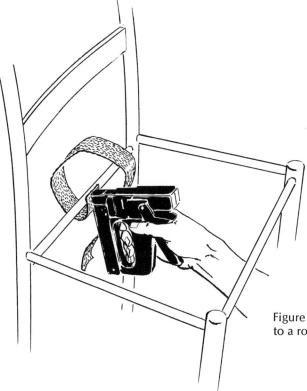

Figure 8-13. Stapling plastic webbing to a round rail

tack them. When the strips are all in place, evenly spaced and equally taut, pound all the tacks all the way in.

SEATS WITH ROUND RAILS. Webbing can also be used on chairs with round rails. Paint the chair or refinish with a natural finish. Be sure the chair is thoroughly dry before you weave the seat.

Mark the centers of the four rails as directed on page 202. Plan the number of strips you will use each way and cut those for back to front.

Since both back and front rails are straight on this chair, first fasten the strips to the back and stretch them toward the front. The wood neither takes nor holds tacks easily, so use a heavy stapler gun to fasten the strips. Use 3 strong 5/16-inch staples across the width of each strip of webbing. There is little room for cardboard strips on round rails, so omit them and turn the webbing under a generous 1/2 inch. Otherwise, the seat is woven in the same way as the one with flat rails.

BACKS OF CHAIRS. Webbing may also be used for the backs of chairs. Mark the centers, and plan and cut strips as for seats. Allow enough length so the laced webbing will shape to the back of the person using the chair as well as to the back of the chair. Strips are first fastened up and down, then other strips are woven from side to side.

Tack the end of the strip first on the front of the lower crosspiece. Then pull the strip over the top of the crosspiece, down the back, under the crosspiece, and then up the back of the chair and over the top crosspiece, tacking the end on the underside.

The tacking of both ends of side-to-side strips is more difficult to conceal. The illustration here, at the left, shows tacks fastening the upper two strips. The two lower strips are stapled to the chair and are less conspicuous than tacks.

In the illustration at the right, two fastenings are covered by folds of webbing. Weave the strips first. About 2 inches in from one end, tack near the front of the post. Turn the end under and insert a strip of cardboard. Use 3 3/4-inch wire brads to hold this fold. The top of these brads can be concealed by forcing apart the mesh of the web-

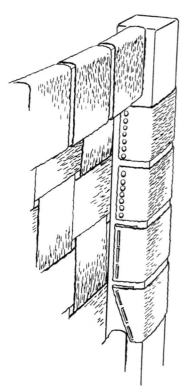
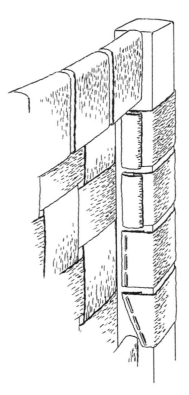

Figure 8-14. Two methods of finishing webbing on backs

bing. The cardboard prevents the brads from going all the way through and also keeps the edge of the fold smooth.

Fasten the other end of the strip to the opposite post in a similar way.

FURNITURE UPHOLSTERY REPAIRS

Upholstered furniture consists basically of a frame, strip or cleat webbing, padding, and cover. Some furniture also has spring upholstery. Repairs needed on upholstered furniture generally include recovering, replacement or redistribution of padding, replacement or refastening of webbing, and regluing, reinforcement or replacement of frame parts. With spring construction, replacing, anchoring, and retying springs may also be necessary. Loose cushions may also be repaired; for this information, see pages 228–34.

Recovering

Replace the entire cover if the covers on seat, back, or arms are torn, soiled, or worn beyond repair. Even with fairly new furniture it is usually impossible to match new material to worn or faded fabric, so all sections must usually be recovered when one is damaged.

Procedures for recovering upholstered furniture vary with furniture design, but the following general procedure applies to almost all types:

1. Remove the old cover carefully, taking out all tacks.

2. Using the old cover as a pattern, cut a piece of new material to the approximate shape and size.

3. Smooth out and replace any lumpy or torn padding and lay the new cover in place, making certain all four sides have the same amount of surplus material.

4. Tack the center of the opposite sides, stretching the material lightly but firmly. Don't drive the tacks all the way in. Work from center to edges, stretching the material evenly. If wrinkles develop, remove the tacks and work the wrinkles out. Note how the old covering was folded and fitted at corners and around legs and arms. If this was satisfactory, fit the new cover the same way. When the covering fits smoothly, drive the tacks all the way in.

5. After the covering is tacked to the side of the frame, cover the tack heads with an edging or gimp. Fasten the gimp with large-headed upholstery nails spaced about 2 inches apart.

Replacement or Redistribution of Padding

Padding tow, cotton batting, excelsior, or moss is used over the springs in the case of spring construction, or on the webbing in the case of padded construction. When padding shifts or becomes lumpy, remove the cover and redistribute or replace the padding. To replace padding:

1. First, remove all old padding and tack a piece of burlap smoothly over the entire surface to be padded.

2. Spread padding evenly over the burlap, forming a compact cushion about 1 1/2 inches thick.

3. Cover this with a second piece of burlap or muslin, tacked down securely, and place a 2-inch layer of cotton batting on top. Pull off surplus cotton

around the edges; don't cut the cotton, since this will make a ridge under the cover.

4. Tack a cambric cover over the frame bottom to keep the padding from working through to springs or webbing and falling out.

5. Replace the cover as described previously.

Repairing the Frame

Tighten loose frame joints with glue blocks, pins and screws, or angle irons. Repair any frame damage. Full details on this type of work may be found in Chapter Two.

Repairing Webbing

Check strip or cleat webbing for signs of wear or breakage whenever the cover

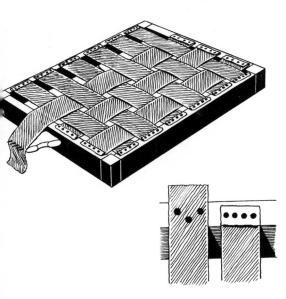

Figure 8-15. Method of attaching webbing to a framework

is removed. Replace damaged webbing and refasten loose strips. To insure that webbing will hold securely, double it over at the ends to give the tacks more gripping power, tighten, and tack so that stress is at right angles to tack length. Run the webbing in two directions, at right angles to each other. Closing the entire bottom with webbing is not necessary, but too much webbing is better than too little. If springs are to be anchored to the webbing, space the webbing to support the spring bases. Similarly, anchor metal strips or wood cleats securely and space them for springs.

Adjusting Springs

Springs may shift, bend, or become otherwise damaged. Reanchor and retie loose springs; replace those that are damaged.

Springs are usually attached differently on webbing, on metal strips, or on wood cleats. Fasten spring bases to webbing with heavy flax cord about 1/8 inch in diameter. Anchor springs to metal strips with clamps. If the clamps loosen, rerivet them. Fasten springs to wood cleats with staples or metal straps and nails.

After the springs are anchored, retie them with heavy flax cord like that used to anchor springs to webbing.

1. Nail the cord to the center of one side of the frame. Pull it over the top of the springs to an opposite anchoring nail. Allow enough cord to tie two double half hitches to each spring and cut to this length.

2. Bring the cord up to the top of the first coil spring and tie it with a double

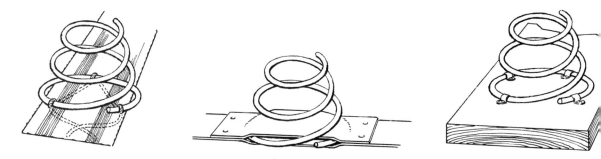

Figure 8-16. *Left to right:* Tying a spring to webbing, fastening a spring to a metal strip, and fastening a spring to a wood cleat

half hitch to the nearest rim of the first spring. Before drawing the knot tight, pull the spring down to shape the seat or back. Continue to the opposite side of the top on the same spring and tie it.

3. Continue in like fashion, tying two points on each spring and finally anchoring the cord to the nail on the opposite side of the frame. Run cords in both directions (side to side and front to back) at right angles to each other, until all springs are tied in two directions.

4. Tie springs diagonally in the same manner, beginning at one corner of the frame and anchoring the cord on the opposite corner.

5. Repeat with the cord at right angles to the first set of diagonal cords. Tie this cord to the spring with two double half hitches and also tie it to the other three cords at their junction in the center of the coil. Each spring is now tied in eight places, and the crossing cords are tied together as well.

6. Replace the padding.

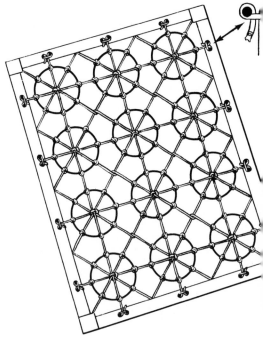

Figure 8-17. *Above:* A spring tied lengthwise. *On facing page:* crosswise and diagonally in place.

Repairing Innerspring Cushions

A sagging or lumpy seat cushion with an innerspring unit can be repaired in a few hours. With a new case for the springs and a little extra padding, you can make the cushion look as good as new.

Place the cushion on the table, top side up, with the front toward you. Insert a safety pin near the front. Using a stiff rule, measure and write down the height of the boxing between the seam cords.

Open the outside cover by ripping the back and side seams of the bottom of the outside cover to within an inch of the front corners. Throw back the loose flap.

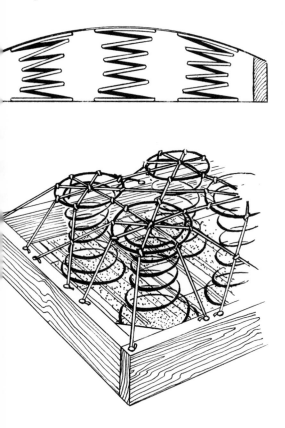

OPEN THE PADDING. Manufacturers use different methods to lay the padding around an innerspring unit. Examine the padding of the cushion, disturbing it as little as possible, to find out how the cushion has been padded.

If the padding is wound several times around the innerspring unit, usually the springs can be pulled out through one of the easily opened ends of the padding.

If the padding is badly torn, take out the springs through a hole on the top. When the old padding is in this condition, usually most or all of it has to be replaced with new padding.

REMOVE THE SPRINGS. Before taking the springs from the padding or before tearing the unit apart, count and write down the number of springs from back to front and from side to side so that they may be placed in the same order in the new case. Then take the springs out of the padding. If some of the rows of springs are crushed together so the count can't be made in this way, lift out the springs and, if they can be seen, count the number of circles on the bottom padding. But if the material covering the springs is badly torn and all the springs are tangled, pull them apart, count them, and determine the number that should be in each row.

All springs should be the same height and should stand erect. If they are not the same height or don't stand erect, pull the bent ones into shape. To shorten them, hold the top coil down with one hand and pull the next coil upward. You may need to follow this pro-

MEASUREMENTS YOU NEED

	Sample Cushion	Your Cushion
Height of the boxing in the cushion (inches)	3 1/2	——
Number of springs from back to front (case)	6	——
Number of springs from side to side	4	——
Total number of springs	24	——
Diameter of the widest part of the springs (inches)	3	——

cedure at both ends of the spring. To straighten the spring, use one or more of the following methods:

1. Pull sidewise, toward you on one wire and away from you on an adjacent wire.

2. Or twist the coils around and bend them, if necessary.

3. Flatten the spring and then twist the coils between the palms of the hands. Test each spring to be sure it stands erect from both ends.

MAKE THE CASES. The new inner-spring unit is made of several long cases of firm, nonstretching material, such as muslin, feed-bags, or burlap, in which are stitched the pockets for the springs. When these cases are filled, the springs and cases are tied together.

Make one case only, to test your measurements before making the rest of the cases. Tear or pull a yarn across the material to get a straight cutting edge.

Pull the material if necessary to get it straight and to make it lie flat.

See table on facing page for measuring width and length of one case before proceeding.

Cut off this measured strip on the grain of the material and fold it in half lengthwise. Draw pencil lines 1/2 inch in from each end, then stitch on these lines. Make a test pocket before stitching all the pockets. Differences in quality and weight of the cloth may make the pockets too loose or too high for the springs. Starting from the seam, mark off the width of one pocket, draw a line from that point parallel to the seam, and stitch along this line, backstitching each end for about 1 inch. Now fit a spring in this pocket, inserting it sidewise, and turning it upright after it is in the pocket. The spring should fit the pocket easily. If the pocket is too tight or too loose, the material will wear out quickly. Make the necessary change in measurement now if it is necessary and restitch the pocket. Starting from the line of the first pocket measure and mark accurately as many other pockets of the same width as are needed, drawing parallel pencil lines from top to bottom and stitching all the way through on these lines.

Next test the pocket for height. Insert the spring sidewise and turn it upright as before. Then put a row of pins along the top of the pocket 1/2 inch down from the open edge. Measure the height of the spring as it stands in the pocket; if it is higher than the height of the boxing of the outside cover (measuring

For the width of one case (cut on the width of the material), add together:

	Sample Cushion	Your Cushion
The diameter of the widest part of a spring	3 inches	——
The height of the boxing	3 1/2 inches	——
Seam allowance	1/2 inch	1/2 inch
Total	7 inches	——
Multiply by 2 for the width of one case	× 2	
Total	14 inches	——

For the length of one case (cut lengthwise of the material), add together:

The diameter of the widest part of a spring	3 inches	——
One-half of this diameter	1 1/2 inches	——
Total	4 1/2 inches	——
Multiply the above total by the number of springs in one row from back to front		
4 1/2 inches × 6 springs	27 inches	——
Add 1 inch, for 1/2-inch seam at each end	1 inch	1 inch
Cut the case this length	28 inches	——

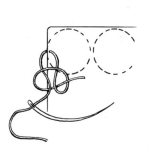

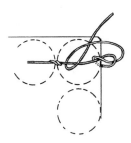

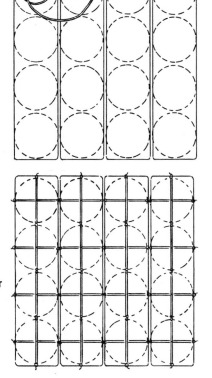

Figure 8-18. Cases tied together

from seam to seam or between the cord-ings), lower the pins for the distance needed to make the measurement the same as that of the boxing. Mark this pinned line at one point and remove the pins and the spring. Measure from the bottom or folded side of the case up to this point to determine the height the pockets should be. Using this measure-ment, from the folded edge mark the height of all the pockets, then draw a line.

Make the rest of the cases like the first so there will be one case for each row.

INSERT THE SPRINGS. Press the springs flat and insert them sidewise into the pockets, pushing each one to the bottom. If there is a poor spring, place it where the cushion has least wear. Hold the springs down by placing a pin in the cloth close to each spring, and hold the two sides of the case to-gether by inserting two or three pins at right angles to the edges. Stitch on the line. Remove the pins and turn the springs upright in the pockets, with the seam running through the middle of the spring-tops.

SEW THE CASES TOGETHER. Arrange the filled cases with the long side to-gether, squaring them up against the corner of a table. Insert a few pins to hold them in place. Fasten them by tying the tops and bottoms of the springs right through the cloth as fol-lows: Cut a length of mattress twine a generous 1 1/2 times the distance to be sewed. Thread a curved or straight needle with the length of mattress twine. Insert the needle through the

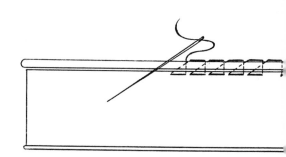

Figure 8-19. How to sew together the pinned edges of the cover

cloth and under the top wire of an out-side spring. Tie a slip knot. Then con-tinue by passing the needle through the material and under *two* top wires of each pair of springs, using the knot shown in the drawing here. End the row with a square knot. Tie the front row next, in the same way, and then the other rows from side to side. Repeat the tying from back to front. Turn the unit over and tie the bottom side in the same way.

SEW THE UNIT INTO THE CUSHION. To replace the finished spring unit in a cushion that has an open flap, lay the spring unit back in the padding in its former place without crushing the side pads. See that this side padding is pulled up around the sides of the spring unit and that it is of the same thickness all the way around, that it fills the cor-ners, and that it is smooth on the out-side. Draw the loose top padding back over the spring unit. To insert the spring unit into a cushion that has pad-ding wound around it, bend the sides of the unit inwards, push it through the

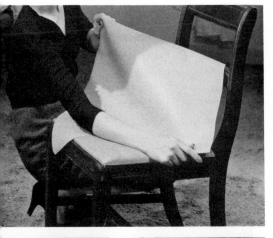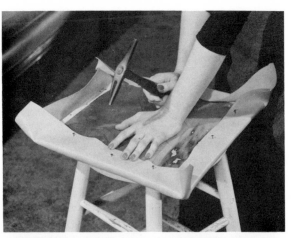

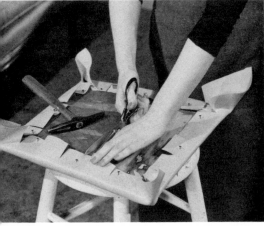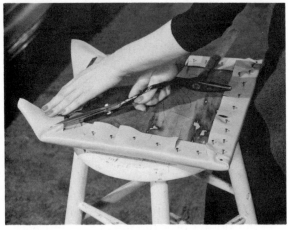

Figure 8-20. Steps in covering a leather or plastic seat

hole at the end of the padding, then flatten the unit.

In both types of cushion make the corners square and well filled; cover any holes in the padding by laying pieces of upholsterer's felt under them, or place a new layer over the entire top and bottom. If this material is not available, use layers of cotton batting, or cut pieces from an old blanket, smooth quilt, or mattress pad, large enough to fit over the top and bottom of the old padding. With such pieces the cushion will not be so soft nor look so well as when the upholsterer's felt is used.

If all new cotton padding is to be used, lay 2 or 3 thicknesses of the upholsterer's felt in the bottom of the outside cushion cover. Use pieces large enough to come up to the top of the side walls. Then lay the spring unit in place on the bottom, usually a little nearer the front of the cushion than the back, and bring the padding up around the sides. Cover the top of the unit with the same amount of felt, tucking it over the sides down to the bottom. This makes two or three thicknesses of cotton over the top and bottom of the unit and four or more in the space between the sides of the unit and the side walls of the cushion cover. Add more if needed, particularly in the corners. There should be enough padding so that you cannot feel the springs on the outside when you press the cushion with your hand.

Pull the loose top of the cushion cover back into place. Make sure that all raw edges are turned in and that the cording, if the cushion has cording, is stitched securely to the edge of the cushion-cover top. Pin the open edges together first at the corners, then at the middle of the back and the middle of the sides. Continue to pin first from a center and then from a corner on each side of the cushion. Pull all the seams into their proper places on the cushion.

To sew the pinned edges together, use a linen thread matching the color of the cushion. First fasten the end of the thread into the material, then run the needle straight upwards through the two open edges. Insert the needle again a little ahead, push it diagonally through. Insert the needle again and repeat the sewing procedure. The completed cushion should look flat, should have sharp corners, and be firm and comfortable.

CHAPTER NINE

Care of Furniture

Today's miracle furniture finishes have new and desirable qualities and characteristics. They are more durable and more resistant to scratches, stains, and extremes in temperature. Coatings industry research programs have made it possible to bleach and apply uniform color finishes to even low-price hardwoods—something that was impossible a few years ago.

However, even these amazing new finishes need to be cared for properly. There are right and wrong ways to even the simplest care of furniture, and the following hints will help you in protecting the beauty of *all* your furniture.

Of course, the patina of furniture, which develops a mellow richness of color and texture, is purely a surface condition, and a great asset in antique furniture. Unfortunately, it's not only the surface of furniture that needs to be dusted regularly, and occasionally washed or polished, and perhaps waxed or treated with oil; it is also important that the wood should not become too dry or absorb too much moisture, thus causing it to shrink or swell.

It's not difficult to keep furniture in excellent shape, providing it is not neglected. Frequent care will help to keep wood furniture in good condition. This chapter will give you information regarding its upkeep (some of which methods have alternates), as follows:

DUSTING

Furniture should be dusted frequently. Unless fine particles of dust are removed often, they will act as abrasives and become ground into the finish. Always follow the grain of the wood while dusting—wiping across the grain is likely to cause scratches, since dust contains grit. A few drops of quality furniture polish on your dustcloth will help pick up the dust, instead of just pushing it around the surface.

For dusting, use soft cheesecloth, silken rags, or chemically treated dust mittens or cloths, which can be readily purchased.

WASHING

Furniture sometimes acquires a coat of grime, which dusting won't remove, because its home is in a smoky city, or because it is exposed to greasy fumes or smoke from a fireplace or kitchen. The furniture is then best cleaned by washing or using materials prepared for cleaning. Furniture should also be washed when waxes have gradually built up and have created a thick film. This film streaks, smudges, and hides the natural beauty of the wood grain. Additional waxing can only add to this accumulation, and you will only be polishing the old wax, not the finish.

Wash a section at a time, dipping a cloth (such as toweling) into a sudsy solution of warm water and a good detergent or soap flakes. Rinse the cloth often and again follow the wood grain with your strokes. More than one washing may be needed to get down to the original finish. When the furniture surfaces have dried thoroughly, they are ready to be properly waxed or polished. Furniture finished only with oil should never be washed. More on washing furniture can be found in Chapter Three.

WAXING AND POLISHING

It's the belief of many professional refinishers that an occasional rubbing with furniture polish is beneficial to a finish, but that excess use of oil polishes should be avoided, since they have a tendency to cause a dull and lifeless surface that collects dust more rapidly.

When using commercial furniture polishes, follow the directions on the container closely. In using most polishes, it is best to saturate a piece of cheesecloth with hot water and wring it out. When the cloth is cold, shake the polish thoroughly, apply sparingly to the cloth, and clean the furniture by brisk rubbing. Turn the cloth as it becomes dirty. When the piece is clean, rub the surface with a soft dry cloth until a fingerprint will no longer show on it.

A mixture of 1 part commercially boiled linseed oil and 1 part turpentine makes an excellent polish for use once or twice a year on varnished and highly polished surfaces. This polish brightens a dull, foggy finish and helps either to stop surface checking or make existing checking less obvious. The oil feeds the wood; the turpentine loosens dirt and helps the oil to penetrate the wood. Apply the mixture with a soft cloth, wipe off excess with a dry one, and polish with the grain of the wood until no fingerprint will show on the surface.

Waxing furniture properly with a quality product has a more lasting and softer effect than treating it with furniture polish does. Once wax is correctly applied, it lasts a long time, and its polish can be revived by rubbing the surface with a soft and lintless cloth. Additional wax should be applied only when needed. This is indicated by the refusal of the surface to polish, after a firm rubbing with a dry, soft cloth. Applying wax thickly, or building up too many coats, is a detriment to a good finish, causing surfaces to become slippery and to have too high a shine, instead of the desired soft mellow appearance; and, under damp conditions, it may become sticky. The same conditions prevail when wax is used as a floor polish. For types of wax and application, see *Wax Finish,* page 174.

DOS AND DON'TS WITH WOOD FURNITURE

DO dust furniture regularly—lift lamps, ashtrays, and other objects, too.

DO rub with the grain of the wood when dusting, polishing, or waxing.

DO carefully read and follow the label instructions on all furniture-care products.

DO use a pad under bowls and platters to prevent heat damage on your dining room table.

DO use coasters or pads under drinks, flower pots, and other containers for liquids that are placed on furniture.

DON'T use self-polishing floor wax on furniture.

DON'T wet any of the glued joints on furniture.

DON'T use rubber mats or coasters unless there is a felt pad beneath them. (Some rubber compounds and vinyl films may stain or soften furniture finishes.)

DON'T wash furniture finished only with oil.

UPHOLSTERED FURNITURE

Sofas and upholstered chairs are among the most frequently used pieces of furniture, and are therefore subject to constant wear, tear, and soil. Upholstery will look better and last longer if given frequent light cleaning; once soil is deeply imbedded, cleaning becomes difficult, if not impossible. Remember that upholstery fabrics can be cleaned only on one side, so water and chemicals that soak into the upholstery must be avoided. The best insurance against future soiling is to have all upholstery fabrics processed with one of several chemical materials to repel spots and stains.

There are two kinds of dirt that plague the home. There is dry dirt, particles of dirt that are in the air, a problem generally solved by vacuuming. Then there is the dirt produced by cooking fumes, heating, and floor and furniture wax. This kind of dirt produces an oily film on upholstered furniture and must be removed by wet or dry cleaning.

For weekly care, go over upholstery once a week to remove surface dirt and dust. Use a whisk broom or vacuum-cleaner brush attachment on the entire piece, giving special attention to arms, headrest, and crevices. Clean cushions the same way, unless they are stuffed with down. In that case, use only a cloth or brush; the suction of a vacuum cleaner may pull out the down if the cushions don't have down-proof ticking. Seat cushions will keep their shape better if they are turned frequently. Down pillows and others without spring construction should be plumped daily.

Remove all spots as soon as they occur. The longer a spot is permitted to sit on a piece of furniture, the rougher it will be to get off. Before attempting to remove spots, however, check with the furniture manufacturer for special instructions. There are special upholstery spot removers available, but be sure to read the instructions carefully, and always test them on a concealed area of your furniture. In some cases, spots and stains on delicate fabrics should be treated by an experienced dry cleaner.

Fresh grease spots and lipstick stains can often be successfully removed with absorbent powders, such as French chalk, fuller's earth, cornstarch, or talcum. These powders are safe on all fabrics. For most fabrics you can also sponge the spot with carbon tetrachloride, rubbing with the nap of the material until all trace is gone.

Heavy grease stains can be treated with a commercial dry-cleaning fluid. Use in a well-ventilated room and follow the safety precautions on the label. Incidentally, tar, paint, machine oil, furniture polish, chewing gum, ice cream, shoe polish, and similar stains may be removed with these commercial products. But dry cleaners and solvents

must never be used on foam-rubber upholstery; they cause the rubber to disintegrate. Use only foamy or liquid cleaners.

Food spots, urine and perspiration, mildew, and cosmetic marks can be removed with a solution of light-duty detergent and water or a commercial upholstery shampoo. Apply the cleaner sparingly with a clean cloth. Work from the outer edge of the spot toward the center so that the stain does not spread. Use a clean part of the cloth for each application.

Never use soap on upholstery fabrics. Since it cannot be properly rinsed, it forms a film that attracts dust and soil. In general, woolen and silk fabrics require a lighter-duty detergent than synthetic or cotton fabrics.

Vinyl plastic upholstery materials require proper care for maximum service. Clean deep-embossed patterns regularly with a damp, soapy brush. Wipe leather-like finishes with a damp, soapy cloth. (Use mild soap and avoid abrasive cleaners.) Rub off lipstick, crayon, or ink with cloth dampened with rubbing alcohol. Rub off shoe polish, paint, or tar with kerosene or a similar agent.

Vacuum or dust the furniture thoroughly. Check the label for fiber content and special cleaning instructions, then prepare your cleaning solution and test an inconspicuous spot of the furniture. A "dry" foam made from a detergent and water (use only the foam) is a simple cleaner you can make at home. Apply the foam to a small area with a soft brush or a sponge. Work in a circular motion and wipe immediately with a dry towel. The process should go quickly with as little moisture as possible. Excessive moisture can cause shrinkage and mildew. As you begin each area, overlap the previous one so that the entire piece will dry evenly. It's a good idea to begin with armrests or other heavily soiled areas so you can go over them again, if necessary.

Dry as quickly as possible. Furniture can be dried out of doors in the shade, indoors with the windows open, in the draft of an electric fan, or in a heated room. The furniture may feel damp for a day or so, depending upon the atmospheric conditions.

CHAPTER TEN

Furniture Repairing and Refinishing Tools

It is surprising how much can be accomplished with only a few simple hand tools. However, those should be of the best quality. It is difficult and often impossible to accomplish good work with hand tools that are cheaply constructed, are made of poor materials, are out of balance, or won't retain a cutting edge.

Good tools are the delight of every mechanically minded person, and to use them is a fascinating, often profitable, hobby. You realize a profit when you construct a needed article in spare time, or when repairs, which you complete in a satisfactory manner, would otherwise have had to be done by a professional.

In practically every household can be found a hammer, saw, screwdriver, pliers, rule or yardstick, and perhaps a chisel and plane. These are fine for a starter if they are quality tools that can be used for good workmanship.

This chapter will give you a list of those hand tools that are deemed adequate for the work you will first attempt. When purchasing tools (hand or power), it pays to buy those of a size, weight, or kind suitable to the worker or the work to be done. Don't hesitate to ask for information from a competent sales person. Buy tools of a good brand with years of reputation back of them. A friendly carpenter or cabinetmaker could be of great assistance.

In the list to follow, the tools are shown singly or in groups, according to the type of work for which each is to be used. Referring to the classification will make it easier to select a tool for a specific purpose.

If you desire to add electric power tools, it is suggested that the first you purchase be a grinder (also with wire brush and cloth buffers), a small hand sander, and a hand drill (1/4-inch capacity).

BASIC TOOLS SUGGESTED FOR PURCHASE

Boring

Bit braces, 8-inch ratchet type
Auger bits, 3/8-, 1/2-, 3/4-inch
Countersink, rose head, to fit brace
Hand drill, 1/4-inch chuck capacity
Twist drills (drill bits), straight shank, 1/8-, 3/16-, 1/4-inch

Clamping

Mechanic's bench vise
"C" (screw) clamps, 2 each, 3- and 6- or 8-inch
Clamp clothespins, 6
Pliers, combination step-joint, 6- or 8-inch
Pliers, long-nose, side-cutting, 5- or 6-inch
Screwdrivers, 6- and 8-inch or 10-inch
Screwdriver bit, to fit brace, 3/8- or 1/2-inch

Cutting

Pocketknife (Scout), with strong, pointed blade
Old knife, blunt
Razor-blade holder, with blades
Diagonal cutting pliers, 7-inch

Filing

Half round wood rasp, 10-inch
Smooth mill file, 8-inch
Shoemaker's rasp
Nail file

Gluing

Patching tool

Hammering

Carpenter's nail claw hammer
Tack hammer, claw type, lightweight
Nail-set, 1/16-inch
Mallet, rubber-headed

Marking

Center punch
Pencil

Measuring

Rule, steel roll-type, 6-foot
Rule, straight, wood, 6- or 12-inch
Try square, 6- or 8-inch

Painting	Paintbrushes, 2-inch
	Paintbrushes, artist's, for touchup
Removing Finishes	Putty knife, stiff blade, 2-inch
	Toothbrushes, old
	Meat skewers, wood
Sawing	Handsaw (panel), crosscut, 26-inch, 8 points per inch
Shaving	Plane, "block" (7-inch), or "smooth" (8- to 10-inch)
	Chisels, 1/2-inch plain type (straight edges) and 1-inch beveled edge
Miscellaneous	Ice pick, for marking and holding
	Oil can, small
	Dusting brush and pan
	Teaspoon and tablespoon, 10¢-store type
	Clothesline, cotton and strong

ADDITIONAL TOOLS SUGGESTED FOR PURCHASE

Boring	Auger bits, 5/8-, 7/8-, and 1-inch
	Bit depth gauge, adjustable
	Expansive bit, 7/8- to 3-inch capacity
Clamping	Woodworker's bench vise, quick-acting type
	Hand-screw wood clamps, 2 each, 5- and 12-inch jaws
	Furniture bar clamps, 2 each, 3 and 5 feet long
	Spiral ratchet screwdriver
	Monkey wrench, 12-inch
	Pipe wrench, 14-inch
Cutting	Scissors or shears, 6- to 8-inch
	Tinner's snips, combination type
	Cold chisels, 1/4- and 7/8-inch
Filing	Rattail file, slim and tapered
	File brush

Hammering

Mechanic's ball-peen hammer, 13 to 16 oz.
Nail set, 1/8-inch

Marking

Wood-marking gauge
Scratch awl

Measuring

Carpenter's combination square
Slide "T" bevel square
Steel square (framing), 16 by 24 inches
Rule, 2-foot, folding
Spirit level, 18 to 24 inches long
Calipers, both inside and outside types
Dividers

Painting

Putty knife, 2 inches wide, flexible blade

Sawing

Ripsaw, 26-inch, 7 points per inch
Dovetail saw, 8-inch, 17 points per inch
Keyhole or compass saw
Coping saw, 6 1/2-inch
Miter box
Backsaw, 12- to 14-inch, 13 or 14 points per inch
Hack saw, type adjustable to length of blades

Shaving

Plane, block (7-inch), or smooth (8- to 10-inch), whichever you do
    not have already
Plane, junior jack 11 1/2-inch, or jack 14-inch
Plane, fore or joiner, 18-inch
Spoke shave, 2 cutters, blades curved and straight
Drawing knife, medium size
Cabinet scrapers

Miscellaneous

Carpenter's bar, gooseneck 18-inch (commonly called a *wrecking
    bar* or *pinch bar*)
Electric soldering iron
Staple machine and staples, 1/4-inch size
Spatula, artist's or druggist's with flexible 3- or 4-inch blade
Spirit lamp
Cutter and chisel grinder
Combination oilstone

CARE OF TOOLS

The care of tools is of great importance in keeping them in proper working order. Those with cutting edges may become dulled easily by careless handling or by being stored in the wrong manner, or they may become rusted, which can be prevented. Instruction on the proper care of tools can be divided into four parts, as follows:

Handling Tools

More tools with cutting edges are dulled or damaged by the way in which they are handled (or stored) than through actual use. *Example:* Many workers lay a plane on a surface with the cutting edge down, instead of upon its side. If they had stopped to reason, they would have realized that the blade will not cut unless it extends below the bottom of the plane. When it is laid on that surface, the blade is dulled.

Also, chisels, saws, cabinet scrapers, knives, etc.—in fact, all tools with a cutting edge—should always be handled with the utmost care when being laid down, for fear of damage.

A good rule to follow before any work is done with a cutting tool is to examine carefully all wood for hidden pieces of metal, such as broken nails, screws, etc.

Storing Tools

Saws should seldom be laid down because of dulling the offset teeth, but should rather be hung on a peg or nail, immediately after use. If they must be stored by being laid down, the cutting edge should be protected by wrapping the saw blade in a paper, or by placing a narrow U-shaped strip of wood over the teeth and tying it in place with a string. This strip may be made on a power saw in a few minutes.

If there is a chance of damage to chisels, make a small hood for the point by folding a piece of thin cardboard and tying it with a string, so that it may be slipped on and off easily.

Sharpening Tools

Many workers are careless about keeping their cutting tools sharp and their other tools in shape to do good work. Quality work is largely dependent on properly sharpened, edged tools, together with the manner in which they are handled.

A worker should learn how to sharpen chisels, plane irons, and cabinet scrapers, since they need attention often, but sharpening saws is a very difficult task. A saw, made of good steel and correctly sharpened, will remain sharp a long time unless abused, and should never be sharpened by an amateur, unless he is trained to do the work properly.

Oiling Tools

Tools become rusty from being stored in a damp place and from being handled. This may be prevented by cleaning and oiling them before they are stored away. And while there are products especially made for this purpose, a mixture of 1 part of no. 10-grade motor oil and 1 part kerosene works perfectly. Keep some in an oil can and apply with a piece of cheesecloth. Wipe the tool with this cloth, and then lightly with a dry cloth, thus leaving a thin film of oil. Store the tool and, under normal conditions, it shouldn't rust. No tools should ever be stored in a damp place.

Slight rust on the surface of a tool can often be completely removed by being rubbed with a pad of 3/0 steel wool dipped in kerosene. Care should be used not to injure the cutting edge. When a tool is badly rusted, it is impossible to remove all the rust by this method, but it should be followed to remove as much as possible.

PAINTBRUSHES

Paintbrushes play an important part in restoration work. Here are several thoughts with which many experienced workers in this field may not agree, but which have proven practical and may save time and money:

Selection of Brushes

A good brush is one that picks up a good amount of paint and lays it on smoothly with almost no drag, pull, or brush marks remaining in the paint film. A good brush is one that doesn't lose hairs or wear out after a few paint jobs and repeated cleanings. It is also one that works with less arm weariness, gives better coverage, is more fun to use, and saves you money.

Paintbrushes are made of pure bristle, or a mixture of bristle and horsehair, or pure nylon, or a mixture of bristle and nylon. If you look at any brush, you will see that the bristles are combined in several sizes. Compared with another brush, you may see that there are different weights or thicknesses of the bristle. It is the thickness, length, mixture of filament or bristle shape of the end, and soft flag or split ends that make a good brush and determine its cost.

Larger bristles may have two or three wedges, or dividers, where the bristles are seated in the ferrule. But the total wedge thickness should not be over half the thickness of the brush at the ferrule. Very cheap "giveaway" brushes usually have thick wedges and thin layers of bristle, in addition to short bristles of inferior quality.

When you go to buy a new brush, check the total thickness of the bristle, the length, and the general shape. Separate the bristles down the center with a knife or stick and inspect the size and placement of the block insert. Hold the brush by the handle and feel the bristle ends against the back of your other hand. A good brush will feel elastic and springy, and the bristles will not fan out excessively.

Look next at the tips of the bristles to see that they are both tapered and flagged. Flagged ends will show tiny splits and shoots very similar to those of a young plant. Finally, check the setting by reading the manufacturer's label or guarantee. It is impossible to see the vulcanized setting in a good paintbrush without breaking it apart. If you can see the rubber base below the edge of the ferrule, it is a poor brush.

It is seldom that any brush other than a 2-inch width is used in most wood finishing, and they can be of the same grade and type. The only real occasion for the use of 1/2-inch and 1-inch brushes is for the application of stains to a small area. Turnings and carvings can often be worked over better with a 2-inch brush than with a narrower one. It is also necessary to have one or two sizes of small, fine-pointed artist's brushes for touchup work, especially for stains.

Any type of old and worn brush is satisfactory for applying paint and varnish removers.

It is an excellent plan to mark a letter on both sides near the top of the handle of each brush to indicate a single use for that brush. This letter may be made by hitting a screwdriver lightly with a hammer, making straight-lined letters. Having the letter near the top of the handle makes it easy to identify when the brushes are stored with paper wrapped around the bristles (see page 248–49). Typical markings could be as follows:

V—Varnish
Z—Shellac (Z looks like S)
N—StaiN
L—Lacquer
P—Paint

(It is not necessary to mark brushes used for paint remover, since they are hung on a nail.)

There are other single-purpose brushes used in a well-equipped shop:

1. A large scrub brush to be used with lye as a remover.

2. A small hand scrub brush for abrasive powders on finishes.

3. A long brush, with a horizontal handle, used for removing dust (with added wiping) before finishes are applied. A standard product in most paint stores.

4. A brush for cleaning workbenches. A cheap 7-inch paintbrush with coarse bristles is perfect for this work.

5. A shoe brush for use in applying paste furniture wax.

Preparing Brushes

A new paintbrush almost always has some loose hairs that should be removed before the brush is used. This may be done by rolling the brush rapidly between the hands, then beating it lightly across spread fingers. This also removes any dust.

Many professional painters prepare their new paintbrushes for use by suspending the bristles in raw linseed oil for 12 hours. The surplus oil is squeezed out with the fingers, then brushed on a clean lintless cloth, and the brush is ready for use. It is said that this preparation keeps paint from sticking to the bristles too much.

Another method of preparing a paintbrush before use is to wash it in cleaning fluid, such as carbon tetrachloride, which evaporates quickly and won't catch fire.

Using Brushes

Standard paintbrushes are composed

of three parts: the bristles, the ferrule, which binds them into shape, and the handle. This type of brush should be held by the handle and near the ferrule, very much like a pencil, for ordinary use. When applying varnish or similar products, it is better to hold the brush further down, so that the fingers and thumb rest on the upper part of the ferrule.

Most brush work should be done with a short and quick, easy motion of the wrist, and with little movement of the arm. The reason for the lower grip on the brush, when applying varnish, is to take advantage of the V shape of the special varnish brush. Varnish should be literally "flowed" on a surface with very little brushing, except to smooth it out and pick up snags or runs.

A brush should not be used unless it is clean, the bristles flexible and free from dust. The bristles should never be dipped more into a material than one-half their length, and, before it is applied to a surface, the brush should be wiped lightly on the edge of the container. When using materials that are difficult to work with, it is well to get the brush shaped, and the material flowing properly, by stroking the wet brush a few times on a dust-free old newspaper.

Cleaning Brushes

A brush that is thoroughly cleaned, immediately after use, by a proper method will avoid the necessity of using a solvent at a later date after the material has hardened. This weakens the bristles and is not good for them. (See note 3 following.)

Under no circumstances should a furniture finishing brush be left or stored in a container filled with water. This makes the bristles soft and flabby, destroying their spring and resiliency, and often swells and splits the ferrule. It is a common habit in households, and is the result of carelessness, want of time, or lack of knowledge of brush cleaning. It would save time and be better to throw away the brush after use.

Cleaning a brush immediately after use is a simple matter; it is easy to do, takes little time, and, when completed, the brush can be stored. The brush will then be ready for future use and will be as good as ever, except for ordinary wear.

The method for cleaning a paintbrush is as follows:

1. Wipe the brush on the top edge of the container to remove as much of the paint material as possible.

2. Remove more of the material from the brush by stroking it on clean newspaper.

3. Then clean the brush in the type of solvent, as recommended below, for the paint material used. Fill 3 containers about one-third full. For this purpose the larger-sized cans (about 2 quarts) in which fruit juices are sold are ideal, when their tops have been so removed as to leave a perfectly smooth edge.

4. First hold the brush in one hand and manipulate the bristles with the

fingers while submerging the brush in the solvent in the first can.

5. Then remove the brush from the can and continue to manipulate the bristles, while holding the brush upwards at an angle of about 45 degrees, so that the solvent fluid will flow from the bristles at their juncture with the ferrule, bringing with it any paint material that has worked deep into the bristles.

6. Repeat operations 3 and 4, using the *same* can, until the bristles and metal on the ferrule are relatively clean. Then repeat those operations in the *next* can, until the metal and bristles are thoroughly clean.

7. Finally wash the brush in the third can to remove any paint material remaining. Then shake the brush to remove surplus solvent.

The solvents to be used for the cleaning of paintbrushes are listed below.

Sometimes the solvent recommended will not take the stickiness out of a brush completely. This often happens when attempting to clean a brush that has been used with a material (sometimes synthetic) that doesn't indicate on the label what thinner to use. (A proper thinner for a paint material will always clean a brush.) In such cases, experiment either with other solvents or try to complete the cleaning with warm water and mild soap.

Paint that has hardened on brushes may be removed by the use of products sold for the purpose.

Storing Brushes

The simplest way of storing brushes is to wrap a few thicknesses of news-

MATERIAL	SOLVENT
House paints, enamels (varnish base), and varnish (oil type)	Turpentine, painter's thinner, or mineral spirits
Synthetic varnish and other similar materials, including plastic	As directed on the can for thinning or, if questionable, try turpentine or mineral spirits
Shellac	Denatured alcohol
Lacquer and lacquer sealer	Lacquer thinner (Sometimes benzol may be used.)
Oil stains	Turpentine, painter's thinner, kerosene, or naphtha
Spirit stains	Denatured alcohol
Water stains	Warm water and soap
Paste wood fillers	Mineral spirits
Paint and varnish removers	Denatured alcohol

paper around the bristles and ferrule, fold it back so that the bristles will not be bent, tie with a string, and lay the brush away in a clean place where there is a free circulation of air.

When you store a brush that has been cleaned with kerosene in this manner, do so while it is somewhat wet, and allow the kerosene to soak into the paper. Before the brush is used, wash it in turpentine to remove any remaining kerosene, as kerosene is harmful to paint materials.

Paintbrushes that are frequently used are often stored by being suspended in a container partly filled with either raw linseed oil, painter's thinner, or a mixture of the two. It is best that only enough of the material be used so that the bristles alone are in the liquid. A brush should never touch the bottom of the container.

There are several ways of adapting a container for this purpose. Painter's thinner will evaporate, so that when the mixture is used, the container should be covered. A mason jar is best for this purpose, since it is transparent. Cut a hole in the lid the size and shape of the brush handle. Drill a small hole through the brush handle, put the handle through the hole in the lid, insert a nail through the hole in the handle, which will hold the brush suspended in the jar, which should then be filled to the proper level with the solvent. Another method is to use a tall tin can with a lid. Drill or punch holes through the sides of the can at a height where a wire can be inserted through the holes in the can and in the brush handle.

Many professionals who wish to store a number of brushes that they use frequently make containers from gallon paint cans. For a closed-top type, a thin disk of plywood is cut to a size that will just go through the can opening. Another is cut but slightly larger. The two disks are temporarily tacked together, and several holes, slightly larger than the width of brush handles, are bored through the disks. The disks are then taken apart and a piece of rubber (an inner tube is good), cut to the size of the smaller one is placed between them, and the disks are secured together with screws. Slots are then cut through the rubber at the holes. When a brush handle is inserted through the hole from the underside, the rubber holds the brush suspended in the lid.

A way of using a gallon can with an open top is to drive short nails or screws through the sides of the can, near the edge, on which brushes are hung by holes in their handles. Another method is to suspend brushes from a stick in which several oval-shaped notches have been cut to fit the brush handles where they are narrow. These elongated holes are cut along both sides of the stick and are shaped in such a manner that there is a narrow opening on the stick edges to permit the brush handles to pass through.

With these open-can methods, only the raw linseed oil should be used, and the cans should be covered with a piece of cheesecloth to prevent dust from getting into them.

SPRAY GUNS

Whether finishing new furniture from your own workshop or refinishing older pieces from around the house, you can get professional results with the spray method by following a few simple instructions.

The basic equipment needed for spray painting is a gun, air compressor, and hose. There are two types of spray guns to choose from, suction or pressure feed. The pressure-feed gun will spray heavy materials like those used for outside finishes with a low volume of air and is ideal for use with a small compressor.

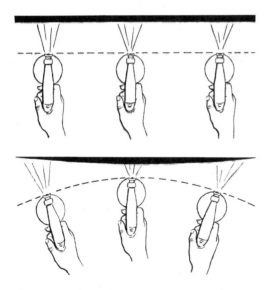

Figure 10-1. *Top:* Right way—move the gun parallel to the work surface, keeping the wrist flexible. Hold the gun 6 to 10 inches from work. *Bottom:* Wrong way—keeping the wrist too stiff causes arching and poor distribution of the finish.

However, the suction-feed gun is best suited for the lacquers and light synthetics used in furniture finishing, since it is easier to clean and allows quick changes of color and materials.

If you expect to do a great deal of high-grade finishing, you may require an oil and moisture separator that filters water, oil and other particles out of the air supply.

It is always a good idea to get the feel of the gun before doing any actual finish spraying. Practice with some inexpensive finishing material until you have adjusted the gun properly and mastered the techniques explained below. Use old cartons or sheets of newspaper tacked to a carton or box for practice spraying.

The spray-gun stroke is made by moving the gun parallel to the work and at a right angle to the surface. The speed of stroking should be about the same as brushing. Gun distance from the work should be between 6 to 8 inches. Each spray stroke should overlap the previous one by one-half to assure a full wet coat without streaks.

Never tilt the gun up or down away from the surface or angle the gun at the end of the spray strokes. Both of these practices result in an uneven spray pattern that coats some areas heavier than others.

The fluid flow is regulated by the fluid-adjusting screw on the gun. You start with the adjusting screw nearly closed, then gradually open it until the spray seems right. A distorted spray usually indicates a dirty air cap. To

Figure 10-2. The correct pattern is shown at the top, while poor fan patterns—result of incorrect pressure, a dirty spray gun, etc.—are also detailed.

remedy the situation, take the cap off and wash it carefully in clean solvent. If it is necessary to ream the air-cap holes, use a matchstick or a broom bristle—never an instrument that is hard or sharp.

It is a proven fact that 90 percent of spraying ailments can be traced to lack of cleanliness. Clean your gun immediately after use. If the paint dries in the gun, it will be almost impossible to get out.

Triggering the spray gun is the heart of spray technique, since proper triggering prevents excessive overspray from being deposited on adjacent surfaces and conserves material. To "trigger" the spray gun properly, start the stroke with a dry gun, pull the trigger when the gun is opposite the edge of the work, release the trigger at the end of the work and continue the dry stroke a few inches before reversing for the second stroke. The main point to remember is hitting the exact edge of the work, maintaining full coverage without undue overspray.

An important factor in spraying furniture expertly is setting up the job beforehand to get it done with the least effort and without overspraying parts already coated. Work on such parts as legs, stretchers, and other slender members is best done with a small spray pattern 3 to 5 inches wide. This small pattern is dense at the edges, permitting close control of overspray.

Chairs and tables are easily handled if mounted on a pedestal turntable. If you have an outboard turning stand for your lathe, it can be used as a base. Chairs are usually turned over for the legs to be sprayed, especially if you use the bench setup as shown in figure 10–

8 *above*. Some sprayers also work table legs upside down since this position gives the best spray angle.

There are three common methods of painting chair and table legs. Most beginners like the four-square method, in which the operator stands opposite each of the four sides in turn and sprays everything facing him.

A faster method is the diagonal system, which employs two work positions. The operator faces the corner of the chair or table and aims the gun at the corner of each leg, covering two of the facing surfaces with one stroke. Then the table is turned and the other two surfaces of each leg are sprayed in the same manner. If the work has round legs, the usual system is to spray the inside of all legs first and then spray each leg complete.

To spray an entire table, use a vertical fan pattern and spray all the inner sides of the legs first. With the inside of all legs sprayed, the general procedure is to spray four-square, that is, you spray all of the other outer surfaces and edges facing you in a systematic manner. The top is sprayed last. If you are using lacquer, take care not to overspray surfaces already coated. If you like the faster system of spraying legs two sides at a time, use a horizontal fan for good coverage. In this case, spray the legs inside and out and then change to the vertical fan required for the rest of the job.

In casework and cabinet jobs, the inside is always sprayed first. Then the outside is worked four-square, the right end first, followed by the front, left end, and top. On some jobs it is practical to

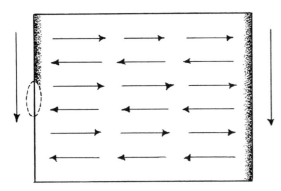

Figure 10-3. Overlap strokes one-half.

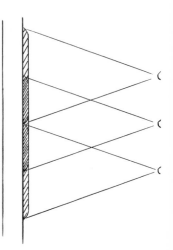

Figure 10-4. Spray bands at each end.

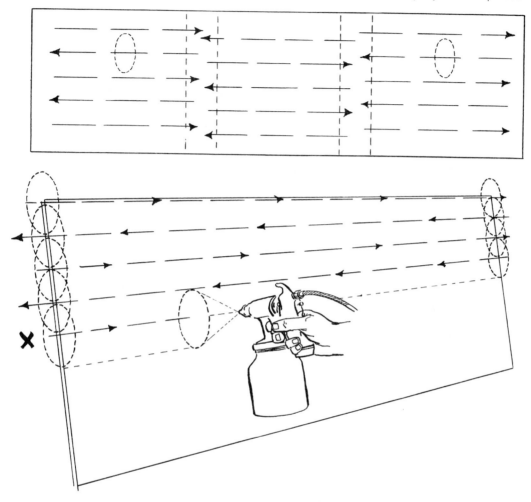

Figure 10-5. On level surfaces start at the near edge to avoid overspraying on coated work. Any overspraying then falls on uncoated work.

leave drawers in place, although the usual practice is to remove them for spraying separately.

Any brushing material for furniture finishing can be applied by spraying. However, the gun is at its best when used with quick-drying materials. Both nongrain-raising and pigment stains can be obtained in quick-drying products, which can be recoated in 10 to 30 minutes.

So far as surface stains—that is, pigment stains—are concerned, almost identical effects can be obtained by simply spraying the work with a thin coating of diluted lacquer enamel.

Good quick-drying fillers can be obtained that dry for recoating in 2 hours. In top coats, nothing beats lacquer for speed—you can finish maple natural with a double coat of lacquer and the work will be dry to touch in a manner of minutes. Spraying synthetics, too, are fast, with many good 1- and 2-hour air-dry products available.

A final word on finishing materials— always strain them through fine screen or cheesecloth before spraying. Also, if you're using a spray gun to apply the paint, add 2 tablespoons of mineral spirits to thin the mixture enough to insure an even flow of paint.

SPRAY-CAN PAINTING

From a modest beginning, aerosol paints have grown to a sophisticated line of products. Today you can buy aerosol paints in flat, semigloss, or high gloss finishes, in frosted finishes, in antique glazes, in metallic finishes, and in specialized primers.

There are four basic components in aerosol paints: the container, the valve, the propellants that produce the pressure, and the paint itself. The principle which makes aerosol painting work is a simple one. With the injection of the propellant, the pressure within the container becomes greater than that in the atmosphere. Thus, when the valve is opened, the pressure produces a fine spray of paint.

Most aerosol paints are stirred by the movement of small balls within the container. When you shake the can, you cause the balls to move and stir the contents, mixing in any pigment that may have settled at the bottom of the can. Remember that this pre-painting "shake-up" is a very important step. Without a thorough shaking, the paint may come out too thin, or you may use up the pressure before you use up the paint.

Here is another important suggestion. When you have shaken the container well, hold the can at its top and swirl the container around until the ball is at the bottom. This trick will insure blending of the pigments, which often settle at the bottom of the container.

Here is a worthwhile precaution: Try your hand at spray painting on a piece of scrap cardboard or newspaper. Once you get the hang of it—which you will in no time—you'll find how simple spray painting can be.

Application

Place the piece on a horizontal surface when possible to avoid running, and even distribution of paint. After the preparations are completed, and your aerosol paint is completely shake-blended, you're ready to go. Hold the container at least 10 to 12 inches away from the surface you are painting, keeping the nozzle parallel with the piece. Press the button all the way down and move the can evenly over the surface. Release pressure on the button before you end each stroke—the trick is to follow through. That is, work across the piece starting before its left edge, beyond its right edge. Overlap the first stroke with at least one-third of the next. Keep your distance equal always, the angle 90 degrees. Be sure to use rapid, smooth strokes as you spray. If you stop the movement of the can, or go too slowly, you can cause streaking.

If you've never used aerosol paints before, you are likely to hold the valve down too long, as if you were using some other aerosol product. This "freezing on the button" will cause dripping and running. Don't forget to turn the can upside down when you are through painting. Press the trigger once or twice with the can in this position. It clears the nozzle, and keeps it clear for the next job.

If you are painting cabinets with drawers, it's a good idea to open the drawers 1/4 inch so that the spray will cover the sides, top, and bottom to that distance. Spray chairs upside down first, working along legs and rungs, then reverse it to spray the top.

Only when spraying openwork—wick-

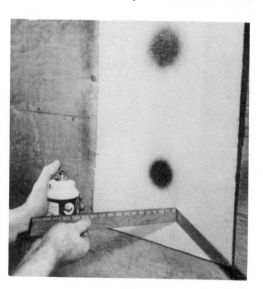

Figure 10-6. How to spray with aerosal paints: (1) Test the spray pattern against cardboard before starting work. Measure the distance from the target and note the spread of the sprayed pattern. (2) Start coverage of the surface at the left and work to the right evenly. Carry spray on past the end of the piece and then release the button to stop the spray.

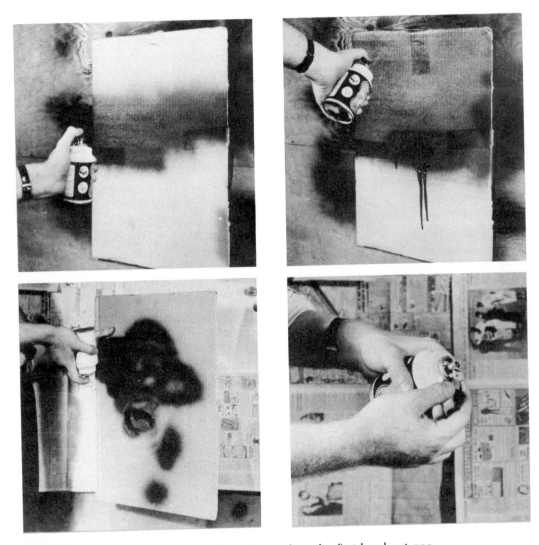

Figure 10-6 *continued*. (3) The second stroke overlaps the first by about one-third. Maintain equal distance from the work at all times for uniform application. (4) If the spray can is tilted at an angle while spraying, paint "piles up" and runs badly. A right-angle position is best for flat work. (5) After spraying, turn the can upside down and press the button once or twice. This frees the feeder tube and valve, and prevents the can from clogging. (6) A removable trigger on some cans insures nonclogging, since the trigger can be cleaned after use. Thinner or solvent will clean the trigger.

er chair seats, screens, or radiators—do you turn the spray can at an angle. Tilt to 45 degrees then, to prevent too much paint from passing through the openings. Here, spray the first coat left to right, the second top to bottom to be sure you are painting all surfaces.

Anyone who has had trouble applying lacquers will appreciate the spray-can method. The thickness of each coat is easily controlled. Brush marking is done away with. The same applies to the application of several varnish coats to fine pieces of furniture. Those who suffer from bubble-and-brush-mark defeat can now make a successful job of varnishing.

If you wish to have a particularly smooth-finished product, it is helpful to sand the surface between each coat of paint. A fine grain of sandpaper is best for this job, and one should apply two or three coats of spray paint for maximum coverage. Shake the container frequently throughout your job to insure consistency of the paint.

Although ventilation is an important safety factor in spray painting, attempt to find a spot that is both well ventilated and yet not in a draft. Wind gusts can catch the paint particles and deflect the spray. Work in a room where the temperature is about 70 degrees F. or higher. This rule applies to all painting, but the spray can works better, won't clog at this temperature.

If you are planning a touchup rather than a complete repainting, it's a good idea to spray a swatch of paper, let the paint dry, and then compare the spray

Figure 10-7. In spraying a finish on wickerwork, the can should be held at a 45-degree angle so that the finish is not forced through the weave openings.

paint with the covering that was originally used on the piece. Sometimes even a small color difference will be glaring when the job is done.

Stenciling with a spray can is fun. Make a stencil cutout and paste it to the wall or other surface with a paste made of soap flakes and water. Spray through, and when the paint is thoroughly dry, remove the stencil. It picks off easily, and the wall can be wiped down to remove the paste.

Safety Hints

Label instructions on aerosol products

Figure 10-8. *Above:* Turn chairs upside down to spray the inner surfaces of legs and rungs, then the outer edges. Then spray the upper portion. *Below:* In spraying a chest of drawers, open the drawers about ¼ inch so that all the edges are completely painted.

have safety hints as well as instructions for the user. Remember, these products have been tested and tried by their manufacturers, and instructions are well founded and should be followed. The manufacturer knows his product, so try it his way.

Aerosol paints are flammable mixtures, so perhaps one of the most necessary safety precautions is keeping these products away from open flames, particularly during use. The nature of the container also requires the user to store the aerosols in areas that are not too sunny and warm. Absolutely *never* keep them where temperatures are warmer than 120 degrees F.—even when empty. And do not incinerate these products.

Puncturing containers is another don't, but *do* find a spot with good ventilation when applying the paint.

If by now you are wondering how one does safely discard these products—without incinerating or puncturing—there is a way. Turn the can upside down, press the nozzle, and allow every bit of the propellant to be released. When nothing further comes out, the can is empty and you may discard it. Incineration is still a hazard, however, so let the community sanitation service deal with the empty containers.

HANDY FINISHING ITEMS

There are several items that you can make that will simplify wood finishing. These include:

Tack Rags

A tack rag is used for the final wiping of a piece to be varnished. Dry brushing and wiping with a clean soft cloth will not remove all foreign particles and dust. A tack rag must be used for a smooth finish, and will save much sanding and rubbing. These rags may usually be purchased in paint and automotive parts stores.

1. The best material for this purpose is a piece of finely woven cheesecloth about 2 feet square. This should be washed in several changes of tepid water and wrung out slightly to prevent drip. (The back panel of a man's shirt, hemmed to turn in raw edges, also can be used to make a tack rag.)

2. Apply pure turpentine to the moistened cloth and shake it out loosely. Then sprinkle varnish freely over the cloth, fold all edges to the center and twist it into a tight roll to force out the water and saturate the cloth fibers with the varnish and turpentine. Refold the cloth and wring it as tight as possible. Then unfold the cloth, wave it in the air a few moments, and refold it, being sure all raw edges are turned inward to avoid threads coming loose. Enough varnish should be used to make the cloth quite yellow. It should be sticky enough to pick up dust but dry enough so it won't deposit moisture.

3. A tack rag, when properly cared for, may be used almost indefinitely. It should never be allowed to dry out— even for a few minutes. It should occasionally be unfolded, sprinkled with a few drops of water and turpentine, refolded and wrung out. Under this treatment a tack rag improves with age and is kept soft and flexible.

4. Store a tack rag in a mason jar, sealed tight with a rubber washer. Never store the rag in a metal container, since the water in the rag will rust the metal. Always add some turpentine and water to the rag (as outlined above) before storing it. A tack rag left in the open air for some time becomes a fire hazard through spontaneous combustion.

Pick Sticks

A pick stick is used to remove small particles from a freshly varnished surface by touching the varnished surface with a ball of burned varnish and "lifting" the speck of dust, lint, etc., upward with a stick. They can be made as follows:

1. Swab sticks used by doctors and sold by drugstores are the best for this purpose.

2. Place 1 part of liquid varnish (less than a teaspoonful) and about 6 to 8 parts of dry brown varnish (crushed) in a small, clean tin can. Place this can in a larger one, a quarter full of water, and then heat.

3. Stir and cook until a drop of the melted mixture will form a stiff pill when cooled on glass and rolled between the fingers.

4. Dip a stick end into the melted mixture and, with fingers moistened with saliva, form a small pear-shaped ball.

5. For use as directed above, tap the ball on the hand and, if the consistency and cooking is correct, the ball will become sticky.

It is a difficult problem to store pick sticks for future use. They may sometimes be softened by heat but, as they are easy to make, it is best to make fresh ones for each job.

Strike Wires

Professional wood refinishers use a strike wire in a small can (or tin cup) when brushing varnish. Surplus varnish can be wiped from the brush after it has been dipped in the can, by "striking" (wiping) the brush on the wire, rather than against the side of the can.

A strike wire may be installed in a small can (or tin cup) by punching a hole in each of the opposite sides, just below the rim. A wire is then run through the holes, cut off about an inch from the outside of the can, and the ends turned down. The holes should be spaced in such a way that the wire will be off center and closer to one side of the can than the other.

It is always good practice to varnish from a small can rather than from the container in which it was purchased. The greatest detriment to successful varnishing is small particles, like dust, which must be avoided by every possible means. When the job is completed, any varnish left in the small can should be thrown away, as it may contain dust, or be damaged by exposure to the air.

The greater the pains taken when varnishing, the more success will be attained in the final finish.

Rubbing Blocks

A rubbing block is best made of flexible material, like sponge-rubber pad, or a block (about 1/2 inch thick) of hard rubbing felt. This should be cut slightly narrower than the abrasive paper and placed over it for rubbing. Two types of rubbing blocks may be purchased. The first is of a size for an eighth cut of abrasive paper and is made of thin sheet metal, with an inverted U-shaped grip and a padded rubber bottom. It is cheaply made but good. The second is made of an aluminum casting about 2 inches by 6 inches, with springs holding a rubber padded bottom and with a coil of abrasive paper attached, which may be drawn out as needed. Naturally, this tool is more expensive. Both may usually be purchased in paint and hardware stores.

Rubbing Pads

A rubbing pad is used for the final smoothing or polishing of a finish, with the use of abrasive powders (pumice stone or rottenstone) and oil and water. Professional shops seem to prefer a block of hard rubbing felt about 1 inch thick (of the type recommended for a rubbing block). One may be made of several layers of an old felt hat or several pieces of felt padding sewed together, of the kind that is used under rugs and carpets, or a blackboard eraser.

STORAGE OF PAINTS

There is no necessity for the great waste of paint, enamels, varnish, lacquer, or synthetic materials used for refinishing that is so commonly met with. All of these may be saved for future use with a little care.

When not properly stored, the surface of the material left in the can usually thickens into a skin, even though the lid is secured tightly, but this can be prevented. This skin can't be dissolved merely by adding solvent or thinner, and thus a part of the material is wasted. The proper storage of these materials is a very simple matter and will save much money. Proceed as follows:

1. Clean most of the material from the groove in the top of the can but leave a small amount so that the lid will seal. If the material is heavy or dried, it must be removed until the surface is clean and even. This may be done with a screwdriver, followed by a knife blade, but care should be exercised in order that none will drop into the can.

2. Clean off all dried material from the underside of the lid with the same tools and wipe it clean with a cloth.

3. Pour on the surface of the material in the can a small amount of the thinner used with the material. Use just enough so that it will spread to a thin film; the amount to be used is dependent upon the size of the can. Use turpentine or painter's thinner for house paints, enamels, and all types of varnishes. Use a lacquer thinner for lacquers. Use the type of thinner directed on the can for synthetic and any other type of material. If no directions are given, smell the material and use a thinner that you believe will be satisfactory.

4. Place the lid on the can and set the can on the floor. Step on it. Move it back to the workbench, place a piece of paper over the can, and drive the lid down to a tight fit by tapping around the edges with a hammer. (The paper over the can keeps excess material from spattering.)

5. Move the can to the storage place, using care not to rock or shake the can, to prevent the film of thinner from mixing with the material.

The film of thinner can't evaporate in a tightly sealed can since there is not enough air. It is lighter than the material and will remain on top almost indefinitely, thus preventing the formation of a coating or skin. When the material is needed again, remove the lid; after stirring, it will be ready to use. It must be remembered that thinners evaporate, and it is often necessary to add much thinner before storage. Materials stored in this manner may be used without being strained.

A method employed by some in storing paint materials is to cut a piece of heavy paper the size and shape of the can, placing it on top of the remaining material in the can. This is helpful, but not as satisfactory as the thinner suggested above.

Materials such as linseed oils, shellac, etc., need no liquid film coating for protection. Depend upon the tightness of the container top for their proper storage.

Reviving Old Paints

When a can of paint material has a dried skin on its top, this can best be removed by cutting around its edge with a sharp knife blade and then picking it out by taking hold of the center of the skin with two fingers. House paints and enamels should then be thinned by the addition of some raw or commercially boiled linseed oil, turpentine, or painter's thinner, with a little japan drier to increase its drying power. It should also be strained through cheesecloth or a sheer stocking.

Varnishes and lacquers often thicken to a point where they are worthless for further use. If thin enough to use, add pure turpentine to varnish and lacquer thinner to lacquers.

Paints, enamels, varnishes, and lacquers made over in this manner are seldom satisfactory. It pays to use care and store these materials in a manner that will keep them without deterioration or destruction.

THE HOME WORKSHOP

A person who enjoys tinkering with tools is indeed fortunate if he has a home workshop. Here one may relax and gain pleasure and profit, whether it be the restoration of furniture or building something. Creative hobbies may be practiced and minor repairs completed for the upkeep of the home. There is no better-known cure for a tired, worried mind than working with tools.

Unfortunately, many homes do not have the space in which such a shop can be set up. That should not be a discouragement. A removable bench top may be made that can be clamped to a kitchen table, or a portable cabinet bench can be designed that may be stored. The floor around such a workshop can be covered with a mass of old newspapers, over which can be spread an old piece of canvas. Many a piece of furniture has been repaired and refinished and something useful created under such conditions, without damage to the furnishings or the room.

When there is ample space in which to create a workshop, many things must be considered. There must be a good circulation of air to get rid of the fumes from volatile materials. The place should be dry, for dampness ruins tools. Electric current must be available for any power tools, and work can best be done in a strong light, such as that from 100- and 150-watt lamps. The place must be of adequate size for the type of work to be done, and it must be heated for winter use.

Under certain conditions a basement is an ideal place for a shop. Attics are fine so far as space is concerned, but most of them are hot in summer and cold in winter. The side or end wall of a garage may often have sufficient space, but in most climates there is a heating problem in winter. The same is true of a barn. A small service room or bedroom may often be made available for a shop, and those with light and heat often make an ideal place in which to work. Under ordinary circumstances anyone who wants to work with tools can find a place where it can be done, even if it is necessary to set up a temporary platform out of doors on sawhorses.

A shop centers around the workbench. It is needless to give directions for building one since a bench must be built to suit the available space and personal needs. A workbench for hard service must be made of sturdy material with a thick plank top. Most of the work at a bench is done while standing. A workbench with the top 36 inches from the floor is ideal for a tall person, but should be made lower, to a convenient height, for shorter people. Hard maple is the best wood for workbench tops. Many plans are available in technical books for the construction of workbenches, but most of them are too elaborate in design for the needs of the amateur worker.

The following are a few practical ideas given with the thought that they might be helpful in the construction of a home workshop.

1. Measure any space available and draw plans prior to any construction. Make a list of materials of the kind and size necessary for the complete construction program. Don't deviate from the plan unless unforeseen conditions arise. Start with the workbench construction, followed by shelves and racks, unless prior work must be done on the space or room available. Construct one thing at a time and take plenty of time.

2. When laying out this plan, there are a number of things to be taken into consideration. The workbench should be against a wood wall or one on which a sheet of plywood can be fastened so that loops or racks may be fastened to it, into which tools can be placed.

3. It is convenient and makes working at a bench easier if the most frequently used tools are on the wall back of the bench. Flat strips of heavy woven cloth, used for lacings under automobile hoods to stop rattles and called hood lacings or hood gaskets, are available at auto supply stores at low cost. They are perfect for holding tools when nailed or screwed, in proper-sized loops, along a wall.

To hang such tools as hammers, hatchets, mallets, putty knives, etc., on the wall, drill a 3/16-inch hole through the handle near the end, and use finishing nails (small-headed) to hang them on. It is well to countersink the holes in the handle slightly on both sides with a "rose drill," which makes it easier to match the hole with the nail when hanging up the tool. If the workbench has an exposed end, it is a good plan to place nails there for hanging saws temporarily while working, rather than laying them down and dulling the teeth.

Some workers prefer to lock up their tools and yet have them hanging on the wall back of the bench. This may be done by making two large, shallow boxes of the same size. One is secured to the wall and the other is hinged to the first, so that it may be swung around as a cover and locked.

For those who wish to make their shop a bit dressy, there are enameled metal fixtures on the market that make a perfect tool rack. These come in sheets (usually white) with many small square holes in them, and with short and longer square rods, turned up at the end, or loops, that fit into the holes and may be spaced for many sizes. Of course, one of the most popular tool racks is made from perforated hardboard or pegboard, plus the tool holders that are available with this material.

4. The question of light in a shop is very important. When a workbench is short, it is best not to place it directly in front of a window, since it is difficult to face the light and see the work on a bench clearly. It is better to have strong lights over the bench and near shelves for supplies. Plug outlets for power tools are handy.

5. Ample storage space on shelves is also important. Shelves 5 inches wide for storage and easy display of small items and about 10 inches wide for the larger ones are satisfactory. Vertical space will not be wasted if the height of the various-sized containers is measured in advance of the laying out of shelf spacing. It is of great convenience if a shelf about 5 inches wide is run along the wall about 10 inches above the workbench and for its full length.

6. When there is space for a horizontal lumber rack to be placed on a side wall, it is a great convenience. When the ceiling is of rafters that are within reaching distance, as in a basement, very convenient racks may be made for the storage of dowel rods, abrasive papers, long tools, short lumber, etc., by nailing narrow cleats across the beams. Convenient triangular-shaped racks for short lumber may be built in a corner. It is well to store very old lumber in a separate place.

7. There is one method of keeping track of tools that may be missing from their space on a wall or have been borrowed and not returned. This is by painting an outline of the tool on the wall where it is customarily kept.

8. It is a good plan to keep all edged cutting tools (chisels, planes, saws, etc.) in a locked cabinet or drawer if you expect to keep them sharp, particularly if there are children in the household.

9. The storage of small items such as brads, screws, staples, corrugated nails, etc., is always a problem. Keeping them in small "jelly glasses" with tops and storing them on narrow shelves, permits visibility and easy access. Likewise, nails of various sizes and types, solder, stick shellac, powdered stains, etc., which are larger in size or kept in greater quantities, may be visibly stored in "peanut butter" jars or other glass jars with tops and wide openings.

For better identification of sizes of materials thus stored, it is a good plan to make notations on small gummed-paper labels and stick them on the jars. A good light should be near the shelves.

Then there is the problem of storing various types of materials that are useful for the type of work done in the shop or for repairs about the home, such as light cords and sockets, hinges, locks, and door knobs, etc. Labeled coffee cans, both the 1- and 2-pound size with lids, make ideal containers.

Good Shop Practice

The workshop is considered by most workers as a sanctuary, with a warning to others that "Thou shall not trespass, nor touch a thing, nor use a tool, nor clean up the place." This is not because the worker is selfish, but because he doesn't like work once started to be disturbed, and tools taken without permission injured, not returned, or lost. He likes to clean up the place himself, so that tools and materials may be put back in order where they belong and odds and ends of lumber, etc., not thrown away but put in a special place for safekeeping and future use.

All these thoughts are natural and logical, for when a person turns out work that is admired, not only are the shop, tools, and equipment held in high respect, but more credit is given to the material things than to oneself.

Experienced workers get into bad habits, so beginners will profit if they start out with good shop practice. A few examples are as follows:

1. Arrange the tools that are most often used on a wall or in a cabinet in a position from which they may be easily reached. When a tool is used, put it back where it belongs, unless it is to be used again soon.

2. Have great respect for edged cutting tools. Always lay a plane on its side and handle a chisel or saw with care. More tools are dulled or damaged by careless handling than by normal use.

3. Prevent rust on tools before it starts by wiping them with a half and half mixture of kerosene and light oil.

4. Keep the workbench neat and reasonably clean while work is in progress and brush up the entire shop as necessary.

5. Good receptacles for the disposal of sweepings from the bench and floor are 50- and 100-pound metal lard containers, which may usually be purchased for very little from bakeshops. They will be greasy, so they must be washed. When disposing of trash, it is best to separate all metal things from the burnables. The 50-pound cans are a good size for the metal trash and for storing clean rags and burlap.

6. A shop is certain to get full of dust from use of tools and sanding. Shelves and workbench should be dusted and the floor well swept before using finishing materials.

7. Regardless of how clean a shop may be, always spread clean old newspapers under pieces that are being worked on. The paper will catch drippings from finish removers, glue, or finish materials and prevent dust; and the work can be seen better against a lightened background.

8. Oil power tools at regular intervals. Stores that specialize in the sale of electric motors sell a type of oil that is best for motors and that will not burn if the motor should become overheated.

9. Two or more jobs may often be worked at the same time by dovetailing the work on one piece in with another, instead of waiting for glue, finishes, etc., to become completely dry.

10. Teach children proper respect for tools.

11. Lending tools is a bad practice unless it is kept under control.

12. Take all possible precautions against fire. It is a good plan to have a fire extinguisher in the shop.

13. The best products and tools are the cheapest from every standpoint.

14. Standing on floors is hard on the legs and feet. Very often sufficiently large scrap pieces of thick wallboard may be bought at a most reasonable price at builders' supply stores. These may be placed on a floor like a rug before a workbench or work table and make standing easier.

15. It is difficult to do fine, close work at a bench while standing. A flat, sturdy wooden box of the proper height makes a fine seat. It may also be used to stand on for high work (a flat box, longer than it is wide, gives 3 levels).

Index